Cindy Hill
252-2180

$ 3.75 10771

Used

PRINCIPLES OF
ECONOMICS
Macro

$ 2.81

THE IRWIN SERIES IN ECONOMICS

Consulting Editor
LLOYD G. REYNOLDS
Yale University

PRINCIPLES OF ECONOMICS
Macro

WILLIS L. PETERSON, Ph.D.
University of Minnesota

1971

RICHARD D. IRWIN, INC.   Homewood, Illinois   60430

Irwin-Dorsey Limited, Georgetown, Ontario

First Printing, April, 1971
Second Printing, July, 1971
Third Printing, October, 1971

Library of Congress Catalog Card No. 72–149900

Printed in the United States of America

PREFACE

The general philosophy of this book probably is best expressed by Alfred North Whitehead in *The Aims of Education and Other Essays:* "Whatever be the detail with which you cram your student, the chances of his meeting in afterlife exactly that detail is almost infinitesimal; and if he does meet it, he will probably have forgotten what you taught him about it. The really useful training yields a comprehension of a few general principles with a thorough grounding in the way they apply to a variety of concrete details. In subsequent practice the men will have forgotten your particular details; but they will remember by an unconscious common sense how to apply principles to immediate circumstances."

In line with this philosophy, the book has three main objectives. The first is to improve understanding of how a market economy operates. What are the causes of unemployment and inflation? What can the government do to mitigate these problems? The book addresses itself to these basic questions. The second objective is to help the student acquire an understanding of the major tools or principles that have proved useful in making economic decisions or solving economic problems. The third and most important objective, but also the most difficult to attain, is to help the student acquire a skill in using these tools or principles to conduct economic analysis.

Hopefully, the student will not be so unfortunate as the economist who decided to build his own house. After acquiring the necessary tools—hammer, saw, level, etc.—he proceeded to go about his task. After finishing the house, it didn't look quite right to him so he asked a carpenter friend to take a look at his accomplishment. A quick glance at the structure prompted the carpenter to reply, "Of course it doesn't look right, you've built it up-side-down"; to which the economist replied, "Oh, I thought something was wrong, I kept falling off of the porch." Unfortunately, "up-side-down" answers to economic questions are much less recognizable than up-side-down houses. To avoid such answers, it is necessary to be able to use the tools of economic analysis as well as just to learn of their existence.

This book is a twin. It is linked to a micro volume in style and is complementary in content. Yet either can stand alone or be used with another principles text. Both volumes were written to be used interchangeably. Some instructors prefer to teach macroeconomics first, others prefer micro first. In addition, the many new "current economic issues" books that have come on the market in recent years can serve as excellent complements to either book.

No book, of course, is the product of just one person's thinking, least of all this one. Credit must go to all those who have influenced my thinking in economics—my teachers, my colleagues, and my students. I am especially indebted to Professor Conrad Caligaris of Northeastern University for his perceptive comments and suggestions on the first draft of the manuscript. Also I have benefited from discussion with my colleagues and fellow principles teachers, Dale Dahl, John Helmberger, Emiel Owens, Jerome Stam, and John Waelti. Special thanks also go to Mrs. Kay Perry for her long hours of typing the manuscript, and to Dorothy Peterson for her assistance and cheerful endurance as a "writer's widow."

March, 1971   WILLIS L. PETERSON

CONTENTS

of Money. Velocity of Money. Quantity Equation of Exchange. The New
Quantity Theory of Money. Motives for Holding Cash Balances. Cost of
Holding Cash Balances. A Demand Curve for Money. Shifts in the Demand for Money. Factors Shifting the Demand for Money. Relationship
between Velocity and the Demand for Money. Changes in Velocity.

CHAPTER

1

INTRODUCTION TO MACROECONOMICS

"MICRO" VERSUS "MACRO" ECONOMICS

During its relatively short history, economics has evolved into two major subdisciplines: microeconomics and macroeconomics. As its name implies, microeconomics is concerned mainly with small segments of the total economy—individual consumers and producers, or groups of consumers and producers which are known as markets or industries. The subject matter of microeconomics deals in part with allocating resources to their most valuable uses so as to maximize the total output of the economy. Also considerable emphasis is placed on wage and price determination which bears upon the distribution of the total output.

Macroeconomics, the topic of this book, is concerned mainly with economic aggregates, or the economy as a whole. The subject matter of macroeconomics deals to a large extent with the problems of unemployment and inflation. In large part, these problems also bear upon the total output of society and upon the distribution of this output.

The existence of unemployment implies that the total output of society is smaller than it need otherwise be. Unemployment also has an effect on the distribution of society's output in that the unemployed suffer a reduction in income which in turn means that they cannot place as large a claim on society's goods and services. Inflation also has distributional effects. Those whose wages or assets rise less rapidly in value than the price level suffer a real loss during inflation. Unfortunately, the lower income people tend to suffer the most during inflation, as we will see more clearly in the following chapters.

1

At any rate we can say that both micro and macroeconomics deal with the size of society's output of goods and services and the distribution of this output. After completing the study of the micro and macro areas, however, it will become apparent that the methods of analysis used in each differ to a considerable degree.

We should also say at this point that macroeconomics can itself be divided into two major subdivisions. One is sometimes referred to as a study of income and employment theory; the other, the study of monetary theory. The first deals to a large extent with the effects of government spending and taxation on the level of economic activity. The second is concerned mainly with the effect of the quantity of money and interest rates on the economy. As you might expect, then, the actions of government are very important in the study of macroeconomics.

POLITICS AND ECONOMICS—POLITICAL ECONOMY

In view of the importance of government in the study of macroeconomics, we should not be surprised to learn that politics and economics are closely related. Indeed, economics has sometimes been called the study of political economy. This was especially true during the 19th century. With the passage of time, political science and economics gradually emerged as separate, although closely related, disciplines.

We would expect too that much of the disagreement and controversy inherent in politics would carry over into economics, particularly in the macro area. This cannot be denied. People of a more conservative political outlook tend to prefer a society with a minimum of government intervention. Although it is unwise to generalize too much here, it seems reasonably safe to say that economists of a more conservative political philosophy also prefer a minimum of government intervention, particularly in the economic activities of society.

All, or virtually all, economists would probably agree on the need for a certain amount of federal government intervention. For example, there is little question about the need for government regulation of the money supply or the provision for certain public goods such as national defense or roads. Moving towards the liberal pole, which we should recognize by various degrees of liberalism or conservatism rather than an all-or-none situation, we find people who are more willing to delegate more decision-making authority to government. Again, the more liberal economists would tend to fall within this category. Although most economists make a sincere attempt at being objective or "scientific" in their profession, it is important to recognize that their political philosophies may, to some degree, carry over into their economic analysis.

There are, of course, exceptions in each group. We find some economists, probably a growing number, who would be labeled as fairly conservative because of their objection to increase government intervention in the marketplace. But these same economists might at the same time appear quite liberal on other issues such as their support of a more equalitarian distribution of income or for advocating a more active role of government in civil rights issues, etc. Thus, it is often misleading to label someone, particularly an economist, conservative or liberal solely on the basis of one or two criteria.

POSITIVE VERSUS NORMATIVE ECONOMICS

Economists, recognizing that they do have different political philosophies and that these divergent points of view may influence policy recommendations have attempted to sort out as much as possible the "positive" from the "normative." We can think of positive economics as "what is" and normative economics as "what should be." For example, an economist may determine that a tax increase will take X billions of dollars away from the private sector. But it is a different matter to say that the X billion dollar tax increase is the best thing for the economy. The first statement would be considered positive economics while the latter would be of a normative nature.

We should not conclude from this example, however, that all positive statements are devoid of value judgments and as such are purely objective. For in the process of formulating a study, there is a great deal of value judgment involved. For example, the researcher must decide what data to collect, how to organize and analyze the data, etc. Beware of the person who says "let the facts speak for themselves." What the facts say depends a great deal upon which facts are used and how they are presented.[1]

THE INDIVIDUAL VERSUS SOCIETY

Most of us are accustomed to looking at the world from the perspective of the individual. However, we find in our study of macroeconomics that what is true for the individual person need not hold true for society, or even for groups of people. Standing up to watch a touchdown run at a football game provides a good noneconomic example. If just one person stands up, he can gain a much better view, but if everyone in the stadium stands up, no one is much better off.

The distinction between the individual and society is especially important in monetary policy. Any individual would consider himself much better off if the amount of money he held were doubled. For this would

---

[1] For an entertaining little book on the use of statistics, see Darrell Huff, *How to Lie with Statistics* (New York: W. W. Norton & Co., Inc., 1954).

mean he now has access to twice the amount of goods and services. But if the total quantity of money in the entire economy were doubled, the total quantity of real goods and services available to the people need not necessarily change. As we go along we will encounter other situations where circumstances are much different for the individual than for society.

CAUSE AND EFFECT

If two events happen in proximity to each other, there is a temptation to conclude that the second event was caused by the first. But whenever we observe two events such as these, we should always inquire whether there might have been a third event that caused both to occur. A good example is the stock market crash of 1929 and the ensuing Great Depression of the early 1930's. This order of events has prompted some people to argue that the stock market crash caused the Great Depression. But as we shall see later a third independent event probably offers a better explanation for the Great Depression than the stock market crash, although the crash probably contributed to the depressed state of the economy once unemployment began to increase.

A rather interesting phenomenon that is somewhat related to this general topic is the relationship between women's skirt lengths and the state of the economy. With amazing regularity, women's skirts have shortened during economic booms and lengthened during periods of increased unemployment. The relationship again became evident during the 1960's. In the middle and latter part of the decade the economy boomed along with high employment, rising prices, and rising hemlines. Then as the economy experienced a slowdown in 1969 and 1970, the "maxi" and the "midi" appeared on the scene. Indeed, the aesthetic value of the "mini" provides incentive enough for maintaining a healthy, full-employment economy!

Seriously, though, there is no economic reason to expect a relationship between the state of the economy and women's fashions. It has been argued that with depressed economic conditions people become gloomy and turn to "dowdy" fashions but this is mainly speculation. But perhaps there is a good lesson here. When attempting to explain economic phenomena it is always a good idea to look for economic reasons. Some of the early economists forgot this simple idea and attempted to explain business cycles (ups and downs in economic activity) by sunspots, which strikes us as quite silly today.

UNLEARNING PRECONCEPTIONS

One of the characteristics of studying economics, particularly macroeconomics, is that most people bring with them at the start at least some preconceived ideas of how the economy functions. In fact it is almost impossible not to form economic opinions in view of the vast amount of reporting of economics by the news media. This is both good and bad. It is good because people are becoming more aware of the importance of government economic policy in their lives. But it is bad to the extent that people form erroneous ideas of how the economy operates and the effect of government policy. Unfortunately there are many myths, half-truths, and misconceptions about the economy that appear over the news media just about every day.

One of the major reasons for this problem is that there are many influential people both in government and in private industry who are carrying out economic analysis without the benefit of economics training. Few if any professional occupations can make this claim (or excuse). To practice law or medicine one must have the appropriate degree from an accredited college. Indeed to be a plumber or electrician a person must complete a number of years of apprenticeship training. Not so in economics. Economics is practiced by everyone, and the importance of one's practice increases with his influence over the nation's affairs. Nations have paid a dear price for having leaders who have had little or no understanding of economics.

Throughout this book it is more than likely you will come across ideas that are quite different from what you had previously learned and accepted. Understandably it is difficult to unlearn old ideas, but economics training will be of much greater value if you approach it with an open mind, allowing the new ideas you encounter to at least compete with your old preconceptions.

ECONOMIC MODELS—A FRAMEWORK FOR THINKING

Needless to say the economy is very complex. Each day millions of economic decisions are made by millions of people. Some of these decisions, especially those made by the government, have far-reaching and long-lasting consequences. To study each decision, however, even the major ones, would be a hopelessly complicated task. We would soon be bogged down in a maze of dull and uninteresting detail. Thus, economists have found it useful to construct economic models of the economy. In a sense economic models provide a framework for thinking. They help us to identify and separate the important information for making economic decisions from the trivial or unimportant.

In Chapters 4 and 7 we will develop what has come to be known as the Keynesian model of the economy, named after its founder, a famous English economist, John Maynard Keynes. Here we will focus our attention on the effect of private and public spending decisions and the quantity of money on the level of employment and prices in the economy. We will see that the model makes it possible to explain the causes of economic events such as the Great Depression of the 1930's or the inflation of the 1960's. Perhaps even more important, the model enables us to predict future levels of unemployment and inflation under certain government policies. In short, economic models facilitate explanation of past events and help us to predict future events.

Economic models also are known as economic theories or principles. Essentially all three mean the same thing. Thus, we could refer to the Keynesian model as the Keynesian theory or the Keynesian principle.

Unfortunately the word "theory" has suffered from a bad press for a long time. To students, the word often brings to mind abstract material, devoid of any practical application. The feeling is probably justified if theory is learned purely for the sake of learning theory. But economic theory is not developed for its own sake; it is developed because it can be useful to explain and predict events. As we proceed, you will find that an attempt is made to apply the theories (models or principles) to "real world" situations. Thus if you do not find the world dull, you should not find theory dull.

We should point out, too, that just about everyone utilizes theory of one kind or another from the time they are old enough to think. To take a very simple example, we know that if we touch a hot stove we will burn a finger. Essentially this is a theory. In essence, the "hot stove theory" both explains and predicts. It explains why you might have a sore finger and it predicts that should you touch another hot stove you will again burn a finger.

In the main, theories or models are developed by observing events and then generalizing from these events. Most of us formed the "hot stove theory" by touching a stove and observing (and feeling) what happened. From one or two observations we were able to generalize that touching all hot stoves results in burned fingers. Economic theories or models are developed in a similar manner. By identifying the prime causal factors of economic events, economists attempt to explain these events and thus predict future events.

A PREVIEW OF THINGS TO COME

We are now ready to begin our study of macroeconomics. First, we will become somewhat better acquainted with the two basic problems at hand: unemployment and inflation. Then in Chapter 3 we will look at some measures of national output, particularly at GNP. Here we will be especially concerned with the biases of GNP when it is used as a measure of economic well-being. From here we move on to the development of what we call the Keynesian model without money—the simplest model of the overall economy. With this model we will be able to shed some light on the causes of unemployment and inflation and what can be done to avoid these problems.

Although the simple model without money provides a useful starting point for the study of the economy, it is somewhat incomplete in that it does not explicitly incorporate the effects of changes in the quantity of money on the economy. Thus we turn next to a study of money, first looking at the factors that influence peoples' decisions to hold part of their wealth in the form of money—the demand for money. Then we will move on to a discussion of the supply of money, looking mainly at the banking system.

After making our acquaintance with money, we will in Chapter 7 incorporate money into the Keynesian model to develop a more complete model of the economy. Then in the chapters on fiscal and monetary policy, we use these models to analyze the effect of government action on the economy, particularly how government policy influences the level of unemployment and inflation. In the remaining three chapters we will cover some related topics starting with the problems of poverty and the distribution of income. We end up on the international scene, first discussing international trade and finance, then economic growth and development.

MAIN POINTS OF CHAPTER 1

1. Economics has evolved into two major subdisciplines: "micro" and "macro" economics. Macroeconomics, the topic of this book, is concerned mainly with economic aggregates, or the economy as a whole. The problems of unemployment and inflation constitute the major part of the subject matter of macroeconomics.

2. Because macroeconomics deals to a large degree with the actions of government, political considerations become important, which helps explain why economics is sometimes called the study of political economy.

3. Positive economics is concerned with "what is" while normative economics emphasizes "what should be."

4. When studying economics, especially macroeconomics, it is important to recognize that what might be true for the individual need not be true for groups of people or for society as a whole.

5. The fact that two events may occur in proximity to each other does not necessarily mean that one is the cause of the other. Both might be caused by some third event.

6. Unlike many other disciplines, people undertaking the study of economics often bring with them preconceived ideas of how the economy functions. Unfortunately some of these ideas are erroneous or only partly true and therefore should be discarded or unlearned.

7. Economic models or theories provide a framework for thinking and as such they are useful to explain past events and help to predict

future events. The words "models," "theories," or "principles" all have about the same meaning.

QUESTIONS FOR THOUGHT AND DISCUSSION

1. Scan an edition of your daily newspaper and try to identify all the news stories that have some economic content.

2. Try to classify each of the news stories referred to above according to whether the economic content would be primarily macro or micro.

3. Try to classify the news stories in Question 1 according to whether they would be considered statements of a positive or normative nature.

4. Try to remember from your experience two events which happened within a very close time span but which were both caused by a third event or circumstance.

5. Would you classify yourself as a liberal or a conservative? On what basis?

6. List some of your currently held ideas or opinions in the area of macroeconomics. Where did you acquire these ideas? Are you convinced they're correct?

7. Think of a situation in your daily life where you use a theory. It need not be economic in nature.

CHAPTER

2

UNEMPLOYMENT AND INFLATION

UNEMPLOYMENT DEFINED

Although we all have a general idea of what unemployment is, it will be useful, nevertheless, to look a bit more closely at its meaning. Perhaps the best way to begin our discussion is to define what is meant by the absence of unemployment, i.e., full employment. Full employment is defined as a situation where everyone who is willing and able to work at the prevailing wage rate can find a job in the line of work for which he is qualified.

There are several points that are worth noting in this definition. First, full employment, or unemployment, as used in the context of macroeconomics generally refers to people rather than machines, buildings, land, or other forms of capital. As a rule society has not been greatly concerned with the unemployment of nonhuman inputs. It is not hard to understand why. Machines or buildings do not become hungry or cold if their income stops nor do they suffer from the psychological ills of being idle.

A second point to note about the definition of full employment is that at full employment not every adult need be gainfully employed. For example, full-time college students, housewives who choose not to work outside the home, and most retired people would not be considered unemployed. Of course, this is not to say that these people are idle or "nonproductive." It is just that they are not considered part of the labor force. Also there are a few people who have decided that work is too distasteful and have removed themselves from the labor force.

To be sure, it is an enormous task just to determine those who are included in the labor force as well as to determine who are the unemployed.

Figures on labor force participation and unemployment in the United States are gathered each month by the Bureau of Labor Statistics by means of a sample survey of about 50,000 housholds. Employed persons include all those who during the survey week did any work at all as paid employees, worked in their own business or profession, or worked 15 hours or more as an "unpaid" member of a family enterprise. Also included are those who did not work during the survey week but who had jobs from which they were temporarily absent.

The unemployed include those who had not worked during the survey week but had made specific efforts to find a job within the past four weeks (of the survey) and were available for work during the survey week. The total labor force, then, is defined as the employed plus the unemployed. During the latter part of 1969, the U.S. labor force consisted of about 80 million people of which 2.8 million were considered unemployed.

The extent of the overall unemployment in the country at a given time generally is given by a percentage figure—the percent of the labor force that is unemployed. Of course, we should not lose sight of the fact that even a rather modest percentage figure implies a large absolute figure from the standpoint of people unemployed. For example, the 3.5 percent unemployment rate in 1969 meant that on the average over 2.8 million people were out of work at any given time during the year. Add to this figure the dependents of the unemployed and we gain an appreciation for the total number of lives affected.

A third subtle but fairly important point in the definition of full employment relates to the willingness of people to take jobs that are available. For example, consider the case of a $200 per week construction worker who is laid off. If there are no other construction jobs available in his area, he files for unemployment insurance and is considered unemployed.

The fact that he is unemployed, however, does not mean he is unemployable. There may be other comparable jobs available that he would be qualified for such as janitor, factory worker, etc., but which he chooses not to accept. Rather than work in a different occupation, he chooses to be unemployed.

This is not intended to be a criticism of the construction worker or anyone who decides on this line of action. For the individual it can be the most rational thing to do. If he expects to be back at work again in a week or two he may not wish to seek another job. Or if a person's unemployment compensation approaches the take-home pay of another lower paying job, there isn't much incentive to take such a job. Of course, if a person is unemployed for a prolonged period of time so that his unemployment payments run out, then he might be more willing to accept a comparable or even a less desirable job. The main point is that a certain amount of unemployment may refer to unemployment from a specific job or line of work rather than not being able to find any job at all.

We should also be aware that some unemployed people probably would be willing to work at their previous jobs for a lower wage rather than being out of work altogether. For example, the construction worker may be willing to work for $175 or $150 per week rather than being forced to accept say $50 to $60 per week unemployment compensation or even a $150 per week alternative job.

Unfortunately for the unemployed, wage rates tend to be rather inflexible on the down side. If there is a choice to be made between an across-the-board wage cut and a laying off of the most recently hired people, both employers and labor unions tend to favor the latter alternative. For a reduction in wages affects all employees of a firm or industry and needless to say does not make them very happy. And both employers and labor unions are reluctant to antagonize the rank and file of the labor force. No firm with disgruntled employees can prosper nor can a labor union be a very effective bargaining agent if its members have the feeling of being "sold out."

The other alternative, laying off the youngest and least skilled workers, affects only a small part of the labor force. Once they have left, they no longer are disgruntled employees that can cause disruptions in production. Nor do these people have much of any power within labor unions; many are not even members.

The main point to remember here is that there is somewhat of a built-in incentive for both employers and labor unions to choose unemployment over lower wages. At least some unemployed people likely would choose to work at their old jobs at less than the prevailing wage rather than be unemployed but seldom do they have the opportunity to make this choice.

U.S. UNEMPLOYMENT RECORD

It will be useful to look briefly at the long-run record of unemployment in the United States. Looking at the past 40-year period, 1929 through 1969, we can observe a substantial amount of variation in the overall U.S. unemployment rate. As shown in Figure 2–1, 1929, with an unemployment rate of 3.2 percent, was a year of relatively high employment. Then came the crash. Just four years later in 1933, the United States reached the depth of the Great Depression suffering from an astronomical unemployment rate of 24.9 percent. We will have much more to say about the Great Depression as we go along in later chapters.

The Great Depression was no overnight sensation, however. In fact it lasted just about all the way through the 1930's. In 1940, just before the U.S. entry into World War II, unemployment still was at a high 14.6 percent. Then at the height of World War II, 1944, unemployment fell to an almost unbelievable low of 1.2 percent. The drain of manpower into the military and the strong demand for labor undoubtedly contributed to this low figure.

FIGURE 2–1.   U.S. unemployment rates, 1929–69

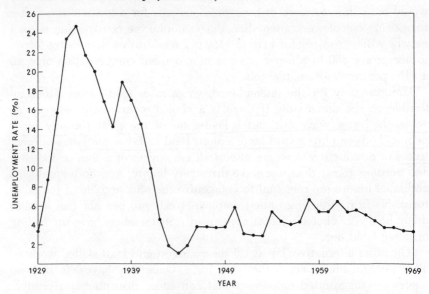

Source: *Economic Report of the President, 1970*, p. 202.

The return to a peacetime economy was accompanied by a rise in unemployment, reaching a postwar peak of 5.9 percent in 1949. The Korean
conflict reduced the rate to 2.9 percent in 1953. But towards the end of the
1950's, the country found itself in the "1958 recession" with an unemployment rate of 6.8 percent. Unemployment tended to drift downward during the 1960's particularly during the latter part of the decade.

It is fairly evident from these figures that war and low rates of unemployment tend to be positively correlated. During this 40-year period the
United States was involved in World War II, Korea, and Vietnam. In all
three cases the onset of hostilities was followed by a decrease in unemployment while the return to a peacetime situation, both after World War
II and Korea, was accompanied by a rise in unemployment.

Is war, therefore a necessary condition for full employment? We will
be better able to answer this question in later chapters. For now about
all we can say is that government policies during wars no doubt were
conducive to full employment. But we should not conclude that it is necessary to have war in order to implement policies that promote full employment. We shall return to this subject in later chapters.

FRICTIONAL UNEMPLOYMENT

From our discussion thus far it might appear that any unemployment
at all is undesirable and that we should not be satisfied until we attain a

goal of zero unemployment. Would such a goal be reasonable, or even desirable, to attain? Probably not. We should bear in mind that the economy is continually changing and adapting to new opportunities. Very few business activities continue to remain unchanged month after month, much less year after year. As a result we may observe a temporary loss of work for certain employees because of short-term fluctuations in business activity, changes in employment opportunties, or a voluntary termination of work because of a desire to change jobs. Economists sometimes refer to the loss of work in these situations as "frictional" unemployment.

We know that many occupations experience busy and slack seasons during the year. Construction work, for example, typically has experienced a seasonal decline during the winter season. People who work in this industry expect temporary layoffs, and their salary during the busy season generally compensates them for this. Another example occurs in the auto industry where a company may lay off part of its labor force for a week or two in order to bring its inventory back to a desired level.

It is a common occurrence as well in a dynamic, growing economy for employment opportunities to change. Because of changes in consumer demand, some firms or industries tend to decline and fade away only to be replaced by others. Workers who find themselves in declining industries or firms must relocate to other growing industries. Even though there may be other comparable jobs available, most people prefer to take some time to search out the best.

Related to this is the frictional unemployment brought about by employees who quit their jobs in order to search out more desirable ones. In many cases people cannot take time off to interview, etc., while holding down a full-time job. Anyone who has gone through the job searching process knows that it can be very time consuming. Sometimes a new job requires travel, buying and selling a house, or finding a different apartment. Probably most people who quit a job for one reason or another are reasonably certain of finding another. And in most cases they succeed within a few weeks or a month. Their earnings may have been temporarily interrupted, but in the long run they are able to make up the loss in their new and better jobs.

In the main, frictional unemployment has not been a major concern of economists and government. In fact we might be concerned if frictional unemployment did not exist. For this would imply a stagnant, unchanging economy, or one in which people were not free to change jobs. Both would be undesirable situations. At the present time, most economists probably would consider a 3.0 to 3.5 percent unemployment rate as a reasonable level of frictional unemployment. An unemployment rate that rises much above 3.5 or 4.0 percent, however, might be an indication that the economy is headed for a downturn and that there is a need for some kind of government action to stimulate business activity.

DURATION OF UNEMPLOYMENT

So far we have been concerned mainly with the total amount of unemployment in the economy. But we should also consider how long the unemployed are out of work. It is one thing to be out of work for a week or two but quite another to lose one's main income for several months. The first case might result in a strained budget, but the second could mean the loss of home, car, or even hunger for the family. Thus we should be concerned about the duration of the unemployment existing at any point in time as well as about the total number of people unemployed.

In Table 2–1, we present the average duration of those unemployed during 1969 and 1958. We chose these years for comparison because 1969

TABLE 2-1. Duration of unemployment, 1969 and 1958

	1969		1958	
Duration of Unemployment	Number of People (1,000)	Percent of Unemployed	Number of People (1,000)	Percent of Unemployed
Total	2,831	100	4,602	100
Less than 5 weeks....	1,629	57	1,753	38
5–14 weeks..........	829	29	1,396	30
15–26 weeks.........	242	9	785	17
27 weeks or over.....	133	5	667	15

Source: *Economic Report of the President, 1970*, p. 206.

was a year of relatively low unemployment, 3.5 percent, whereas 1958 was one of fairly high unemployment, 6.8 percent. Notice first that even in 1969, when the unemployment was within the "acceptable" range, 133,000 people had been unemployed for 27 weeks or longer. On the brighter side, we should point out that the bulk of the unemployed during 1969, 57 percent, had been out of work five weeks or less.

Looking at the figures for 1958 we see that as the overall rate of unemployment increases, there is a tendency also for the duration of the unemployment to increase. Notice for 1958, the five weeks or less category is substantially less than the 1969 figure, but that the remaining three categories, especially the last two, are substantially higher. We might expect such to be the case since the more depressed the state of economic activity the more difficult it is for people to find suitable jobs to replace the ones lost.

We should bear in mind too that even at fairly low levels of unemployment such as 2.0 to 2.5 percent, there will likely be some people who have been out of work for long periods of time. These might include people from "depressed areas" or those with few skills to offer in the job market. Unfortunately, it is not likely that government policies or programs to stimulate the entire economy can do much for these people.

What is needed often are measures to improve employment opportunities in specific areas and/or job training programs that will increase the marketable skills that the long-term unemployed can offer in the job market.

DISGUISED UNEMPLOYMENT

We should also be aware that employment figures may disguise a certain amount of unemployment. Consider the case of an aeronautical engineer who is laid off and accepts employment as a parking lot attendant, which for the sake of argument is his best alternative at least for the immediate time. Although he is no longer unemployed, his income and his contribution to society's output is considerably less than it might otherwise be. This is not meant to demean any occupation, much less parking lot attendants, but when people have no choice but to work in jobs that do not fully utilize their capabilities, they are in part "unemployed" or underemployed as economists might say. Thus a reduction in unemployment accomplished by people taking less desirable jobs may in fact overstate the true reduction that takes place.

The manner in which unemployment statistics are collected also may result in a downward bias to the true unemployment figure. Recall that for a person to be unemployed, he must have made specific efforts to find employment in the past four weeks. For a person who has been out of work for months and has been turned down repeatedly in his quest for work there will likely come a time when he gives up looking, at least until some concrete opportunity presents itself. A person who has given up trying to find a job would according to the unemployment survey not be included in the labor force and hence would not be considered unemployed. However, he (or she) still would not be working. This kind of situation probably would be most prevalent among the minority groups, and among those with the least amount of skills, i.e., the poor.

WHO ARE THE UNEMPLOYED?

Although average unemployment figures such as 3 or 4 percent are useful in providing an indication of the seriousness of the unemployment problem, they do not tell us anything about the differences in employment between individuals or groups in society. As you might expect, not all employees face an equal chance of being laid off or finding a new job.

As shown in Table 2–2, unemployment is more prevalent among the young, among minority groups, and among people with the least amount of skills. Note that in 1969 when the overall unemployment rate in the United States averaged 3.5 percent of the labor force, young people between the ages of 16 and 19 experienced an unemployment rate of 12.2 percent. Part of these unemployed came from high school dropouts and part from the 1969 high school graduating class who were not able to find a job after graduation.

Notice also that in 1969 women had a somewhat higher unemployment rate than men. We see too that negros and other minority groups tend to have about twice the unemployment rate of white workers. We do not know how much of this increased unemployment is due to discrimination and how much is due to a lower level of education and skills among minority groups.

TABLE 2–2.   Unemployment rates by groups (percent) 1969 and 1958

	1969	1958
All workers	3.5	6.8
Both sexes, 16 to 19 years	12.2	15.9
Men 20 years and over	2.1	6.2
Women 20 years and over	3.7	6.1
White	3.1	6.1
Negro and other minority groups	6.4	12.6
Experienced wage and salary workers	3.3	7.2
Married men	1.5	5.1
Full-time workers	3.1	7.2
Blue-collar workers	3.9	10.2

Source: *Economic Report of the President, 1970*, p. 205.

In general, the more skills a person has the less chance he has of being laid off. We would expect employers to be reluctant to lay off a person who cannot be easily replaced. The employer who lays off a skilled person runs the risk of not getting him back when business conditions improve. If he doesn't come back, then the firm must run the expense of finding a suitable replacement and retraining or breaking him in. For this reason firms may actually choose to lose money on a skilled person for a few months rather than lay him off. The unskilled person, however, is more easily replaced so there is a greater tendency on the part of employers to let him go as soon as he is not producing the value of his wage.

It is interesting to observe the relatively low level of unemployment among married men as opposed to other groups. Part of the explanation, no doubt, is the longer seniority on the job since married men as a group are older than single men. In addition, married men with a family to support are likely to look harder for another job when laid off and also be more willing to accept other less desirable employment on a temporary basis.

Notice also that in times of more severe unemployment, 1958 compared to 1969, the unemployment rate for married men increased relatively more than that of other groups, even though it still remains lower than the overall average. With widespread unemployment, layoffs affect people with longer seniority and also there is less chance of finding even a temporary job at lower pay.

COSTS OF UNEMPLOYMENT

From the standpoint of the individual, the economic cost of unemployment is, of course, the loss or reduction in income from being out of work. Granted, a large share of U.S. workers now are eligible for unemployment compensation which eases the problem somewhat. During 1969, the average weekly unemployment check was $46.10. For a family accustomed to a $125 or $150 per week check, however, this reduction in income comes as a severe shock to the family budget.

We must leave to the psychologists and sociologists the identification and measure of the mental and social problems that result from unemployment. In spite of how much we dislike trudging off to work or school on Monday mornings, most people find a life of idleness even more distasteful especially when they have little or no income to buy recreation. Living off of the "dole" may keep one alive, but it doesn't lead to a very enjoyable or interesting life.

It is necessary as well to look at the economic costs of unemployment from the standpoint of the total economy or society. Unemployment means that the economy is producing a smaller amount of real output of goods and services than it could otherwise enjoy. For this reason, nearly everyone loses from unemployment because there is a smaller output to be distributed among the members of society. The President's Council of Economic Advisors estimates that a 5 percent unemployment rate reduces the annual output of goods and services by almost $50 billion from what it would be if unemployment were on "acceptable" rate of 3.8 percent. Dividing this $50 billion loss by 203 million people, the approximate U.S. population, we obtain a per capita loss in real output of almost $250 per year.

Payment of unemployment compensation to the unemployed, of course, does not reduce the loss in total output. However, it is a method of redistributing the claims to society's output. Essentially, society by introducing unemployment compensation is saying that employed people are willing to give up a part of their claims on the output of the economy and share it with their less fortunate neighbors who are out of work.

MEASURES OF INFLATION

Inflation, the second major problem area of macroeconomics, is defined as a sustained rise in the general price level. The most commonly used measure of prices in the United States is the Consumer Price Index (CPI). This index is constructed by the U.S. Department of Labor, Bureau of

Labor Statistics, and is intended to reflect the prices of goods and services purchased by consumers.

We will not go into a detailed study of the CPI or its construction; these topics are covered in more depth in intermediate statistics courses. However, in order to better understand the meaning of the CPI and its uses, it will be helpful if we constructed one from a very simple example. Let us consider just three items: a loaf of bread, a jug of wine, and a theater ticket—the cost of eating, drinking, and being merry.

What we want to do is construct a number that will tell us how much, if any, the prices of these items have changed over a period of time. Essentially we will represent three prices by just one number. The official CPI, of course, represents the prices of thousands of items with just one number, but the technique of construction is still the same. Assume that the time period we are interested in is from 1960 to 1969. Let 1960 be the so-called "base year," the year we use for comparison. The average prices of the three items for 1960 and 1969 are shown below:

Item	1960 Price	1969 Price	1960 Quantity
Loaf of bread............	$0.25	$0.30	50
Jug of wine..............	1.75	2.25	10
Theater ticket...........	1.85	3.00	20

The next thing we must determine is quantity of each item that is consumed. If we just add raw prices then the theater ticket, for example, carries 10 times as much weight as the loaf of bread in 1969. This could be misleading if the person did not go to the theater very often. Therefore, in constructing a price index, we have to assign a quantity to each item so that it reflects its importance in the budget.

The Department of Labor CPI uses "base year" quantities; let us do the same. Some plausible quantities of these items that might be consumed by an average person during 1960 are shown in the right-hand column of the above table.

The next step is to multiply price times quantity of each item for each year. The results are shown below:

Item	1960: P × Q	1969: P × Q
Bread	$12.50	$15.00
Wine	17.50	22.50
Tickets	37.00	60.00
Total	$67.00	$97.50

These figures tell us that the same bundle of goods and services that cost $67 in 1960 sell for $97.50 in 1969. We can represent this change as an index by dividing the 1969 cost by the 1960 cost and multiplying by 100. We obtain:

$$1969 \text{ index} = \frac{97.50}{67.00} \times 100 = 146$$

The 1969 index of 146 tells us that the price of this bundle of goods and services increased 46 percent from 1960 to 1969. Thus the price index allows us to combine the movement of many prices into a single number.

The general formula for constructing this index is as follows:

$$I_p = \frac{\Sigma_i \, Q_{0i} \, P_{1i}}{\Sigma_i \, Q_{0i} \, P_{0i}}$$

where Q_{0i} and P_{0i} represent base year quantity and price, of the ith good or service, and P_{1i} represents the current year price of the ith good or service. The Σ_i instructs us to sum all the $P \times Q$'s as we did above. This formula is essentially the one used by the Department of Labor to construct the CPI for each year. The formula is sometimes known as the Laspeyres formula, after the man who popularized it.

When using the CPI to measure the change in the general level of prices, we should be aware of some possible biases that tend to creep in. Perhaps most important is the bias caused by improvements in quality of goods and services over time. In constructing the CPI, the Department of Labor attempts to hold quality as constant as possible. For example, in comparing automobile prices, they choose prices of comparably equipped cars. It would not be meaningful to take the price of a car with a standard transmission in 1960 and compare it with the price of one with an automatic transmission in 1969, for example.

However, there are certain quality changes that are difficult to hold constant. The 1969 engine may run 100,000 miles while the 1960 engine may only stand up for 75,000 miles before a major overhaul. But this type of quality change cannot be so easily taken account of. Because most durable goods have undergone some quality improvements over the years, many of which are difficult to measure, the CPI probably overstates the true rise in prices that can be attributed purely to inflation. In other words, part of any price rise might be attributed to better quality and part to pure inflation.

Another bias can stem from a change in the relative prices of items purchased. Notice in the above example that the price of theater tickets increased relatively more than the price of bread or wine. When the price of a good or service rises more than other prices, there is a tendency on the part of consumers to economize on the higher priced items, substituting more of the cheaper items for it. In our example, the consumer may substitute wine in place of attending the theater.

But in our construction of the 1969 price index we assumed that the consumer bought the same relative amounts of the items in 1969 as he did in 1960. If in fact the consumer had bought less theater tickets and more wine, as we might reasonably expect him to do, then the 1969 cost, $97.50 in our example, will likely overstate the true cost of the bundle of goods that the consumer actually bought. This second bias, often called the "old index number problem" by statisticians and economists, also tends to make the CPI overstate the "true" rise in prices.

A second commonly used index to measure the change in the general price level is the Wholesale Price Index (WPI). This index, also constructed by the Department of Labor, is the same type of index as the CPI except that it reflects prices at the wholesale level of both consumer goods and industrial products. Also the WPI excludes prices of personal services. Because prices of services have risen faster than prices of goods in recent years, the WPI has not risen quite as much as the CPI.

U.S. INFLATION RECORD

Although we are all aware that prices have been rising in recent years, it will be useful in later chapters to have a general idea of the extent of U.S. inflation and the periods in recent history in which inflation has been most prevalent. In Figure 2–2 we present the United States CPI for the

FIGURE 2–2. U.S. Consumers Price Index, 1929–69 (1957–59 = 100)

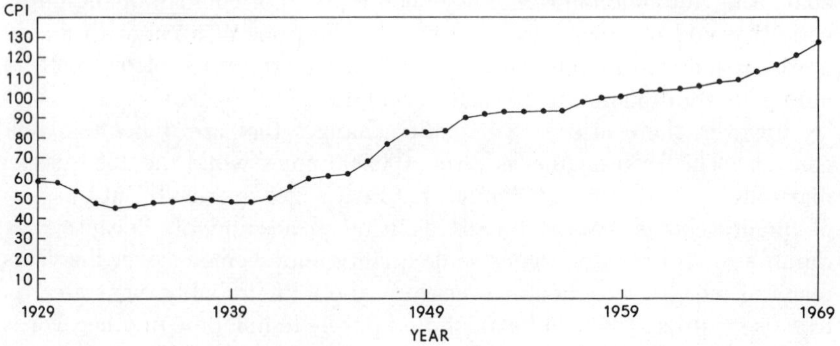

Source: *Economic Report of the President, 1970*, p. 229.

period 1929 to 1969. In this case 1957–59 is used as the base period, i.e., the CPI for this period equals 100.

We observe first that the 1930's was a decade of deflation rather than inflation. It is difficult for us today to grasp the impact of a 24 percent decline in prices as occurred in the 1929–33 period. As you would expect the severe decline in the general price level is closely related to the large

increase in unemployment during that time. We will study this relationship more closely in later chapters.

The 1940–44 World War II years in comparison brought significant
price increases, about 25 percent in this five-year period. However, an
even greater increase in prices took place in the immediate postwar
period. In order to hold down inflation during the war the government
imposed ceilings on wages and prices. When these controls were taken
off after the war, prices increased very rapidly. During the four-year,
1945–48 period, prices increased 34 percent.

The three-year, 1948–50 period was one of stable prices. As a matter
of fact prices actually fell during 1949, but the slight increase in 1950 offset this decline. The Korean War brought another round of price increases. And prices continued to rise during the remainder of the 1950's
and 1960's, with the rate of price increase speeding up during the late
1960's as Vietnam came into the picture.

It is fairly evident, then, that war and inflation go hand in hand. We
should not conclude from this relationship, however, that war per se is a
cause of inflation. We will see in later chapters that war necessitates certain government policies that result in inflation. These same policies if
carried out during peacetime also can result in inflation.

DEMAND-PULL VERSUS COST-PUSH INFLATION

Although we cannot at this point present a rigorous explanation for
inflation, we can present somewhat of an intuitive idea of its causes. Economists and the news media have often times referred to price increases as
demand-pull or cost-push inflation. Evidently these phrases are intended
to explain why inflation takes place.

Demand-pull inflation is said to take place if demanders or buyers of
goods and services wish to purchase a greater quantity than the economy
can produce. Traditionally, demanders have been divided into three
groups: consumers, investors, and the government. If the composite demand of these three groups or sectors increases more than the supply of
goods and services, then prices begin to rise.

The federal government is unique among these three groups because it
has the power to regulate the quantity of money in the economy. At
times, particularly during wars, governments have financed a part of their
increased expenditure by newly created money. Although we will study
the impact of changes in the quantity of money in more detail in later
chapters, at this point it will be useful to present at least an intuitive explanation of its importance.

Let us consider as a very simple example an economy that produces
only 1,000 bushels of wheat per year. Let us assume also that this economy has 1,000 pieces of paper in existence that it calls money. Also sup-

pose that each piece of paper, call it a dollar if you wish, is spent once each year for a bushel of wheat. In this particular case, each bushel of wheat is exchanged for one piece of paper. In other words, the price of a bushel of wheat is one dollar.

Now suppose we double the number of pieces of paper called money to 2,000. Again if each piece of paper is exchanged once a year for wheat and there is no change in the quantity of wheat produced, each bushel of wheat now will be exchanged for two pieces of paper. In other words, the price of wheat now increases to two dollars. This must be true if all of the money is spent for wheat and all the money changes hands (from buyer to seller) just once during the year. The relationship between prices and the quantity of money in this example is summarized below:

Quantity of Money	Quantity of Wheat	Price of Wheat
$1,000	1,000	$1
2,000	1,000	2

We will present a more sophisticated explanation of the effect of the quantity of money on prices in later chapters but we will see then that the same general principle holds true. For a given level of output, the larger the quantity of money, other things equal, the higher the level of prices. Price, after all, just is a measure of how many pieces of paper (or coins) are to be exchanged for a unit of real output.

Cost-push inflation, on the other hand, is said to occur as labor unions and big business demand and obtain successive increases in wages and prices. The process of wage-price hikes allegedly can begin either with labor or business. For example, suppose labor unions demand and obtain a wage increase. Businessmen then point out that costs have gone up so they are forced in turn to increase their prices. Labor unions then point out that the cost of living has gone up so they in turn ask for another wage increase. And so the wage-price spiral goes up and up with each party accusing the other of causing inflation.

At this point, it would not be particularly enlightening to make an attempt at placing the blame either on labor or business. In fact some economists have argued that neither is to blame. Rather they maintain that business and labor are simply responding to circumstances beyond their control. The argument is that individual businessmen have little choice but to ask for higher prices on their goods and services in order to maintain profits as their costs rise. Similarly, it is pointed out that labor unions have no choice but to ask for cost-of-living increases in the face of rising living costs. In other words, should we blame people for trying to maintain their profits or real income? Economists who have argued this line, instead place the major responsibility for inflation on the shoulders of government, and point out that down through history, the major inflations throughout the world have coincided with large increases in the quantity of money in circulation. At any rate, we can conclude that the identification of the major cause(s) of inflation is one of the more controversial issues in economics today.

THE ECONOMIC EFFECTS OF INFLATION

Inflation can be viewed as a tax. Moreover, it is a tax that takes income and wealth away from some people in much greater degree than others. Let us analyze briefly the major economic effects of inflation. First, inflation is harmful to people with relatively fixed incomes. Hurt most by inflation are retired people living off of social security or pensions. Although social security benefits are increased from time to time, along with some pensions, they generally lag far behind the rise in the cost of living.

In fact the same is true for most wage earners. If inflation is unexpected, as it often is at the start, wages cannot be adjusted upwards until prices have risen. Also many union contracts must run their course before new contracts can be negotiated. Many unions now insist on a cost-of-living clause that automatically raises wages as prices go up. Employees that do not have cost-of-living provisions in their contracts may have to resort to strikes to bring their wages in line with the cost of living. It is not surprising then that times of inflation also tend to bring a rash of labor unrest and strikes.

A second effect of inflation is that it tends to hurt lenders and benefit borrowers. A simple example will illustrate this point. Suppose you lend someone $100 to be paid back one year from now. Also suppose that during the year prices increase by 6 percent. The $100 in cash that you are paid back after the year is up will buy only $94 worth of goods and services at the inflated prices. In other words, the borrower obtains from you dollars with relatively high purchasing power but pays you back in "cheap" dollars. He gains, you lose.

Now, of course, you would receive some interest from the borrower. Suppose it is 6 percent. Thus you might be paid back $106 for the $100 loan. But with the price rise, the $106 is equivalent in purchasing power to the original $100 you lent. Taking into account the interest payment, we see that you obtain the same amount of purchasing power back at the end of the year as your money was worth at the beginning of the year. In other words, the borrower was able to use your money free of charge.

If prices had in fact risen 10 percent, then it would take $110 to buy what the $100 would have bought before you lent it. If you still received 6 percent interest, the $106 interest plus principle you receive will buy less than what you lent out.

THE MONEY RATE VERSUS THE
REAL RATE OF INTEREST

The only way lenders can protect themselves in times of inflation is to charge a higher rate of interest. Of course borrowers also are willing to pay a higher rate of interest if they believe the item purchased with the loan will go up in value with the general price level. In borrowing or lending money, it is important to consider the "real" rate of interest. The real rate is equal to the money rate minus the percentage change in the general price level. Expressing this relationship in terms of a simple formula, we obtain:

$$r = i - \%\Delta P$$

where r is the real rate, i is the money rate, and $\%\Delta P$ is the annual percentage change in the general price level.

Because no one is able to predict with certainty future changes in the general price level, the actual real rate of interest may turn out to be different than the expected real rate. In fact, the real rate may turn out to be zero or negative. For example, if you expected a 4 percent increase in prices when lending money at a 6 percent money rate of interest, you would expect a 2 percent real rate. But if in fact prices went up 6 percent during the year, the real rate would turn out to be zero. Or if prices increased by 8 percent, the real rate of interest on the loan would be a minus 2 percent, indicating that the purchasing power of your money was less after you lent it than before. Of course if you had not made the loan and kept your money in the form of cash, it would have depreciated even more.

As yet we know relatively little about how people form expectations. In part they likely reflect recent experience. For example, if prices have been rising 6 percent per year for the past several years, most people would expect prices to continue rising in the coming year. However, expectations also reflect current action. For example, if the government is taking action to slow down inflation, people also take this into account and may expect only a 4 or 5 percent rate of inflation in the coming year. No one knows the actual real rate until the year is past.

Generally it takes time for people to reformulate their expectations. For this reason the money rate of interest tends to lag behind changes in the general price level. When prices are falling, the real rate tends to be high whereas in the early phases of inflation the real rate tends to be relatively low or even negative before it catches up. This is illustrated in Table 2–3.

In the early years of the Great Depression, the money rate fell but not fast enough to account for all of the decline in prices. (Note from the formula that a decrease in prices must be added to the money rate to obtain the real rate). Thus the real rate of interest increased from 1929 to 1933 even though the money rate decreased. In part, at least, this might explain why businessmen were so reluctant to borrow and invest during this period.

Then as we enter the World War II era prices began to rise. The money rate of interest also begins to rise, but again the change is not enough to compensate for the change in prices. Hence the real rate on low-risk, four- to six-month prime commercial loans actually becomes negative. What a splendid time to borrow and invest.

TABLE 2–3. Money rates and real rates of interest in the United States, selected years

Year	Money Rate* (%)	Percent Change in Price Level†	Real Rate (%)
1929	5.85	−0.6	6.45
1933	1.73	−7.7	9.43
1940	0.56	−1.1	1.66
1944	0.73	+3.9	−3.17
1949	1.49	+3.4	−1.91
1953	2.52	+1.5	+1.02
1958	2.46	+3.1	−0.64
1969	7.83	+4.7	+3.13

*Interest rate on prime commercial paper, four to six months' duration.
†Average annual change in CPI over the previous two years.
Source: Columns 2 and 3 from the *Economic Report of the President, 1970*, pp. 229 and 242.

The late 1960's have become known as a time of high interest rates. But this is true only from the standpoint of the money rate of interest. The 7.83 percent in 1969 on prime commercial loans was the highest of the 40-year period. But the real rate during 1969 was only 3.1 percent. Again this presented a fairly good opportunity for people to borrow and invest.

It is somewhat ironic then that during 1933 when the government wanted the business community to invest, there was little incentive to do so because of the high real rate of interest. Then in 1969 when the government wanted to discourage new investment in order to dampen inflationary pressure, the real rate of interest was relatively low, thus encouraging investment. A consideration of the real rate of interest helps explain why businessmen and consumers sometimes act contrary to the way the government would like them to act.

During times of extreme inflation the money rate of interest can reach legal upper limits for certain types of loans because of usury laws. If the inflation rate then continues to increase, the inevitable result is a continued decline in the real rate of interest. And as the real rate declines, there is an increased incentive for people to borrow and buy even more, which in turn adds more fuel to the "fires of inflation."

If the money rate of interest reaches an upper legal limit, then the interest rate no longer can serve as a rationing and allocating device for loanable funds. When the demand for loanable funds becomes greater than the supply, lenders must resort to other means of rationing the available funds. They might lend, for example, on the basis of friendship, first-come first-serve, or some other criteria.

During these times the people most likely to obtain loans are the very large commercial and institutional borrowers. Because of lower lending costs on larger loans, lenders often prefer to do business with a few large borrowers rather than many small accounts. Thus the people who suffer the most from usury laws during times of extreme inflation tend to be small borrowers such as small farmers, small businessmen, or prospective home buyers who are unable to obtain loans.

If the rate of inflation far outstrips, the legal money rate of interest so that the real rate becomes negative, there is a strong incentive to "pay under the table," i.e., bribe, to obtain loans. Indeed such practice is not uncommon in some developing nations where high rates of inflation prevail. Again the loans go out to large, wealthy borrowers who may be either relatives of the bankers or know them on a personal basis.

The third economic effect of inflation is that it lessens the real value of assets that have a fixed monetary value. Such assets include cash, bonds, and insurance policies. During inflation the purchasing power of these assets declines. As you know a dollar spent today doesn't buy nearly as much as a dollar spent 10 or 20 years ago. Also the face value of a bond or insurance policy remains the same regardless of the price level.

During times of inflation it is to the advantage of each individual to convert fixed monetary value assets to assets that rise in value as prices rise. The two most common assets used to hedge against inflation are stocks and real estate. This helps explain why these two assets have enjoyed a very strong market during the late 1960s.

Of course, the stock market is very volatile and the slightest hint of a recession can bring it crashing down. For people who buy high and sell low, entering the stock market to hedge against inflation is like "jumping out of the frying pan into the fire." Real estate offers a slightly safer but less dramatic hedge. Also the trend of rising real estate taxes seems to be reducing the advantage of this asset.

THE UNEMPLOYMENT-INFLATION DILEMMA

You might have noticed in our discussions of the U.S. record of unemployment and inflation that one or the other seemed to prevail during each year of the 40-year period we studied. The 1930's saw falling prices but high rates of unemployment. Except for the last two years of the decade, the 1940's brought full employment but a high rate of inflation. Again in the 1950's and 1960's if prices stabilized for a time the rate of unemployment seemed to increase. This phenomenon was first popularized by A. W. Phillips, an English economist. He found that over the past century in England whenever unemployment fell below 5 percent, wages and prices began to rise.[1]

Many economists and policy makers in government have come to believe, therefore, that full employment is incompatible with stable prices. Before we grant the divorce, however, we should learn more about why they are incompatible.

The conventional explanation for the phenomenon is what might be called the "bottleneck theory." As full employment is approached shortages occur for certain types of labor or other resources resulting in price increases in these markets. It is, of course, reasonable to believe that the economy does not "run out" of all its resources at the same time. Those that are most scarce will exhibit price increases, hence contribute to inflation.

Before we abandon all hope for a reconciliation between stable prices and full employment, we should point out that some economists are not yet convinced that we need to have inflation in order to have full employment. In later chapters we will become better equipped to analyze the issue in greater depth. At this point we might just raise the question, what would happen to unemployment if we were able to have price stability for an extended period of time, say 5 to 10 years? Most of our experience has been with varying rates of inflation with only short periods of price stability. As we will see in later chapters even a slowing down of inflation tends to cause adjustment problems that generally lead to an increase in unemployment.

Some economists advocate a small rate of inflation, say 1 or 2 percent per year, to stimulate the economy. In part at least, the argument for this is that rising prices makes it easier for declining industries or firms to "bow out gracefully." For example, suppose there is a declining demand for the output of a particular firm. With a stable price level, the firm's product would decline in price and its employees may be forced to take a wage cut. We know that the latter is not a very pleasant thing for employees to swallow. But if prices were rising slightly, wages in this firm might remain the same in an absolute sense. Then as the firm's employees see other wages rising relative to their own, many will leave voluntarily without being laid off or harboring bitter feelings.

---

[1]A. M. Phillips, "The Relation between Unemployment and the Rate of Change of Money Wage Rates in the United Kingdom, 1961–1957," *Economica*, 1958, pp. 283–300.

MAIN POINTS OF CHAPTER 2

1. Full employment is defined as a situation where everyone who is willing and able to work at the prevailing wage rate can find a job in the line of work for which he is qualified.

2. Many people who are unemployed choose to remain so rather than accept a less desirable or lower paying job. In reality these people are unemployed from their previous job but are not necessarily unemployable.

3. Both employees and labor unions tend to have a built-in incentive to prefer the alternative of laying off employees as opposed to an across-the-board wage cut. Layoffs tend to affect only a small proportion of all employees, particularly the young, the new with little seniority, and the unskilled. Hence the repercussions of a layoff tend to be less severe than a wage cut.

4. Frictional unemployment refers to a temporary loss of work because of seasonal fluctuations in economic activity, contraction of certain firms or industries, and the voluntary termination of a job to look for a better one.

5. In a dynamic, growing economy, frictional unemployment tends to average around 3.0 to 3.5 percent of the labor force.

6. Fortunately in recent years the largest share of all unemployment has been of relatively short duration.

7. Unemployment is most prevalent among the young, minority groups, and people with the least amount of skills.

8. The United States has experienced a large amount of variation in its overall unemployment rate, ranging from 24.9 percent in 1933 to 1.2 percent in 1944. In 1969 unemployment averaged 3.5 percent of the labor force during the year.

9. Although war has been conducive to a low rate of unemployment, it does not follow that war is a necessary prerequisite for full employment. Government policies that result in full employment could as well be carried out during peacetime.

10. In addition to the loss of income to unemployed individuals, the cost of unemployment also includes a reduction in the total amount of goods and services available to society.

11. The most commonly used measure of the general price level is the Consumer Price Index (CPI). This index combines the prices of many goods and services into one number, allowing us to compare the average prices of these items between years. The formula for constructing the CPI $(\Sigma_i\, Q_{0i}\, P_{1i}/\Sigma_i\, Q_{0i} P_{0i}) \times 100$.

12. Most U.S. inflation in recent times has occurred during war years because war necessitates certain government policies that result in inflation. These same policies can result in inflation during peace time as well.

13. Demand-pull inflation refers to a situation where the aggregate demand of consumers, investors, and government is greater than the productive capacity of the economy.

14. The federal government is unique among the three groups of demanders because it can create additional money to finance purchases of goods and services. Other things equal, the larger the quantity of money, the higher the price level.

15. Inflation is harmful to people on fixed incomes, lenders, and people who own assets with a fixed monetary value.

16. When lending or borrowing it is important to consider the real rate of interest. This is equal to the money rate minus the percentage change in the price level.

17. Because it takes time for people to change expectations, changes in the money rate of interest tend to lag behind changes in the price level. Thus the real rate of interest tends to be high during periods of falling prices and low or negative during the early years of inflation.

18. Figures on employment and prices suggest that full employment is incompatible with a stable price level. Most U.S. experience, however, has been with uneven rates of inflation and the mere adjustment to a slowing down of inflation can create adjustment problems that result in unemployment.

QUESTIONS FOR THOUGHT AND DISCUSSION

1. Suppose you worked for a construction company (either in the office or at the building site) and a period of slack activity came along so you were laid off. Would you search out another job? What factors would you consider in making this decision?

2. Suppose you were the owner of the construction firm referred to in Question 1. Would you prefer to cut the wages of your employees by 25 percent during the slack period or lay off 25 percent of employees? Why?

3. As an employee of this firm would you rather be laid off or take a 25 percent cut in pay? Explain.

4. "The government should not be satisfied until it achieves a zero rate of unemployment." Comment.

5. "If the government would raise the level of unemployment compensation high enough so anyone who became unemployed would not have to suffer an income loss there would be no cost to unemployment." Comment.

6. Construct a Consumer Price Index from the following figures for the year 1969 using 1960 as the base year.

Item	1960 Price	1969 Price	1960 Quantity
Dormitory room	$800.00	$1,000.00	1
Cafeteria meal	1.25	2.00	600
Books	5.00	10.00	20

7. What if any bias might you expect in the Index as a reflector of the cost of going to college?

8. During 1969 the rate of inflation in the United States was about 6 percent. What is the real rate of interest that people earned on money in savings accounts that yielded 5 percent per year?

9. "Usury laws protect small borrowers." Comment.

10. If you expected inflation to continue at the rate of 6 percent per year indefinitely would you hold your assets in a different form than if you expected stable prices in the future? Explain.

CHAPTER

3

MEASURES OF NATIONAL OUTPUT

Throughout our study of macroeconomics we will continually utilize several measures of national output. Some of these measures, such as GNP, have become well known to the public through magazines, newspapers, and the like. But the meaning of these measures and how they are derived are less well known or sometimes misunderstood.

GROSS NATIONAL PRODUCT

Gross national product (GNP) is defined as the total market value of all final goods and services produced in the economy during some period of time. There are several points worth noting in this definition. First, GNP is a dollar figure. Because of the thousands of diverse goods and services that are produced in the economy it is necessary when combining them to utilize some kind of common denominater. As we learned in the first grade we cannot add together unlike items such as apples and oranges or bobby pins and battleships.

However, if we assign a monetary value to each item, we are able to use the dollar, or any other kind of monetary unit, as a common denominator. The next question is, what money value should each item be assigned? Two possibilities come to mind: (1) market value and (2) cost of production. As the definition of GNP indicates, the Department of Commerce in measuring GNP has decided upon market value whenever possible. The decision to use this criterion is not completely arbitrary, however. For the market value of a good or service is an indication of how much the item adds to the well-being or satisfaction of society. If a packet

31

of bobby pins sells for 30 cents and a new pair of shoes sells for $30, we can infer that the pair of shoes contributes about 100 times more satisfaction to society than the bobby pins, else people would not be willing to pay 100 times more for the shoes.

One major problem of using market price as a measure of satisfaction is that not everything that is produced is bought and sold through the market. Military expenditure is one important category. In this situation, the Department of Commerce in computing GNP is forced to use cost of production rather than market price. If a missile system costs $500 million to produce, it is implicitly assumed in the GNP computations that the missiles contribute $500 million worth of satisfaction to society. Of course, some people would disagree with this assumption. To some, assigning $500 million to missiles is much like assigning $30 to a packet of bobby pins, i.e., cost of production may be an irrelevant figure.

Another major nonmarket item included in GNP is the rental value of owner-occupied housing. Even though an owner doesn't pay rent he receives satisfaction from his dwelling. However, it is somewhat easier to impute the rental value of a house than that of a missile system. Because there is an established rental market for homes and apartments, the Department of Commerce can utilize these figures in estimating their worth to society. A third major nonmarket item is food produced and consumed on farms. Here again these prices are estimated from comparable items in grocery stores.

The second point to note about GNP is that it is the market value of all *final* goods and services. Thus GNP excludes the value of goods and services produced for resale or further processing. We might inquire, why doesn't the Department of Commerce include these items? Surely the steel that goes into an automobile or the leather that goes into a pair of shoes contribute to the well-being of society. The reason for excluding these so-called intermediate goods and services is that they are already included in the market price of the final product.

A simple example will help make this clear. Consider the various stages in the manufacture of a pair of shoes. The raw material, i.e. the hide, is produced by a farmer. To simplify the example we assume the farmer is completely self-sufficient so that the sale price of the hide on the animal is equal to the value added by the farmer. Let this be $2.

In the second step, the packing plant buys the hide for $2, separates it from the animal, and sells it to the tannery for $3. But this $3 selling price must include the $2 paid to the farmer. In other words, in order to stay in business, the packing plant must be reimbursed for the original raw material it bought plus something extra for the services it carried out. And so it is for each step in the production process. The series of steps in the production of a pair of shoes are illustrated and summarized below:

Notice that the value of the final product, the $15 pair of shoes sold

Stage of Production	Value of Sales	Value Added
Farmer	$ 2	$ 2
Packing plant	3	1
Tannery	5	2
Shoe manufacturer	10	5
Wholesaler	11	1
Retailer	15	4
	$46	$15

by the retailer, is exactly equal to the sum of all the value added figures in column two. This is not just a coincidence. Each of the various steps in the production process contributed something to the finished product. Thus the selling price of the finished or final product is just an accumulation of the value added in these stages.

Gross national product, therefore, is in reality a value-added figure. Rather than attempting to decide which products are final products and which are intermediate, the Department of Commerce estimates the value added by each industry. This is accomplished by subtracting the purchases of each industry from the value of its sales, just as we did in the example above.

A reasonable question to ask at this point is why make such a big thing out of the value-added figure as opposed to simply using total sales of each industry in the country? Granted GNP would be considerably larger if gross sales were used, but as long as we know why it was larger why should it make any difference? The reason for using value added instead of gross sales is to avoid a bias that would occur through merger or consolidation of firms.

Suppose, in the above example, that the packing plant and the tannery merged to become one firm. Now the $3 sale of the hide from the packing plant to the tannery would be eliminated, reducing the sum of the sales column from $46 to $43. Consequently, if GNP were measured by gross sales, it could be changed simply by a change in the number of firms even though output (or value added) remained the same. Notice that the sum of the value-added column does not change with a change in the number of steps in the production process.

A third point to note about GNP is that it excludes "pure exchange" transactions. These include such things as the purchase and sale of securities, gifts, and secondhand sales. These transactions are omitted from GNP because nothing new is produced. If you buy a $100 stock certificate, for example, the person who sells it to you gains the $100 and you gain the certificate. From the standpoint of the total economy nothing has changed. It must be admitted though that after the transaction both you and the seller should be better off than before it; if not there would be no sense in carrying out the transaction.

About the same reasoning applies to donations and gifts. Here also nothing new is produced or created so these should not enter GNP computations. Of course, one could argue here as well that both the giver and receiver are better off after a gift is made than before, else it would not be made. But it is difficult if not impossible to measure this kind of satisfaction so it is simplest to leave it out of GNP.

A fourth and final point to note about GNP is that it is a "flow" figure as opposed to a "stock." Flows are always given per unit time whereas a stock has no time dimension. As a rule GNP is given in billions of dollars per year. It is virtually impossible, though, to imagine the magnitude of a billion dollars. If you were a billionaire, for example, and invested your money in a 5 percent savings account, you would draw $50 million per year just in interest.

GNP AS A MEASURE OF ECONOMIC WELL-BEING

An important use of the GNP figure is to compare the standard of living or economic well-being of people within a nation over a period of time or between nations at a point in time. The presumption is that the higher is GNP, the greater is the output of goods and services, the better off people are. In recent years, however, more people have begun to question whether people really are better off with more goods and services. Is the modern urban dweller living in the noise, congestion, and pollution of the big city "better off" than his forefather who lived on small farms in peaceful surroundings?

It is up to the individual person, of course, to answer this question for himself. We might, however, point out that modern man has the opportunity to choose among more alternatives than his forefathers. If the high-income city dweller becomes disenchanted with his life of affluence, he is free to reject it and move to a place in the country where he can lead the life of a 19th century small farmer if he wishes.

As soon as we consider the cost of this alternative, however, it becomes clear why so few people choose it. For rejecting modern life also means rejecting the multitude of modern conveniences that go along with it. It means, for example, getting up in the early morning in a small cold, dark house without indoor plumbing as opposed to central heating, an automatic thermostat, lights that respond to a flick of our finger, etc. It means a continual struggle with nature to provide food and clothing as opposed to a leisurely walk down the aisle of a clean, modern supermarket with a choice of thousands of items at our finger tips. It means spending one's life within a few miles of home, spending evenings in the rocking chair, playing checkers as opposed to the opportunity of worldwide travel, the theater, the symphony, big league sports, etc.

It is not necessary to elaborate further. When thinking of years gone by we tend to forget the bad things and remember the good. It is only when faced with the stark reality of the "simple" life that we appreciate the conveniences of modern society. Of course, with still higher output and incomes, more and more people will be able to buy the best of both lives. The "second" home is one example of this, where people can "rough it" in luxury on weekends or holidays.

Also in recent years, many high and upper middle-income people have decided that a cleaner environment is worth the cost of obtaining it. It is not surprising either that we don't see the push for a cleaner environment coming from the ghettos or the lower middle-income, "working-class" people who in fact have to contend with the most polluted surroundings of anyone. It is not that these people have no desire for a clean environment, but there are other things that they prefer to buy first.

The main point of this discussion is that a rich, high-output society has many more opportunities or choices than a poor, low-output society. The rich always have the choice of becoming poor if they choose. But the poor don't have this choice.

BIASES IN GNP

When using GNP to compare the economic well-being of a society over time, or between two societies, there are a number of potential biases that can creep in. The first is a change in the general price level. As we know GNP is a monetary figure. Thus with the inflationary spiral that has taken place in the United States over the past 30 years, it is clear that a dollar of GNP today is not the same in terms of real output as a dollar of GNP 30 or 40 years ago.

As an example, let us compare the years 1929 and 1969 in the United States. Gross national product as measured in the prices of each respective year was $103 and $932 billion, respectively. Because of the rise in the general price level, we cannot conclude that the real output of goods and services was over nine times greater in 1969 than in 1929. In other words, inflation biases the 1969 figure upward, making it appear that people were better off in 1969, as compared to 1929, than they actually were.

It is evident, therefore, that we need to adjust or "deflate" the GNP figures so that both reflect the same general price level. We can do this with the Consumer Price Index (CPI) that we studied in Chapter 2. For example, the CPI for 1969 was 214 with 1929 used as the base year (1929 = 100). In other words, prices of comparable items were 2.14 times greater in 1969 than in 1929.

If we choose we can adjust, or deflate, the 1969 GNP to 1929 prices simply by dividing by the 1969 CPI (1929 = 100) and multiplying by 100.

The computations follow:

Deflating 1969 GNP to 1929 prices:

$$\frac{1969 \text{ GNP}}{1969 \text{ CPI } (1929 = 100)} \times 100 = \frac{\$932}{214} \times 100 = \$436$$

Here we see that if the same price level prevailed as in 1929, the 1969 GNP would have been only $436 billion.

If we wished we could adjust or "inflate" the 1929 GNP into 1969 prices. It is sometimes easier to visualize what happened in years past if we make things more comparable to our current situation. The first thing we have to do is change the CPI so that 1969 becomes the base year, i.e., 1969 = 100. To accomplish this, we divide the original 1929 = 100, CPI figures for each year by the 1969 CPI figure and multiply by 100. The computations follow:

Converting 1929 = 100 CPI to 1969 = 100 CPI:

$$\frac{1969 \text{ CPI}}{1969 \text{ CPI}} \times 100 = \frac{214}{214} \times 100 = 100$$

$$\frac{1929 \text{ CPI}}{1969 \text{ CPI}} \times 100 = \frac{100}{214} \times 100 = 47$$

These figures tell us that prices in 1929 were 47 percent as high as in 1969. Now we can inflate the 1929 GNP to 1969 prices by the same procedure we used to deflate 1969 GNP to 1929 prices.

Inflating 1929 GNP to 1969 prices:

$$\frac{1929 \text{ GNP}}{1929 \text{ CPI } (1969 = 100)} \times 100 = \frac{103}{47} \times 100 = 219$$

Here we see that if the same price level prevailed in 1929 as in 1969, the 1929 GNP would have been $219 billion. Of course, we could have used any other year as the base year to deflate or inflate GNP. In most current publications that give the CPI, the years 1957–59 are utilized as a base period. Using a three-year average period as base mitigates the problem of any abnormalities of a single year coming in to distort the long-run trend. In a few years the CPI probably will be published with 1967–69 as the base period. The computational procedure for deflating or inflating, of course, remains the same regardless of the base year or period used. The base period or year tells us what year's or period's prices are being used to inflate or deflate.

Secondly, we can obtain a biased impression of improvement in the economic well-being of people if we only look at the aggregate GNP of the entire economy. Taking into account the change in the general price level, we see that the U.S. GNP increased somewhat over fourfold during the 1929–69 period. Does this mean that the average American was able to enjoy four times as many goods and services in 1969 as in 1929? No.

We must consider also the growth in the population. Even though the size of the pie (GNP) is growing, there are more people around to claim a slice of it. If the fourfold increase in real GNP were accompanied by a fourfold increase in population, there would, of course, be no increase in the economic well-being of the individual. A more relevant figure, therefore, is GNP per capita. It turns out in the United States that population did not increase as much as GNP between 1929 and 1969 so GNP per capita increased as shown below:

Year	Real GNP (Billion $) (1969 Prices)	U.S. Population (Million)	GNP per Capita ($)
1929..........	219	122	$ 1,795
1969..........	932	203	4,587

In many developing nations, however, the picture is quite different. In the post–World War II era most have been able to increase their total real GNP. Unfortunately, for many, population growth has kept pace, or in some cases outrun, GNP growth so the average individual is no better off than before. This is not to say, though, that accomplishing an increase in GNP has been a wasted effort. For without an increase, the relentless growth in population would have resulted in an actual decline in the output of goods and services per capita.

Governments, of course, still are interested in the aggregate GNP of nations because of its military significance. A nation with a small GNP, even though it may have a very high GNP per capita, doesn't stand much of a chance against a nation with a GNP several times its size even though the large nation may have a low GNP per capita. History has shown that total productive capacity of a nation is a more important factor in waging war than the number of people in the military. Of course, a nation with both a large population and a large productive capacity is an even more formidable opponent in war. The United States and Russia fall into this category.

So far we have adjusted GNP for (1) a change in the general price level and (2) a change in population. In the United States the unadjusted, aggregate GNP figures suggest a ninefold increase in the output of goods and services between 1929 and 1969. Adjusting these figures for a change in the price level reduces the increase to a fourfold change. Further adjustment for population growth results in about a 2½-fold increase in GNP per capita. Without these adjustments in the GNP, the economic well-being of people in recent years compared to years gone by is made to look better than it really is.

A third source of bias comes in because GNP does not include many nonmarket activities in the economy. In a previous section we alluded to the fact that the government in estimating GNP attempts to impute a value to food produced and consumed on farms and to owner occupied housing. There are, however, other things that people value which are not in GNP.

A major item is leisure time. As we know most people now work less hours per week than people did 40 to 50 years ago. For example, the average workweek in manufacturing in 1929 was 44.2 hours compared to 40.6 hours in 1969—a reduction of 3.6 hours per week. There can be no doubt that the average manufacturing worker places some value on this extra time that he has to himself but this value is not included in GNP.

Or if we wish, we can look at it another way. If workers in manufacturing were forced to work 44.2 hours per week, the measured GNP would be higher than what we now have. This would not mean, however, that society would be better off with the higher GNP. The fact that people voluntarily shorten their workweek is an indication that they prefer a bit more leisure to a larger paycheck. The wages that they willingly forego is an indication of the value of the extra leisure to them.

We should not be led to believe, however, that the United States will soon become one large leisure class, working perhaps 20 to 25 hours per week. Some people have been predicting this to happen for some time now. But the facts do not correspond to their predictions. With the exception of the period following the World War II years when people worked long hours, the major reduction in the workweek of manufacturing workers came during the 1930's. In fact their workweek in 1941 was exactly the same length as in 1969—40.6 hours.

Indeed some occupations have shown an increase in the length of the workweek since the 1930's. These include telephone and communications workers, railroad workers, coal miners, and workers employed by durable goods manufacturers. The length of workweek of construction workers and wholesale trade employees has remained about constant over the past 30 to 40 years. The only occupation that has shown a downward trend in hours worked in the post–World War II period is retail trade, declining from 40.3 hours in 1947 to 34.2 hours in 1969. But we should keep in mind here that retail trade has become a major source of part-time employment for students and housewives.

It appears, therefore, that the bias in GNP due in increased leisure only becomes important when comparing current year GNP with a year in the 1930's or before. Although when comparing U.S. GNP with that of other countries, it is still a good idea to determine the length of their workweek.

Related to the leisure bias is the bias caused by the entry of women into the labor force. With the coming of laborsaving devices in the home and increased job opportunities for women, a larger proportion of the nation's females now hold down full or part-time jobs than was true 30 to 40 years ago. For example, in 1947, about 32 percent of all women in the United States participated in the labor force, whereas in 1969 this figure increased to 42 percent. Instead of making clothes, baking bread, minding children, washing dishes, etc., more women nowadays are using part of their salary to purchase these services in the market. When these tasks were done in the home they were not a part of GNP, but now when more are purchased in the market they are caught by the GNP measure. Because of this bias the current year GNP measure of economic well-being as compared to years ago is made to look better than it really is.

The bias caused by leaving out nonmarket activities also becomes important when a society changes from a rural, self-sufficient economy to an urban market-oriented economy. Years ago rural people were much more self-sufficient than either rural or urban people are today. They built and repaired their own utensils and tools, wove cloth, sewed their own clothes, built some of their own furniture, grew their own fuel for transportation (feed for horses), etc. Even though much of these goods and services never came through the market, hence were not caught by GNP, the people living in those days nevertheless benefited from their use.

To summarize briefly, we have mentioned three possible biases that can affect GNP because of the fact that it excludes many nonmarket activities. These include (1) the increase in leisure time, particularly in comparison with the 1930's and before; (2) the entry of women into the labor force; and (3) the decreased self-sufficiency, or increased market orientation, of our modern society. The increase in leisure makes the recent GNP figures look worse than they really are in comparison with the 1929 GNP figure, for example. The second and third biases have the opposite effect of making recent year GNP figures look better than they are in comparison to years back.

The inclusion of military expenditures together with police and fire protection costs in GNP represent a fourth source of bias when using it to measure economic well-being. In the Vietnam War, for example, the federal government has been forced to devote a larger share of the nation's resources to the production of military goods than would otherwise be true. As a result the nation's production of nonmilitary goods and services is smaller than it would otherwise be.

Even though GNP may not have been changed by the war, the goods and services available for consumption or investment have been decreased. The World War II years provide an even better example. During this war military output cut much deeper into the output of nonmilitary goods and services. Here GNP increased markedly, but the economic well-being of society certainly did not increase. Thus in times of war, the GNP will overstate the economic welfare of society.

The same reasoning applies to police and fire protection, although the resulting bias is not as severe. Suppose the nation is plagued with an increase in lawlessness, riots, burnings, etc. As a result society decides to devote a larger share of its resources to police and fire protection at the expense of other goods and services. Again GNP does not change, but clearly society is worse off from an economic point of view because it is enjoying fewer goods and services than it otherwise could if the riots, etc., had not come about. Hence it would be of some help if the nation's expenditure on the military, police, and fire were taken out of the GNP figure and presented separately. We would then be given a better measure of the goods and services that people are able to enjoy. Later in the chapter we will present GNP per capita excluding the military portion of GNP.

A fifth and last source of bias that we should be aware of is a difference in the distribution of the GNP. When we computed per capita GNP, we simply divided total GNP by the number of people in the country. We obtain the same figure regardless of how GNP is distributed. But most people feel that society as a whole is better off if everyone is able to share somewhat equally in the nation's output as opposed to the case where the nation's income and wealth is concentrated in the hands of a few very rich and powerful families. The oil rich kingdoms of the Middle East provide a good example of the latter case.

We will study in more detail in Chapter 10 some of the major problems and issues in the areas of poverty and income distribution. For now, it is sufficient that we become aware that the GNP per capita figure does not tell us anything about how the GNP is distributed. We might say, however, that this problem is less severe in the United States than in many other countries of the world. Although U.S. output is not by any means shared equally, neither is it concentrated in the hands of a select few. Also the United States has not experienced a drastic change in income distribution during its history.

TWO SIDES OF GNP

Up to now we have discussed GNP largely in terms of the output of final goods and services in the economy. There is another way of viewing GNP and that is by the income that people receive for producing the goods and services. It is just the other side of the coin, so to speak.

To appreciate this dual measure of GNP, we need only to remember that every dollar that is spent on a final good or service is income to someone, i.e., for every dollar of expenditure, there is a dollar of income. Thus if we measure income we obtain exactly the same total figure as when we measure expenditure on goods and services.

An advantage of measuring GNP in terms of income is that it provides us with a means of determining who is most able to enjoy the fruits of the nation's output. Understandably, the high-income people can claim a larger share of the goods and services available.

Traditionally the Department of Commerce has divided the nation's income into four categories: (1) wages, (2) interest, (3) rents, and (4) profits. The first category, wages, represent the income of wage and salary workers. Interest and rents represent the income earned by capital (machines, buildings, land, etc.) which in turn is claimed by the owners of capital. The fourth category, profits, is the income of management for its efforts in initiating, organizing, and carrying on production.

Representing income by these four categories is often referred to as the functional distribution of income. As the name implies, this distribution categorizes income by the function of its recipients—workers, owners of capital, and management. Income also can be categorized according to its personal distribution. With this scheme, income is divided up according to the level of income of its recipients. It tells us, for example, what share of the nation's income flows to the upper 10 percent of the nation's income recipients, what share flows to the next 10 percent, etc. We will study measures of income distribution in more detail in Chapter 10 where we discuss poverty and the distribution of income.

UNITED STATES GNP, 1929–69

We now have a better idea of what GNP is and the biases that can distort it as a reflector of economic well-being. Next let us review briefly the actual GNP figures for the United States for selected years during the past four decades. The years selected represent milestones in economic activity and coincide with the years selected in Chapter 2 with regard to the discussion of unemployment and inflation. To illustrate the difference between GNP in current year prices (unadjusted for changes in the general price level), GNP in constant prices, and GNP per capita, all three measures are presented in Table 3–1.

TABLE 3–1. United States GNP, 1929–69 selected years

Year	GNP (Billion $) Current Year Prices	GNP (Billion $)* 1969 Prices	GNP per Capita ($)* 1969 Prices
1929.......	103	220	1,806
1933.......	56	159	1,266
1940.......	100	263	1,991
1944.......	210	438	3,165
1949.......	256	394	2,641
1953.......	364	499	3,115
1958.......	447	567	3,242
1969.......	932	932	4,587

*Adjusted by Consumer Price Index, 1969 = 100.
Source: *Economic Report of the President, 1970*, p. 177.

Although in recent years the United States has enjoyed continued growth in GNP, this has not always been the case. Both the total and per capita measures of GNP in constant 1969 prices declined during the Great Depression of the 1930's and again during the period of adjustment following World War II. The biases that we discussed in a preceding section also become more vivid when we consider the actual GNP figures. Note that there is considerably more fluctuation in GNP when it is measured in current year prices than when changes in the general price level are taken into account. Also, as we pointed out earlier, the long-run growth in GNP is much less when measured in constant prices and is reduced even more when measured in GNP per capita.

MILITARY EXPENDITURES

If we are using GNP as a measure of the economic well-being of people, then we ought to look also at the bias caused by military goods and services. As we pointed out, GNP may increase during war, but this does not mean that people have more nonmilitary goods and services to enjoy. We present in Table 3–2, figures on U.S. expenditures for national defense, along with the resulting GNP figures when military expenditures are excluded.

TABLE 3–2.   United States military expenditures and nonmilitary GNP, selected years

Year	Military Expenditures Current Year Prices (Billion $)	Nonmilitary GNP Current Year Prices (Billion $)	Nonmilitary GNP 1969 Prices* (Billion $)	Per Capita, 1969 Prices* ($)
1929.....	1	102	219	1,800
1933.....	2	54	153	1,218
1940.....	2	98	258	1,953
1944.....	87	123	256	1,850
1949.....	13	243	374	2,507
1953.....	49	315	432	2,697
1958.....	46	401	509	2,910
1969.....	79	853	853	4,198

*Adjusted by Consumer Price Index, 1969 = 100.
Source: Economic Report of the President, 1970, p. 177.

As shown in Table 3–2, the record of United States GNP after the 1930's is changed considerably when military expenditures are excluded. Notice that on a per capita basis the 1944 GNP is smaller than the 1940 figure and is not greatly different than the 1929 per capita GNP. Also note that the 1949 GNP per capita now exhibits an increase over the World War II years instead of the decline as shown in Table 3–1.

We should be aware as well that the growth in real GNP per capita from 1949 to 1969 has been smaller when the military is excluded. The difference between these two years in terms of real GNP per capita was $1,946 when the military is included in GNP, but this figure is reduced to $1,691 when the military is excluded.

This is not to argue, of course, that the United States or other nations should abandon all expenditures on the military. Most nations find it necessary to protect the life and property of their people from outside aggression or internal insurrection. Rather the main point is to show that the more peaceful the world can be, the more goods and services there will be for people to enjoy.

Government as a Separate Sector

Traditionally GNP has been represented by the expenditures on final goods and services by consumers, investors, and the government $(C + I + G)$. It is perhaps unfortunate that this breakdown came into such general use because it implies that goods and services purchased by the government are separate or different from the goods and services produced for the private sector. From this breakdown it is easy to get the impression that goods and services purchased by the government are not available to the people. But this, of course, is not true.

Aside from the military together with police and fire protection, government goods and services can be classified as either consumption goods or investment goods. For example, expenditures on public parks and recreation areas, assistance to the poor, etc., would be considered consumption goods. Government expenditure on roads, flood control projects, etc., would be investment goods. The main point is that the public benefits from government consumption and investment expenditures just as they do from private consumption and investment. Even though we will follow the tradition of separating government from the private sector throughout the remainder of this book, we should not fall into the trap of thinking that government goods and services somehow are lost or not available to the people. Aside from the cost of running the government bureaucracy, it doesn't "consume" any goods or services; the people do.

Net Exports in GNP

In our discussion so far we have talked about the three main components of GNP—consumption, investment, and government $(C + I + G)$. To be strictly correct we should include a fourth item—net exports. Net exports are defined as total exports minus total imports. For example, if the country sells $50 billion worth of goods and services to foreign countries and buys $48 billion in return, net exports would be $2 billion.

Again it is somewhat unfortunate that foreign trade enters GNP in this manner particularly if we wish to use GNP as a measure of economic well-being. For it implies that the more we can sell to foreign countries and the less we buy from them the better off we are. But, again, this is not true. Goods and services we use that are produced abroad benefit us as much as things produced in this country.

The effect of subtracting imports from GNP is reduced to an absurdity if we use an extreme example. Suppose we (the United States) were able to sell everything we produced to other countries but did not buy any-thing in return, i.e., zero imports. In this case we would not be able to enjoy any of the fruits of our labor because we would have sold it all abroad. Granted we might have a high GNP and would obtain a lot of foreign currency or gold bars in exchange for real goods and services, but not many people receive much satisfaction from the gold buried at Fort Knox. The mentality that views exports as "good" and imports as "bad" would have us believe, then, that gold is to be preferred to automobiles, crude oil, food, steel, radios, television sets, and the host of other products that are produced in other nations but consumed in the United States.

From the point of view of economic well-being, it would make more sense to add imports and subtract exports from GNP instead of the oppo-site as is actually done. At any rate, exports and imports tend to balance out, so GNP is not affected very much by net exports. In 1969, for exam-ple, net exports were only $2.1 billion out of a total GNP of $932 billion.

Net National Product

In addition to gross national product, the Department of Commerce computes a number of other measures of national output or income. A second measure is net national product (NNP). Net national product dif-fers from GNP in that the depreciation of capital is subtracted. Deprecia-tion of capital is often referred to as "capital consumption allowances." In a sense it is the capital that is worn out or "used up" during the year in the production of goods and services.

As we stated in a previous section, GNP is referred to as the total ex-penditure on final goods and services by consumers, investors, and gov-ernment agencies. These expenditures generally are abbreviated by $C + I_g + G$, where I_g stands for gross investment.[1] Net national product, on the other hand, generally is denoted by $C + I_n + G$, where I_n repre-sents net investment. Net investment, therefore, is equal to gross invest-ment minus depreciation. We can summarize these relationships as follows:

$$GNP = C + I_g + G$$
$$NNP = C + I_n + G$$
$$I_n = I_g - D$$

---

[1] We delete net exports to simplify the discussion.

In most years gross investment is larger than depreciation so that there is a net addition to the productive capacity of the economy. Two periods in which this was not the case, however, occurred during the Great Depression of the 1930's and again during the World War II years. In both of these periods, depreciation was greater than gross investment, resulting in a negative I_n or a drawing down of the productive capacity of the economy.

The main use of the NNP measure, as compared to GNP, is that it is a bit more accurate reflector of the net output or income of the economy. The rationale for deducting depreciation from GNP is similar to why it is deducted from the net output or value added by a business firm. Depreciation represents a cost of production, i.e., the capital that becomes worn out or obsolete. Thus we overstate true output of a firm or an economy if the stock of capital is not replenished or kept intact.

NATIONAL INCOME

National income (NI) is equal to NNP minus "indirect business taxes" (T_{IB}). By in large these are the sales, excise, and property taxes. National income is supposed to be a more accurate measure of income to labor and owners of capital because these taxes, of course, are siphoned off by the government. We must remember, however, that the national income measure became institutionalized before the income tax was very important or deducted from paychecks, so years ago it was a fairly accurate indicator of incomes to resource owners.

PERSONAL INCOME

Personal income (PI) is defined as the income received by households before personal income taxes. It is computed by subtracting social security taxes (T_{ss}), corporate income taxes (T_{CI}), and corporate savings (S_c) from NI and adding transfer payments (T_R) to this figure. Transfer payments represent income payments from government to individuals other than for services rendered, i.e., gifts. Because personal income requires four adjustments to national income, it will be useful to summarize what we have done.

$$PI = NI - T_{ss} - T_{CI} - S_c + T_R$$

DISPOSABLE INCOME

Disposable income (DI) is equal to PI minus personal income taxes (T_{PI}). This measure represents the income that people have to spend or save. In other words, there are only two things that people can do with their disposable income; they can spend it or they can save it. The Department of Commerce separates these two components of DI as well and publishes the annual expenditure on consumption and on personal saving.

SUMMARY OF OUTPUT OR INCOME MEASURES

We have in this chapter derived five different measures of output or income. These tend to be a bit confusing and next to impossible to remember but a brief summary might be helpful. Also we present the 1969 U.S. figure of each measure.

		1969 Measure (Billion $)
1. Gross national product.................		$932
Less: Depreciation	78	
2. Net national product..................		854
Less: Indirect business taxes........	82	
3. National income.....................		772
Less: Social security taxes..........	54	
Corporate income taxes........	44	
Corporate savings.............	26	
Plus: Transfer payments...........	101	
4. Personal income.....................		747
Less: Personal income taxes........	117	
5. Disposable income...................		630
Consumption	592	
Personal saving..................	38	

MAIN POINTS OF CHAPTER 3

1. Gross national product (GNP) is defined as the market value of all final goods and services produced in an economy over some period of time.

2. The market value of an item is an indication of how much the item adds to the satisfaction of society. Thus GNP is an indicator of the economic well-being of society.

3. Gross national product is the measure of value added by each industry in the economy. This is equivalent to measuring the value of final goods or services.

4. The main advantage of measuring value added is that GNP is not changed simply by a change in the number of firms in the economy or the number of steps in the production process.

5. Although more goods and services may not necessarily lead to happiness and contentment, the members of a high GNP economy have many more choices open to them than people in a poor economy. Most people, if they have the choice, choose to be rich rather than poor in spite of the costs involved.

6. Because GNP is a monetary figure, it is biased by any change in the general price level. To avoid this bias, GNP can be adjusted (inflated or deflated) for a change in prices by a price index such as the CPI.

7. To assess the economic well-being of the individual, it is necessary to look at GNP per capita.

8. Gross national product as a measure of economic well-being can also be biased because it excludes many nonmarket activities that people nevertheless value. Among these are included: (1) the value of increased leisure time, (2) the effect of increased labor force participation by women, and (3) the change from a more self-sufficient rural economy to a market oriented, urban society. The first item makes recent year GNP look worse than it is compared to years ago, while the other two have the opposite effect.

9. Increased military expenditure also biases GNP as a measure of economic well-being because as a result people have less nonmilitary goods and services to use.

10. Because every dollar that is spent for goods and services represents income to the sellers of these items, GNP can be expressed either in terms of expenditures or in terms of income. Both are two sides of the same coin. The traditional grouping of income includes four main categories: (1) wages, (2) interest, (3) rents, and (4) profits.

11. Although total GNP has grown steadily in recent years, this is by no means true for the entire period since 1929. Adjusting for the increase in the general price level and for the increase in population reduces GNP growth from a ninefold increase down to a 2½-fold increase between 1929 and 1969.

12. Substracting the military component out of GNP reduces the attractiveness of the World War II years, Korea, and the Vietnam era from the standpoint of a high GNP per capita.

13. The practice of separating government expenditures from private consumption and investment gives the impression that government expenditures are somehow lost or not available to the general public which, of course, is not the case.

14. The practice of adding exports and subtracting imports from GNP implies that the country is better off the more it sells and the less it buys from foreign countries. From this logic we are forced to conclude that gold bars buried in Fort Knox are to be desired over real goods and services.

15. Other measures of national output or income include net national product, national income, personal income, and disposable income.

QUESTIONS FOR THOUGHT AND DISCUSSION

1. "Gross national product is equivalent to the total sales in the economy during a given year." Comment.

2. What difference, if any, is there in the way a new automobile is measured in GNP and the way the antiballistic missile (ABM) system is measured?

3. "If all the husbands in the United States divorced their wives and hired them as housekeepers, the nation's GNP would increase substantially." Comment.

4. From 1929 to 1969 the GNP of the United States increased from $103 billion to $932 billion. From this we can conclude that the average person was over nine times better off in 1969 than in 1929. True or false and explain why.

5. "Money cannot buy happiness," therefore, GNP cannot be used as a measure of economic well-being. Comment.

6. From the following information convert the 1965 GNP into GNP that reflects the 1969 price level:

	GNP (Current Year Prices)	CPI (1969 = 100)
1965........	$504	86
1969........	932	100

Next convert 1969 GNP into 1965 prices.

7. During periods of war the GNP of the United States has increased substantially, even adjusting for changes in the general price level. This shows that war is good for the economic well-being of society. Comment.

8. The more goods and services purchased by the government, the smaller the goods and services available to the people. Comment.

9. Exports are added to GNP whereas imports are subtracted from GNP. We should, therefore, strive to increase exports and decrease imports because in so doing we increase GNP and the economic well-being of society. Comment.

10. Explain how each of the following measures of national output or income differs from GNP: (1) net national product, (2) national income, (3) personal income, and (4) disposable income.

CHAPTER
4
THE KEYNESIAN MODEL
WITHOUT MONEY

When undertaking the study of anything new, especially something as complex as an entire economy, it is usually desirable to begin at the simplest level possible. Then as we progress towards a basic understanding of the material we can probe a bit deeper for more detail. This essentially is what we will attempt to do in the following four chapters. In this chapter we begin with a simple "flow chart" of an economy and then briefly present an early view of how an economy might adjust to an unemployment situation. The major part of this chapter will develop what has come to be known as the simplest Keynesian model, or the Keynesian model without money. In Chapter 5 we will study the role of money in an economy, and in Chapter 6 we will take a brief look at the banking system in the United States. Then in Chapter 7 we integrate money into the simple Keynesian model to obtain a somewhat more detailed picture of a market economy.

AN ECONOMIC FLOW CHART

Figure 4–1 is intended to present a very simplified picture of an economy. Here we see that the economy consists of two main sectors, the household sector and the business sector, and that two types of goods are produced: (1) consumption goods and (2) investment goods. Some of these goods, of course, can be purchased and distributed by the government, but this does not alter the fact that these items are still part of the output of the economy.

We should not be led to believe from Figure 4–1, however, that there are two separate groups in the economy: one producing, the other consuming. Certainly everyone must be a consumer to stay alive, but at the

49

FIGURE 4-1.   Illustrating the flow of income and output in an economy

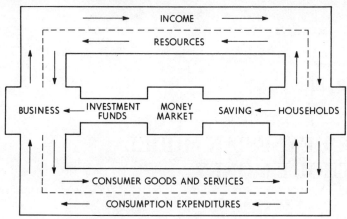

same time most every adult is also a producer. Some, those that are considered part of the labor force, produce goods and services in business places; others such as housewives produce goods and services for themselves and their families at home.

Notice in Figure 4-1 that there are two sets of circular flows. The clockwise or outer flow represents money income and expenditures. The counterclockwise or inner flow represents real resources and consumer goods and services. As shown in the upper part of the diagram, households provide resources (labor, capital, and management) and in return receive income in the form of wages, interest, rents, and profits. The lower part of the diagram illustrates the fact that households in turn spend their income for consumer goods and services.

Of course we know that people, with the possible exception of students, do not as a rule spend all of their income; part is saved. This is illustrated in Figure 4-1 by the small saving flow coming out of the household sector. The two flows coming out of the household sector represent the idea that people can do only two things with their income: they can spend it or they can save it.

The fact that people do not as a rule spend all of their income on consumption goods and services, i.e., part is saved, frees part of the nation's resources for the production of investment goods—buildings, factories, machines, roads, etc. If society insisted on spending every dollar of its income on consumption goods, there would be no resources available to produce investment goods. Thus saving is very necessary if an economy wants to grow and become more productive in the future.

The flow of saving that comes out of the household sector is funneled into a so-called money market where it becomes available to business firms to use for the purchase of resources to produce investment goods. In passing, we should note that business firms also generate part of the saving in the economy by retaining part of their earnings to "plow" back into the firms. But this does not alter the basic idea that saving provides the wherewithal to invest.

To summarize briefly, the income that is generated by the production of consumption and investment flows into the household sector where part is used by households for the purchase of consumption goods and part (the saving) is used by business firms for the purchase of the investment goods. Thus the economy goes rolling along with round after round of income and spending, at least so it would seem.

However, we have made one implicit but very crucial assumption in regard to the saving and investment flows. We have assumed that the business community wishes to invest exactly the same amount that households wish to save. But suppose this isn't true. Suppose businesses become pessimistic about the future and decide to cut back on their investment spending so that desired investment becomes less than desired saving. The result of all this is that there is a reduction in the demand for the total goods and services because of the reduction in business demand for investment goods. This in turn results in a reduction in the demand for resources by business firms so that they begin to lay off employees.

This reduction in business activity might have been avoided if households at the time investment declined would have increased their consumption expenditures, i.e., decreased their rate of saving. Generally the opposite happens, however. When people expect a period of increased unemployment they generally tighten their belts and try to increase their rate of saving. This, of course, just throws more cold water on the economy as consumption expenditures decline along with investment.

THE CLASSICAL ECONOMISTS

The problem of unemployment in the economy has long occupied the attention of economists. However it is by no means true that economists have always agreed on what should be done to avoid or alleviate inflation. In the early years of the economics profession, the predominate views of how an economy functioned seemed to be held by the so-called "classical economists," a name coined by Karl Marx.[1] Of course there were other divergent points of view even at that time such as those of Karl Marx.

How did the classical economists view the economy? To put it very simply, they believed that a market economy if left alone, i.e., little or no government intervention, was capable of generating and maintaining full

---

[1] Three of the better known classical economists include F. Y. Edgeworth, J. S. Mill, and David Ricardo.

employment over the long run. Although the classicists admitted the possibility of short-run or temporary lulls in business activity and the resulting rise in unemployment, they at the same time argued that such conditions would not likely persist. In their view a market economy contained two adjustment mechanisms that would eventually restore it to a state of full employment. These were (1) flexible interest rates and (2) flexible wages and prices.

Regarding interest rates, the classicists argued that a decline in investment and the resulting excess of saving over investment would bring forth a glut of funds in the money market and this in turn would drive interest rates down. The reduction in interest rates would have two effects: (1) it would serve as an incentive for businessmen to increase investment spending because money would be cheaper to borrow and (2) the lower rate of interest would serve as a disincentive for households to save because the income from their saving would be reduced. Thus they reasoned that the decrease in saving, or increase in consumption, together with greater investment spending would stimulate the economy and as a result the economy would move back up towards the full-employment level.

The classical economists used similar reasoning with regard to flexible wages and prices. If unemployment reared its ugly head in the labor market, there would be a tendency for wages to fall as workers competed against each other to get the available jobs. The reduction in wages would in turn serve as an incentive for employers to hire more labor and for some people to remove themselves from the labor market. The market for consumer goods and services would behave similarly. If merchandise was produced that was not sold there would be a downward pressure on prices. And falling prices serve to maintain the purchasing power of people during periods of falling wages.

Thus the classical economists argued that the economy if left alone would return to a state of full employment in the event of temporary downturns in economic activity. In the main, the classical economists did not seem to be nearly as concerned about unemployment as they were with the level of prices. We will return briefly to the classical economists in the next chapter where we present a simple mechanism they used to explain or predict the price level.

INTRODUCTION TO JOHN MAYNARD KEYNES

Up until the early 1930's, the classical economist's view of an automatically adjusting economy appeared to be the predominate view held by economists. But then along came the Great Depression. Astronomical unemployment rates of 15 to 20 percent persisted year after year in the United States. The depression dragged on towards the mid 1930's, and the economy did not seem able to adjust to regain full employment.

Granted, money notes of interest declined and prices and wages fell, but still severe unemployment persisted.

Needless to say many economists began to voice some disenchantment with the classical theory. One in particular, John Maynard Keynes, an English economist was especially influencial. In 1936 Keynes came out with a book entitled *The General Theory of Employment, Interest and Money*, which has since become a classic and greatly influenced economic thinking in the 20th century. The magnitude of the book's influence is illustrated by such terms as the "Keynesian revolution" or the "new economics."

Basically Keynes argued that there was no guarantee of full employment in a free market, "capitalistic" economy. Essentially he argued that in such an economy there is always the possibility that the "effective" demand for consumer and investment goods might not be sufficient to take off the market the entire supply that would be forthcoming from a full-employment economy.

The implication of Keynes' theory, then, is that a free market economy can find itself in sort of an equilibrium in which the level of aggregate demand for consumer and investment goods is not sufficient to generate full employment of the labor force. Keynes argued, therefore, that the government may be needed to influence or augment the level of aggregate demand so as to insure full employment.

You will note, therefore, a basic difference between the classical economists and Keynes. The classicists argued that a free market economy, even though it might experience short-term unemployment, would through flexible interest rates, wages, and prices return to a state of full employment without government intervention. Keynes put less faith in market forces and argued instead for more direct government intervention.

In order to understand Keynes' arguments, it is necessary to construct what has come to be known as the "Keynesian model" of the economy. As we said, we will begin with the model in its simplest form and then expand it a bit in Chapter 7.

CONSUMPTION AND SAVING

The heart of the Keynesian model is aggregate demand. In the traditional method of constructing the Keynesian model, aggregate demand is assumed to consist of consumption, investment, and government spending. Let us look first at consumption.

Keynes argued that consumption was determined mainly by income. This is a fairly plausible argument. People with a $20,000 per year income can be expected to consume more goods and services than a $10,000 per year family, on the average. In addition Keynes argued that as a family's income increased it's consumption increased but not quite as much as the growth in income. In other words, as incomes grow people tend to save a larger fraction of their earnings.

Again this is a fairly plausible argument. In order to maintain a bare minimum of food, clothing, and shelter, low-income people may have to spend their entire income and then some. College students are a good example. In fact most students probably consume more than their income with the difference made up by gifts or borrowing. However, as incomes rise to the $8,000 to $10,000 per year figure and beyond, families can satisfy their basic needs and in addition put something away for a "rainy day."

The figures in Table 4–1 provide a test for Keynes' proposed relationship between income and consumption. Notice that families on the low end of the income scale spend more than they earn. Then somewhere around the $5,000 per year income, a family reaches a break-even point where saving is zero. And as family disposable income grows upwards towards the $10,000 to $15,000 figures, the percent spent on current consumption declines more and more.

TABLE 4–1.   Average annual disposable income and current consumption by income level, United States, 1960–61

Income Group	Average Family Disposable Income	Average Family Consumption	Percent Consumed
Under –$1,000	$ 535	$ 1,276	239
$ 1,000– 2,999	2,014	2,226	111
3,000– 4,999	4,009	4,032	101
5,000– 7,499	6,099	5,649	93
7,500– 9,999	8,554	7,416	87
10,000–14,999	11,723	9,521	81
15,000–and over	21,929	14,208	65

Source: U.S. Department of Labor, Bureau of Labor Statistics, *Handbook of Labor Statistics, 1969*, table 122, p. 331.

It will be helpful to represent this relationship between income and consumption in terms of a diagram. As we proceed we will utilize diagrams a great deal to illustrate ideas or concepts. In a sense, a diagram is a picture of an idea. If a "picture is worth a thousand words" then a diagram is a relatively efficient and concise method of expressing a thought.

In Figure 4–2 (A) we represent the two ideas or hypotheses that Keynes put forth regarding the relationship between income and consumption. First, the upward sloping line tells us that if disposable income increases, then consumption also increases. For example, if disposable income is $2,000 per year, the consumption line tells us that consumption is about $2,750 per year. Then as we move out along the income axis, say to $8,000 per year, consumption increases to $7,250 per year.

Keynes' second hypothesis, namely that consumption does not increase as much as income, is represented by the fact that the consumption line does not rise as rapidly as the 45-degree line. (This line is so named because it bisects the 90-degree angle made by the diagram.) Notice that anywhere on the 45-degree line, income always equals consumption. Thus if consumption increased dollar for dollar with income, the consumption line would be the same as the 45-degree line. The fact that consumption increases less rapidly than disposable income results in a consumption line that is somewhat "flatter" than the 45-degree line.

FIGURE 4-2.   Relationship between income, consumption, and saving

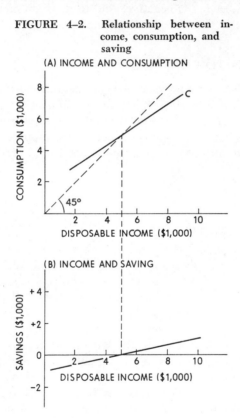

(A) INCOME AND CONSUMPTION

(B) INCOME AND SAVING

The relationship between income and consumption also tells us what kind of relationship exists between income and saving. For as we noted earlier, there are only two things a person can do with his disposable income: spend it or save it. Hence if we know income and consumption, we can easily derive saving. This is illustrated in Figure 4-2 (B) where the distance between the consumption line and the 45-degree line represents the amount saved at that particular level of income. We can, as we have done in Figure 4-2 (B), represent the distance between the 45-degree line and consumption on a separate diagram. The resulting line, call it the saving line, tells us how much is saved at a given level of income.

Also notice the relationship between diagrams (A) and (B) in Figure 4–2. At the point where the consumption line intersects the 45-degree line in diagram (A), consumption is equal to income, i.e., people spend all they take in. Saving, therefore, is equal to zero at this level of income, and this is shown in diagram (B) where the saving line intersects the horizontal axis. In this particular example saving equals zero, or C equals DI, at the $5,000 income level. To the left of this intersection, consumption is greater than income, i.e., saving is negative. And to the right of the intersection, consumption is less than income so saving is positive.

PROPENSITIES TO CONSUME

We can further our understanding of the relationship between consumption and income by developing the concepts of the average propensity to consume (APC) and marginal propensity to consume (MPC). The average propensity to consume is defined as the proportion of disposable income spent on current consumption of goods and services. It is computed as follows:

$$\text{APC} = \frac{C}{DI}$$

If we wish, we would multiply the resulting answer by 100 and express it as a percentage figure—the percent of DI that is spent on consumption goods and services. In the United States the overall APC for the country generally has been in the range of 90 to 95 percent over the past several decades. In 1969 the United States APC was 0.91 or 91 percent.

One interesting thing to note about APC is that it becomes smaller and smaller the further we move out along the consumption line as shown in Figure 4–2 (A). In the region to the left of the intersection of the consumption and 45-degree lines, APC is greater than one. In other words, consumption is greater than DI. At the intersection APC equals one, and to the right APC becomes progressively smaller than one.

You might reasonably ask at this point if disposable income in the United States has been increasing over the years, then is it not logical to expect that we would be moving out along the consumption line so that APC should be steadily declining? Yet we just stated that the U.S. APC has not changed a great deal over the past several decades. We can reconcile this apparent inconsistency between fact and theory by allowing the nation's consumption line to shift upwards over time, as shown in Figure 4–3. At any point in time we can think of the consumption line as being in one particular position. Then as time has gone by, the line has gradually shifted upwards to new, higher positions. An upward shift in the consumption line means that people are willing to consume more at any given level of income. In Figure 4–3 we illustrate the position of the consumption line for three different points in time, 1929, 1949, and 1969. The dot on each line represents about where the county was on the line during each of these three years. We will discuss, in a later section, why the consumption line has been shifting up.

FIGURE 4–3.   Upward shifts in U.S. consumption line

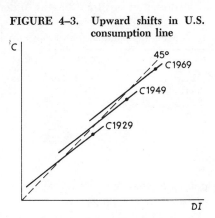

The second propensity relating to consumption, marginal propensity to consume (MPC), is defined as the proportion of *extra* income spent on current consumption. For example, if your disposable income increases by one dollar and you increase your consumption by 75 cents, your MPC would be 0.75. Again, we can express this as a percentage figure by multiplying the figure by 100. Of course, it is difficult to imagine just a one dollar incremental increase in income. Most people when they receive a raise in pay enjoy something more than this. For this reason economists utilize a simple formula for computing MPC that provides sort of an average MPC over a small range of increase in income. The formula is:

$$MPC = \frac{\Delta C}{\Delta DI}$$

where the Δ symbol denotes a "change in."

Let us employ this formula to compute the MPC for a change from one income level to another using the figures in Table 4–1. Suppose we use the figures corresponding to the third and fourth income levels.

$$MPC = \frac{5,649 - 4,032}{6,099 - 4,009} = \frac{1,617}{2,090} = 0.77$$

This figure tells us that if a family in the $4,000 to $6,000 disposable income bracket receives an increase in income they will spend 77 percent of the increase on current consumption and save the remaining 23 per-

cent. Of course, the formula also applies to a decrease in income. Only in
this case MPC tells us what proportion of the decrease will come out of
consumption and what proportion out of saving.

If you were to compute MPC for the other levels of income in Table
4–1, you would find that MPC varies between income levels. In Table 4–2
we present the MPC's for these various income levels. Notice that MPC
rises from the first to second step but then begins to decline.

TABLE 4–2. MPC computation for various income levels

Income Change	Consumption Change	MPC
$ 535–$ 2,014.........	$1,276–$ 2,226	0.64
2,014– 4,009.........	2,226– 4,032	0.90
4,009– 6,099.........	4,032– 5,649	0.77
6,099– 8,554.........	5,649– 7,416	0.72
8,554– 11,723.........	7,416– 9,521	0.66
11,723– 21,929.........	9,521– 14,208	0.45

Source: From Table 4-1.

We should also point out that MPC is equal to the slope of the consumption line. Recall from your geometry or algebra that the slope of a
line is determined by dividing the vertical change by the horizontal
change for a given movement along the line. This is illustrated by the consumption line in Figure 4–4. In this example, the vertical change is equal
to ΔC and the horizontal change is ΔDI. An easy way to remember how
to compute the slope of a line is by the simple formula:

$$\text{Slope} = \frac{\text{Rise}}{\text{Run}}$$

In other words, the "rise" of a line is equal to the vertical change, ΔC in
the consumption line, and the "run" is equal to the horizontal change, or
ΔDI here. But notice that the formula for the slope of the consumption
line is none other than the formula for MPC. Thus the slope of the consumption line is equal to MPC.

In Figures 4–2 and 4–3 and in the examples to follow the consumption
lines are drawn with a slope of 0.75, denoting an MPC of 0.75. This is
probably not too far removed from the actual MPC for the United States.
However we should bear in mind that the nation's actual MPC will depend somewhat on who receives additional income. On the basis of Table
4–2 we would expect the MPC to be higher if the low-income groups receive an addition to their income than would be the case if the added income went to the top-income brackets.

PROPENSITIES TO SAVE

Now that we know about the propensities to consume, it is a fairly
simple matter to apply these same concepts to saving. In a parallel fashion

FIGURE 4–4.   The slope of the consumption line

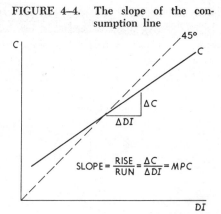

we can talk about the average propensity to save (APS) and the marginal propensity to save (MPS). As you would expect from the preceding section, APS is the proportion of total disposable income that is saved, and MPS is the proportion of a change in income that is saved. The formulas for computing APS and MPS are:

$$\text{APS} = \frac{S}{DI} \qquad \text{MPS} = \frac{\Delta S}{\Delta DI}$$

The fact that people can do only two things with their disposable income, spend it or save it, means that APS and MPS bear a direct relationship to APC and MPC. The proportion that is saved (APS) plus the proportion that is spent (APC) must equal one. Moreover, the proportion of any change in income that is saved (MPS) plus the corresponding proportion that is spent (MPC) must equal one also. Thus we have:

$$\text{APC} + \text{APS} = 1 \qquad \text{or} \qquad 1 - \text{APC} = \text{APS}$$
$$\text{MPC} + \text{MPS} = 1 \qquad \text{or} \qquad 1 - \text{MPC} = \text{MPS}$$

Also the slope of the saving line, as in Figure 4–2 (B), is equal to the MPS.

INVESTMENT

The second major component of the simplest Keynesian model is investment. Investment in this context is defined as the actual construction of productive capacity such as buildings, machines, equipment, etc. In addition, investment in the context of the Keynesian model includes a change in inventories. Thus a building up of inventories adds to total investment and a reduction in inventories is subtracted from investment. We will say more about inventory changes a bit later in the chapter.

In the interest of preserving simplicity we will assume in developing the simplest Keynesian model that investment in the economy is a set or given amount, i.e., does not change at least over a modest range of income.

The term "autonomous investment" is often used to describe this invest-ment figure—a figure that is assumed or imposed on the model. We can represent autonomous investment by a straight, horizontal line as in Fig-ure 4–5 (A). Such an investment line tells us that the level of investment remains constant over the range of income shown.

FIGURE 4–5.   Investment and income

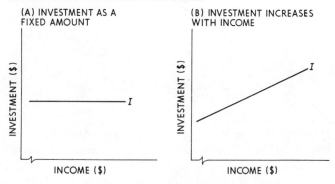

It would be a bit more realistic to assume, of course, that investment would become a larger figure, the larger the income or output of the econ-omy. This would be represented by the upward-sloping line as in Figure 4–5 (B). Although we will develop the model under the assumption of a fixed investment figure, later on we will point out how the model is af-fected by assuming that investment rises with income. At any rate, our major concern will be with changes or shifts in the entire investment line, and not so much with its slope.

GOVERNMENT SPENDING

The third major component of the simple Keynesian model without money is government spending. As we pointed out in the preceding chap-ter, we should not think of the goods and services purchased by the gov-ernment as somehow being "lost" to the private sector. With the exception of the goods and services necessary to run the government bureaucracy, everything the government purchases goes back to the people in the form of either consumption goods, investment goods, or some combination of the two. Granted the economic well-being of the population may not be enhanced by certain types of government expenditure such as expendi-ture on the military.

Again to simplify our discussion we will assume that government spending also is a fixed or set amount, i.e., does not change over a range of income or output. We know, of course, that government purchases of goods and services tends to grow with the rest of the economy. However for relatively small changes in income or output, which we are mainly interested in, it is not too unrealistic to assume a fixed government spending figure.

In terms of a diagram we could represent government spending in exactly the same way we represented investment in Figure 4–5 (A)—by a straight, horizontal line. Instead of drawing a separate diagram for government spending we can visualize it to be the same as the investment diagram, only in this case the horizontal line would be labeled G instead of I.

AGGREGATE DEMAND

We now have developed the three main components of the simplest Keynesian model—consumption, investment, and government spending. The next task is to combine them to form what is called "aggregate demand." To obtain aggregate demand, all we have to do is add these three components together.

In order to make the model applicable to the entire economy we will from now on refer to total consumption instead of consumption per family or per person. Let us assume, as is reasonable, that the overall average MPC for the entire economy is 0.75. Thus the consumption line will have a slope of 0.75. Also to be more specific let us assume that net investment (gross investment minus depreciation) is $60 billion and that government spending is $300 billion. These figures correspond fairly close to actual net investment and government spending at the present time (1969 net investment was $61.7 billion and government spending was $293 billion). The latter figures includes all levels of government spending—federal, state, and local.)

The technique of adding $C + I_n + G$ is illustrated in Figure 4–6. The consumption line represents the total amount that the population wishes to consume at various levels of NNP. (We will now write NNP on the horizontal axis instead of DI because we will be working with net investment. Keep in mind, though, that DI is less than NNP at any given level of NNP.) The consumption line is drawn with a slope of 0.75 indicating that with an increase in income people will want to consume 75 percent of it and save the remaining 25 percent. We are not particularly concerned about the initial level of the consumption line in our construction of the model because we will be mainly interested in studying the effects of relatively small changes or shifts in the consumption line and not in explaining its level at a point in time.

To obtain the aggregate demand line the investment and government spending figures are added to the consumption line. Recall that we assumed I_n equals $60 billion and G equals $300 billion. Thus the vertical distance between the C line and the $C + I_n$ line is $60 billion at any level

FIGURE 4–6. Deriving aggregate demand

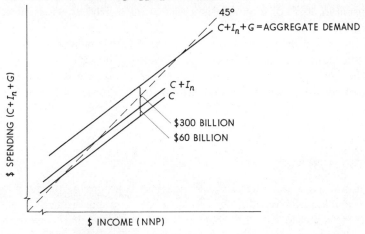

of NNP. This is because we have assumed that investment does not change as NNP increases. Similarly the vertical distance between the $C + I_n$ line and the $C + I_n + G$ line equals $300 billion because we have assumed in this example that G remains constant at $300 billion. The resulting $C + I_n + G$ line has come to be known as aggregate demand. Essentially it tells us how much consumers, investors, and government wish to spend at the various levels of income or NNP.

It is important to realize that in constructing aggregate demand simply by adding G to the $C + I_n$ line, as we have done in Figure 4–6, we have implicitly taken account of the effect of government spending on private consumption and investment. As we would expect, if the government did not provide any consumption or investment goods to the people, then private purchase of consumption and investment goods would be higher than is the case with the government included. Or looking at it another way, the taxes imposed upon the people to pay for government purchased goods and services have the effect of reducing private purchases of goods and services because taxes reduce the purchasing power of the private sector. We must keep in mind, then, that the level of C and I_n are influenced by the level of G. And in Figure 4–6, we have implicitly assumed that the downward shifts in C and I_n caused by the existence of G have already been taken into account.

AGGREGATE SUPPLY

Now that we have combined the basic components of the simplest Keynesian model and derived aggregate demand, the next step is to develop the concept of aggregate supply. In the context of the simple Keynesian model, aggregate supply can be thought of as denoting the

various possible levels of output that the business sector is willing to produce. With this model it is assumed that the business sector will desire
to produce that value of output which they expect to be able to sell. For
example, if they expect to sell $1,000 billion worth of output they will
want to produce $1,000 billion worth.

FIGURE 4–7.   Deriving equilibrium income

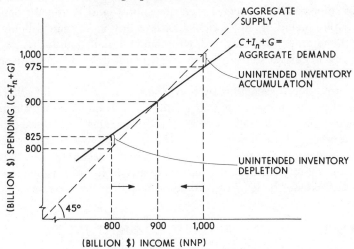

Because aggregate supply denotes a willingness to produce levels of
output that equal the corresponding levels of anticipated spending, the
line representing aggregate supply turns out to be a 45-degree line when
superimposed on the aggregate demand diagram, as in Figure 4–7. This
requires, of course, that the same number scale be used on both axes of
the diagram. In other words, when we graph the points that correspond
to equal values on each axis, we obtain a line that exactly bisects the 90-
degree angle—hence the name 45-degree line.

EQUILIBRIUM INCOME

It is important to recognize, however, that the business sector may not
be able to exactly anticipate the desired level of spending by consumers,
investors, and the government as reflected by aggregate demand for any
given year. For example, the business sector may expect aggregate demand to be greater than it in fact turns out to be. In this case, more goods
and services might be produced than can be sold. This situation is illustrated in Figure 4–7 by the $1,000 level of income or output of the econ-
omy. Notice in this case that desired spending as reflected by the aggregate demand line is $975 at the $1,000 level of output.

The inevitable result of this situation is that $25 billion worth of goods remains unsold which means that inventories rise by $25 billion. The business community, seeing this unintended rise in inventories, cut back on production in the following year. And they will continue to reduce output, or NNP, until they reach the point where they are able to sell all they produce—this point is $900 billion in Figure 4–7.

Just the opposite occurs, of course, if NNP happens to be less than the point of intersection between aggregate supply and aggregate demand. Here people (including government) wish to buy more than is being produced. Inventories are drawn down unintentionally, and the business community begins to step up production which in turn results in an increase in NNP.

As you no doubt recognize by now, there is only one point where the amount of goods and services that people wish to buy is exactly equal to the amount produced. This occurs at the intersection of the aggregate supply and aggregate demand lines. The level of NNP that corresponds to this intersection, $900 billion in our example, is referred to as equilibrium income. For at this intersection there are no forces existing to either reduce or increase the level of income or output in the economy.

EQUILIBRIUM VERSUS FULL-EMPLOYMENT INCOME

Keynes and his followers argued that there is no reason why the equilibrium level of income in an economy must also turn out to be the full-employment level of income. In other words, they were concerned that an economy can come to rest at an equilibrium that is substantially less than the income that will support full employment. The experience of the U.S. economy during the early 1930's is often cited as an example of this possibility.

This situation also can be illustrated in Figure 4–7. If, for example, the level of income necessary to maintain full employment of the labor force is $1,000 billion and the economy comes to rest at the equilibrium of $900 billion, then the workers that would have been employed to produce the extra $100 billion worth of goods and services instead find themselves unemployed. And, if there is no change in aggregate demand, the model predicts that unemployment situation will tend to persist. Therefore, Keynes argued that the government may have to take steps to increase aggregate demand in order to bring equilibrium income up to full-employment income. We will discuss how the government can change aggregate demand in the chapter on fiscal policy.

Of course, the opposite can happen if the equilibrium income is greater than full-employment income. Only in this case there will be an excess demand for goods and services which will give rise to an inflationary situation as demanders bid up the price of the scarce items.

As a third possibility, an economy could at some point in time enjoy the happy situation of being at an equilibrium income that also happened to be full employment. This, of course, is the best of all possible worlds since everyone who wishes to work is employed and there is no tendency for inflation to occur. But would this situation persist for all time to come, or even for several years? Probably not. For during the passage of time, any economy is likely to experience changes that will have the effect of shifting aggregate demand either up or down. Let us now look at some of these changes.

SHIFTS IN AGGREGATE DEMAND

Recall that aggregate demand is made up of three components: consumption, investment, and government spending. Thus a change in the level of any of these three components will in turn have the effect of changing aggregate demand.

1. *Consumption shifts.* From the standpoint of the long-run trend in the entire economy, the consumption line is gradually and continually shifting upwards over time as was illustrated in Figure 4–2. Recognizing that we are now dealing with the entire economy, we would expect the mere growth in population to push the aggregate consumption line to higher and higher levels.

However in addition to the growth in population there appear to be other factors that have contributed to the upward shift of the consumption line over time. One explanation is that peoples' consumption habits depend a great deal on what they observe around them. In other words, it is argued that persons base their consumption decisions on the relative size of their income as much as on its absolute size. As people see their neighbors consuming more, they in turn also wish to consume more.

Another explanation for the continued growth in consumption is the permanent income hypothesis put forth by Professor Milton Friedman. Friedman argues and presents evidence to support the idea that consumption decisions depend largely on long-run expected income or permanent income. Moreover he argues that the propensity to consume out of permanent income is similar for households at different income levels and at different points in time. Thus as income grows there is no reason to suppose that consumption will not continue to increase in proportion. Although the continued long-run growth in consumption is important from the standpoint of maintaining a high level of aggregate demand, our major concern will be with short-term fluctuations or shifts in consumption.

Most economists would probably agree that a prime factor changing the level of consumption is a change in expectations of consumers. For example, suppose people suddenly become pessimistic about the future, thinking perhaps that they might be laid off. As a result they might decide to tighten their belts and reduce their rate of consumption purchases. This is illustrated by consumption C_1, in Figure 4–8 (A). Here it is shown that people wish to reduce their consumption by $10 billion at all possible income levels which in turn leads to a $10 billion downward shift in the aggregate demand line. The opposite might occur if people become more optimistic about the future. An increase in consumption as illustrated by C_2 in Figure 4–8 (A) would have the result of shifting aggregate demand upwards.

FIGURE 4–8.   The effect of changes in C, I, or G on aggregate demand

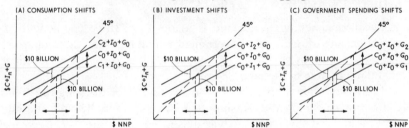

The expectation of the availability of goods and services in the future also tends to influence consumption during a particular period. For example, if people expect war to break out in the near future and as a result expect shortages to occur, some may increase their rate of purchase in order to "stock up" on items that they anticipate will be in short supply or rationed. The periods preceding World War II and the Korean conflict provide examples of this behavior. This can be illustrated by an increase in consumption from C_0 to C_2 in Figure 4–8 (A). Moreover an expectation of higher prices in the future, as commonly occurs during a war, tends to result in an increased rate of present consumption, also illustrated by C_2.

A third factor that is generally considered an important determinant of consumption is the availability of credit. As you might expect this would mainly affect the purchase of consumer durables such as appliances and automobiles. If loans become difficult to obtain, consumers tend to reduce their purchases of these items as illustrated by C_1 in Figure 4–8 (A). Conversely if credit becomes easier to obtain, we might expect consumers to respond by stepping up their purchase of items bought on time.

A factor related to the availability of credit is the size of the interest rate, particularly the real rate of interest. An increase in the rate of interest increases the overall cost of an item purchased on time. If people respond to higher prices by reducing their purchase of these items, there may be a reduction in consumption, again as illustrated by C_1 in Figure 4–8 (A).

A less obvious effect of an interest rate change on present consumption is its impact on the decision to spend or to save. For example, a higher rate of interest means that a dollar of consumption given up at the present and saved will earn a higher return and will buy more in the future. In other words, the higher the rate of interest, the more a dollar saved at the present will buy in the future. Thus a rise in interest rates increases the price of present consumption vis-a-vis future consumption because it means giving up more in the future.

Changes in the stock of goods in the hands of consumers also may affect current consumption expenditures. For example, during World War II, the stock of consumer durables was depleted because of the need to devote resources to war materials production. As a result, during the immediate postwar period consumer expenditures on these items probably were substantially higher than would have been true had there been no war. Even during more normal times, there might be random fluctuations in the stock of durable items that influence consumer expenditures.

2. *Investment shifts.* Because the ultimate aim of investment is to increase the future output of consumer goods and services, we would expect total investment also to exhibit a long-run upward trend in line with a growing economy. However, as in the case of consumption, there is also the possibility of short-run fluctuations of investment spending by the business community.

Again similar to our discussion of consumer spending, we would have to say that expectations by businessmen play a key role in the determination of investment. Because investment by definition is something that pays off far into the future, it is reasonable to expect that the decisions to invest or not to invest depend a great deal on what investors expect the future to bring as far as business conditions are concerned. For example, if investors expect a strong future demand for consumer goods and services, i.e., a high level of employment and spending, it is more likely they will decide to step up current investment spending, as illustrated by I_2 in Figure 4–8 (B). Or if they expect a period of depressed business activity and high unemployment, investors tend to reduce investment spending, as illustrated by I_1 in Figure 4–8 (B). In this example we illustrate a $10 billion change in investment spending.

A second factor that is considered important in determining the level of investment is the rate of interest. A higher interest rate tends to increase the cost of an investment project from what it would otherwise be and thus reduce its profitability. For example, consider a one-million-dollar loan. At a 5 percent rate of interest, the annual interest charge is $50,000. A 6 percent rate of interest increases the annual interest charge to $60,000. This 1 percent increase in the rate of interest reduces profits by $10,000 per year on a one-million-dollar investment project. Of course, if the general price level is rising or falling, then it is important to consider the real rate of interest, although the effect of a change in interest remains the same. Figure 4–8 (B) also can be used to illustrate the effect of interest rate changes: I_1 corresponds to an increase in interest rates, and I_2 represents the effect of a decrease.

3. *Government spending shifts.* Since government spending is included as a separate component of aggregate demand, any decision to change the level of government spending will, of course, change the level of aggregate demand, at least in the short run. Abrupt increases in government spending have come about mainly in wartime, as illustrated by G_2 in Figure 4–8 (C). Then after the end of hostilities, government spending is reduced and G shifts downward as shown by G_1.

In the context of the Keynesian model, the government spending component of aggregate demand takes on special significance because it can be changed by deliberate government edict to offset any changes in consumption or investment. For example, if investors become pessimistic and reduce investment by $10 billion, the government can offset this by increasing its expenditure by $10 billion perhaps on new public works projects and the like. We will consider this topic in more detail in the upcoming chapter on fiscal policy.

THE MULTIPLIER

By now it should be clear that a shift in any one or all of the components of aggregate demand will in turn change the level of equilibrium income. An increase in C, I_n, or G, for example, increases equilibrium income and vice versa. The next question we will consider is how much does equilibrium income change for a given change in aggregate demand? A glance at the diagrams in Figure 4–8 will tell us that the change along the horizontal axis, i.e., the change in equilibrium income, is greater than the vertical shift in aggregate demand. That this must be so is purely a phenomenon of geometry. The closer is the slope of the aggregate demand line to the slope of the 45-degree line, the greater will be the change in equilibrium income for a given shift in aggregate demand.

This phenomenon is illustrated in Figure 4–9. If the aggregate demand line were horizontal, as D_0, then the change along the horizontal axis corresponding to the new intersection would exactly equal the upward shift of the line. This must be true because the slope of the 45-degree line is one, meaning that the horizontal change just equals the vertical change.

But if we increase the slope of aggregate demand line, as in D_0', then the new intersection of the two lines moves further to the right than the upward shift of aggregate demand. In fact, as the slope of the aggregate demand line approaches the slope of the 45-degree line, a small upward shift in aggregate demand gives rise to an almost infinite increase in equilibrium income. When and if the two lines become one, then there is no

FIGURE 4-9. Illustrating the effect of the slope
of aggregate demand on the
change in equilibrium income

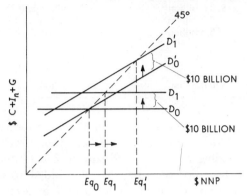

intersection or equilibrium—the system "blows up" so to speak. It will be
easier to understand this phenomenon by drawing some aggregate demand lines of your own with progressively steeper slopes and observing
what happens to equilibrium income when aggregate demand is shifted.

Recall that the upward slope of aggregate demand in this simple model
is due entirely to the upward sloping characteristic of the consumption
line. Thus the steeper the consumption line, the steeper is aggregate demand, and the greater is the change in equilibrium income. However,
recall that we could have also drawn the investment line with an upward
slope as in Figure 4-5 (B). If we would have done so, this would have
added to the slope of the aggregate demand line (making it steeper) and
caused an even greater change in equilibrium income for a given shift in
aggregate demand.

Fortunately there is an economic rationale for the large change in
equilibrium income relative to the shift in aggregate demand—it is called
the multiplier effect. To illustrate the multiplier, let us take as an example
a $10 billion increase in consumption expenditures—i.e., a $10 billion upward shift in the consumption line. The extra $10 billion spent for con-
sumption goods and services (appliances, automobiles, clothes, housing,
travel, etc.) represents extra income for the people who produce and sell
these goods and services. If the MPC of these people is, say, 0.75, they
will in turn spend $7.5 billion and save $2.5 billion. This extra $7.5 billion
of new spending in turn represents $7.5 billion added income for the
people who produce and sell the goods and services sold to the second
group. They, the third group, in turn spend $5.6 billion and save $1.9 billion. And the process keeps rolling along. These first three rounds of new
spending have added a total of $23.1 billion of new spending in the econ-
omy (10 + 7.5 + 5.6 = 23.1). We can summarize the multiplier process by
the following table:

Round	Added Income	Added Spending
One	–	\$10.0 billion = $1 \times \$10$ billion
Two	\$10.0 billion	7.5 billion = 0.75×10 billion
Three	7.5 billion	5.6 billion = $(0.75)^2 \times \$10$ billion
Four	5.6 billion	4.2 billion = $(0.75)^3 \times \$10$ billion
.	.	.
.	.	.
.	.	.
To infinity	.	. = $(0.75)^n \times \$10$ billion
	\$40.0 billion	\$40.0 billion

If we had repeated this process round after round for an infinite number of times (a task that we do not quite have time for), we would find that the added spending column would sum to \$40.0 billion. You might ask, at this point, how do we know that the added spending sums to \$40.0 billion? Surely no one in his right mind, not even an economist, would carry this process out for millions and millions of rounds and add up the total.

Fortunately we can employ a convenient mathematical formula that gives the sum of an infinite, convergent series. The formula is:

$$1 + x + x^2 + x^3 + \ldots x^n = \frac{1}{1 - x}$$

where x is less than one. Notice the similarity between this formula and the right-hand column in the above summary. In the first round the value of added spending is equal to $1 \times \$10$ billion; in the second round it is $0.75 \times \$10$ billion; in the third round it is $(0.75)^2 \times \$10$ billion, etc. If we let x in the formula equal the MPC, 0.75 in our example, the sum of the x's plus 1 equals $1/1 - x$. In our example this would equal $1/1 - 0.75$, or $1/0.25$ or 4. Thus the formula tells us that if MPC is 0.75, the total amount of new spending that will occur after the multiplier process has worked itself out is equal to $1/1 - \text{MPC}$ times the initial increase in spending. Of course we must realize that an infinite number of rounds would never take place. This is not regarded as serious criticism of the multiplier, however, because the major increase in spending comes in the first few rounds. Also the rounds can occur simultaneously as people anticipate changes in business activity and future income.

In this example we considered a \$10 billion increase in consumer spending which led to a fourfold increase in total spending in the economy. In other words, equilibrium income would have increased by about \$40 billion because of this \$10 billion upward shift in the consumption line. Of course, the multiplier process also works in reverse. A \$10 billion downward shift in the consumption line would have decreased equilibrium income by about \$40 billion if MPC is 0.75.

We could go through the very same procedure for a shift in the investment line. The reasoning would be exactly the same. A $10 billion increase, or upward shift, in the investment line would give rise to round after round of spending and respending, again resulting in a $40 billion increase in equilibrium income as shown by the Keynesian model in this chapter. Similarly a $10 billion decrease in the desire to invest leads to a fourfold decrease in equilibrium income assuming an MPC of 0.75.

We can summarize the effect of a shift in the consumption or investment lines by the following formulae:

1. Change in equilibrium income $= \dfrac{1}{1 - \text{MPC}} \times$ change in consumption

2. Change in equilibrium income $= \dfrac{1}{1 - \text{MPC}} \times$ change in investment.

Notice that the size of the multiplier in this simple model, $1/1 - \text{MPC}$, depends only on the size of the nation's MPC. The larger is MPC, the larger is the multiplier, and vice versa. For example, if MPC is 0.80 the multiplier is 5, if MPC is 0.90 the multipier is 10, etc. From an economic point of view the relationship between the multiplier and MPC is reasonable. The higher is MPC, the more people will spend of an incremental increase in income, hence the larger is the amount of income received by the people in the next round, etc. And according to the formula, as MPC approaches 1, a small increase in income to any one person or group will give rise to an infinitely large increase in equilibrium income. Of course, this is not likely to happen as we shall see in later chapters.

A change or shift in government spending, the third component of aggregate demand, also can give rise to a multiple increase or decrease in equilibrium income. Only in this case the multiplier will depend upon how the government spending is financed and the effect of government spending on private consumption and investment. If there is a surplus of funds in the treasury, say from some past year, and there is no change in C or I_n, an increase in government spending will increase equilibrium income by $1/1 - \text{MPC}$ times the increase in G. Similarly, a decrease in G decreases equilibrium by $1/1 - \text{MPC}$ times the decrease. The effect of a change in government spending becomes more complex when we consider accompanying changes in taxation, government borrowing, or changes in the money supply. We will consider these complications in more detail in the chapter on fiscal policy (Chapter 8).

Of course, in order for there to be a multiple increase or decrease in the real output of society, it must be assumed that there are idle resources available. For example, if the economy is already at full-employment income and there is an increase in aggregate demand, there will tend to be an increase in prices, i.e., demand-pull inflation, and an increase in money income but relatively little increase in the real income or output of society. Similarly if equilibrium is greater than full employment and aggregate demand declines, the model suggests that real output should not decline appreciably until the equilibrium falls below full employment.

MAIN POINTS OF CHAPTER 4

1. The fact that people do not spend all of their income on consumer goods and services allows some of the nation's resources to be devoted to the production of investment goods and services. In other words, saving provides the wherewithal to invest.

2. The dominant views on macroeconomics during the formative years of the discipline were put forth by the classical economists. They believed that a free market economy was capable of generating and maintaining full employment over the long run without government intervention.

3. The classical economists granted the possibility of temporary slowdowns in economic activity and resulting increases in unemployment. But they argued that a market economy contains two adjustment mechanisms that would restore the economy to full employment. These are (1) flexible interest rates and (2) flexible wages and prices.

4. According to the classical economists an excess of desired saving over desired investment and the resulting increase in unemployment will result in a glut of funds in the money market, which in turn will drive down interest rates. A reduction in interest rates will in turn make businessmen more willing to invest and people less willing to save. This in turn will have the effect of increasing both investment and consumption spending which stimulates the economy back to its former state of full employment.

5. Also the classical economists argued that unemployment serves to drive down wages. This provides an incentive for business to hire more people while at the same time stimulating some people to leave the labor force. Both effects serve to equalize or pull together the number of people who are working with the number who are willing to work at the prevailing wage rate. Full employment occurs when the two figures are equal.

6. The excess of goods and services in the market during periods of unemployment also results in downward pressure on prices. And falling prices maintain the purchasing power of consumers during periods of falling wages.

7. In contrast to the classical economists, John Maynard Keynes argued that a free market economy could experience prolonged periods of

unemployment, such as the United States in the 1930's, because of insufficient demand for consumer and investment goods. Thus he argued there may be a need for the government to intervene in the economy either to augment or influence the demand for goods and services.

8. The heart of the simple Keynesian model is aggregate demand which has been traditionally defined to include (1) consumption, (2) investment, and (3) government spending. Government spending encompasses both consumption and investment goods and services.

9. Keynes argued that consumption is determined mainly by income, although an increase in income does not bring forth as large an increase in consumption.

10. Average propensity to consume (APC) is defined as the proportion of disposable income that is spent on consumer goods and services. $APC = C/DI$. Marginal propensity to consume (MPC) is defined as the proportion of *extra* income that is spent on current consumption. $MPC = \Delta C/\Delta DI$. MPC is also equal to the slope of the consumption line.

11. The average propensity to consume in the United States has remained fairly constant, fluctuating in the narrow range of 0.90 to 0.95 during the past 40 years in spite of the more than doubling of real disposable income. This has come about because of the upward shift of the consumption line over time.

12. The marginal propensity to consume varies between families with different income levels. At a point in time MPC tends to become smaller the higher the level of family income.

13. The average propensity to save (APS) and the marginal propensity to save (MPS) are exactly analogous to APC and MPC except that they relate to saving rather than consumption.

14. For the purpose of constructing the simple Keynesian model it is assumed that investment and government spending do not change within at least a small range of income, i.e., they can be represented by horizontal lines on the spending and income diagram.

15. Aggregate demand is constructed by added investment and government spending to the consumption line. With this procedure it is implicitly assumed that the impact of taxation and government spending on private consumption and investment is already taken into account.

16. Equilibrium income occurs at the point of intersection of aggregate demand and aggregate supply. At points to the right of this intersection, aggregate supply is greater than aggregate demand, i.e., more goods and services are produced than are sold. This results in an un-

intended inventory accumulation, which in turn results in a reduction in output, income, and employment as the economy moves back to the equilibrium point.

17. At points to the left of this intersection, aggregate demand is greater than aggregate supply, i.e., more is sold than is produced, inventories are drawn down unintentionally, businessmen step up production, and as a result the level of output, income, and employment is increased until the equilibrium is achieved.

18. Keynes and his followers expressed concern that the equilibrium level of income might not be great enough to correspond to full employment of the labor force. Hence there might be a need for government to increase aggregate demand in order for equilibrium income to correspond to full-employment income.

19. Changes in equilibrium income occur because of changes or shifts in aggregate demand. And changes or shifts in aggregate demand are caused by changes or shifts in the level of consumption, investment, or government spending.

20. The fact that equilibruim income changes by a multiple of the initial change in spending is a result of the multiplier effect. The multiplier effect occurs because each additional dollar of spending by one person or group is additional income to another person or group. In each successive round of the multiplier process part of the added income is spent and part is saved. The part that is spent represents added income to its recipients. The multiplier for a shift in consumption or investment in the simple Keynesian model is 1/1-MPC.

QUESTIONS FOR THOUGHT AND DISCUSSION

1. From the standpoint of total society, saving is "bad" because it represents a leakage out of the stream of income and spending. Comment.

2. According to the classical economists, how would a free market economy eventually return to a state of full employment after temporary downturns in economic activity? Explain the effect of flexible interest rates and wages and prices.

3. Explain, as you would to a friend who has had no economics, the meaning of average propensity to consume and marginal propensity to consume.

4. For this past year estimate your APC. If you earned an extra $1,000 next year, what would your MPC likely be? Explain why you think so.

5. We see from Table 4–2 that MPC for the very poor is lower than it is for middle-income families. How would you explain this? Also we see that MPC declines moving from the middle- to the high-income families. What explanation would you offer for this phenomenon?

6. Show why the slope of the consumption line is equal to MPC. Does MPC change at different points along a straight, upward-sloping consumption line? Does APC change along this same consumption line? Explain.

7. Using a diagram, construct an aggregate demand line assuming that MPC is 0.80, I_n equals \$75 billion, and G equals \$325 billion. (Do not be concerned about the level of the consumption line.) What crucial assumption has to be made regarding the level of C and I_n if G is simply added on to these two magnitudes?

8. Using the aggregate demand-aggregate supply diagram, explain what happens if an economy is not at equilibrium income.

9. In the Keynesian model equilibrium income is always full-employment income. Comment.

10. Once an economy settles down at an equilibrium income, what can cause the equilibrium to change?

11. By means of a diagram, illustrate why a shift in aggregate demand brings forth a relatively large change in equilibrium income. What is this phenomenon called? What is its economic rationale?

CHAPTER
5
THE DEMAND FOR MONEY

Let us now turn our attention to the role of money in an economy. At first glance it may appear a bit strange to talk about the demand for money. After all, you might say, money is one item that everyone could use a little more of. Most of us dream about the things we would buy or the places we would go if we just had a little more money. Can we not simply say, then, that the demand for money by most people is for some amount greater than they now have?

Although most of us would like a bit more money than we now have, our discussion of the demand for money will take on a substantially different meaning. Instead we will be interested in the fraction of a person's total wealth or assets that he wishes to hold as cash balances. Although no one has complete control over the value of his assets, we are to a certain extent free to decide how much of our assets we wish to hold as money and how much we wish to hold as "earning" assets, such as stocks or bonds, or durables such as an automobile, house, clothes, appliances, etc.

Before we turn to this topic, however, it will be useful to take a brief look at some of the characteristics and functions of money.

CHARACTERISTICS OF MONEY

Perhaps the first thought that comes to our minds when we consider money is the image of currency and coins in our billfolds or purses. Further reflection might bring to mind the money in our checking and savings accounts at the bank. Of course, from our knowledge of history, we know that man has utilized a variety of objects as money. What was used depended mainly on the resources and technology available at the time. Primitive tribes that "lived off of the land" generally utilized certain bones of agreed upon animals, stones, beads, or other objects that were not overly abundant in nature.

With the coming of animal domestication and agriculture, we read of animals such as cattle or goats, or crops such as wheat being used as money. Then the precious metals, particularly gold and silver came into use as money. These examples by no means exhaust the list. It is interesting to note, for example, that even cigarettes were used as money in some prisoner of war camps during World War II.

One desirable characteristic of money is that it be made out of material that is relatively cheap to produce. For the more resources a society must employ to produce money, the less there are available to produce the real goods and services that sustain life and make it more interesting and enjoyable. For example, if the people of the world insisted on using a costly material such as gold as the only legal form of money, a significant share of the world's population might find it individually profitable to spend their time and effort producing money, i.e., mining. But from society's standpoint the efforts of these people would be for nought. The world would lose the goods and services that these people and their capital resources could have produced instead.

Of course, some gold will always be demanded for industrial purposes and for jewelry. But as we will see in later chapters the main demand for gold at the present still comes from governments as a "backing" for their currency and as a means of settling debts between countries. Gold would likely be much cheaper today were it not for this demand, and the gold-mining interests in South Africa and Russia would not enjoy the prosperity they now do.

Considering the relatively high cost of mining and processing gold, or any other metal, for money, it is fortunate that paper money has come into such widespread use. The cost in terms of resources used for the paper and printing may add up to only a few dollars for millions of dollars produced. If a society decided that the face value of its money should be equal to its value as a commodity, then producers of the money, such as miners, would have an incentive to spend up to a dollar's worth of resources to obtain an extra dollar of the money. Granted, of course, the main motivation for adopting paper money probably came more from a desire for greater convenience than to reduce costs to society.

Going further, modern societies have devised other ways to cheapen the resource cost of money and increase its convenience of use. Checking account money is a good example. Of course, like paper money, the coming of checking accounts probably was motivated more by the increased convenience to the individual than a decreased resource cost to society. Indeed, as a result of a desire for still greater convenience, money as we know it today may someday become obsolete. We will return to this topic in a following section.

Another desirable characteristic of money is that it be reasonably durable, yet easy to carry around. No material, of course, is perfect in this regard. Cast iron may be durable but makes for a weighty change purse. Gold fares rather badly on both counts. Being a rather soft metal, it is not extremely durable, and the fact that it is a metal makes it heavy to carry around. In this regard paper would have to rank ahead of gold as a desirable form of money.

Although money should be cheap and easy to manufacture, it should at the same time be very difficult to duplicate or counterfeit. Gold ranks high on this point which probably explains its popularity in medieval times. An ounce of gold is an ounce of gold. Of course, when gold coins came into use, the possibility of "sweating" was introduced. People soon found out that small particles of gold could be removed from gold coins simply by shaking them in a bag. And by melting the particles together, one might obtain, for example, 51 coins out of a bag of 50. This same problem occurred in prisoner of war camps where cigarettes were used as money. Only here the men found that by rolling a cigarette between thumb and forefinger some tobacco could be extracted without noticeably altering the form of it. Thus, some could smoke their money and have it too.

FUNCTIONS OF MONEY

The fact that money has existed as long as man has populated the earth ought to tell us that money is useful. The word "useful" in this case does not refer to the goods and services that it "buys." Rather it refers to the fundamental reasons for a society to utilize something called money. Money is useful for three basic reasons: (1) it serves as medium of exchange, (2) a standard or measure of value, and (3) a store of value.

Regarding the first use, if it were not for the concept of money we would have to operate under a barter system. In other words, each person would have to exchange the goods or services he produces directly with another person for the goods or services he desires. A little reflection will impress upon us how incredibly inefficient a barter system would be. For example, an economics professor would have to exchange lectures for food, clothing, etc. Not a very easy task if owners of food or clothing did not want to listen to economics lectures. The example becomes even more absurd when we consider what the producers of airplanes or ABM's would exchange for the things they desire. The lesson is clear: were it not for money people would have to spend much of their time shopping rather than producing and as a result society's output would be reduced drastically. Thus, if money did not exist, someone would have to invent it.

Money is useful also to measure the value or price of things. Again with a barter economy we would have to remember the price of each good or service in terms of every other good or service. For example, one economics textbook might be exchanged for a pair of gloves; three textbooks for a pair of shoes, etc. Thus each good or service would in fact have thousands of prices, i.e., the amount of every other good or service that is worth the same as the good or service in question. It doesn't take long to realize that even in a relatively primitive society the task of determining prices would be next to impossible without a common denominator—money. With money, each good or service only has one price, i.e., its price in terms of the monetary unit.

Most people like to put away part of the fruits of their labor for future use. Thus money is useful as a store of value. Without money we would have to save material objects. But what would these objects be? Obviously they could not be things that deteriorated or depreciated with time, else time would erase our savings. Also they should not be items that are costly to guard and store, else a major part of our efforts would be devoted to guarding our savings rather than producing and enjoying life. Money, of course, is a convenient object to save; it doesn't deteriorate with reasonable care, and it is relatively costless to store.

WHAT GIVES MONEY PURCHASING POWER?

We know, of course, that paper money or even coins are worth only a small fraction of their face value as a commodity. A ten-dollar bill, for instance, is worth only a fraction of a cent in the used paper market. But take it to a store and it can be exchanged for a good deal more than that even in today's inflated prices. The same is true of coins.

In fact, it would not be desirable for the commodity value of money to approach or exceed its face value. Indeed this happened in the early 1960's with respect to silver nickels. Shortages of silver drove its price up in the market until the value of the metal in a nickel coin was worth about 7 cents. It soon became apparent to some enterprising people that a profit could be earned by melting down nickels and selling the metal in the market, perhaps even back to the government. Thus money that is worth more than its face value tends to disappear from circulation.

Also as mentioned earlier, if the commodity value of money approaches its face value, it is an indication that the money is far too costly to produce. If a nickel is worth 7 cents, this is an indication that society is devoting 7 cents worth of resources to produce each nickel—not a very good buy for society.

But we are still faced with the question, why can paper money, which has virtually no value in itself, be used to purchase valuable goods and services? We might be tempted to say that the gold in Ft. Knox provides a "backing," hence provides a value to our paper money. But we should realize that the nation's gold reserves amount to only a small fraction of the nation's money supply. In December, 1969, for example, the nation's currency, demand deposits, and time deposits totaled $393.8 billion while the value of gold owned by the government amounted to only $11.9 billion. Thus each dollar of money was backed by only about 3 cents of gold at that time. Although the nation's gold may provide a certain confidence in the value of the dollar, its relatively small amount cannot provide each paper dollar with a dollar's worth of value.

Confidence by the people in the government that issues the paper money takes us part of the way towards the answer we are searching for. If people do not expect the government to exist in the future, it is likely that they will become somewhat reluctant to accept its paper money in payment for real goods and services. However, the basic reason for the fact that paper money has value seems to come down to the confidence of the people in the money itself. In other words, each of us accepts each unit of paper money as having a specified value as long as it is accepted by almost everyone else in society. Thus paper money seems to have value because people accept it as having value. If most people in the United States suddenly decided that they would no longer accept paper money as a medium of exchange, this form of money no longer could be used as such.

Of course, this is not to say that paper money always retains a certain fixed value in the purchase of real goods and services. As we will more adequately explain in later sections, the quantity of money in relation to the real output of goods and services in a country can be expected to have an important bearing on its value or purchasing power.

A CASHLESS SOCIETY

As we noted, money has taken many different forms throughout history. Even within fairly recent times we have seen a gradual transition from the use currency to demand deposits or checking account money. And within the last 5 to 10 years, the credit card has become a convenient tool for making small purchases. However, the use of credit cards does not rule out the use of checks or currency. It is just a means of paying for several purchases with one check or cash payment.

A truely cashless society would be one step removed from the credit card society of today. Each person may have to present the equivalent of a credit card or some form of identification when making a purchase. But instead of billing the customer at a later date, the procedure would be to deduct the amount of the purchase from the buyer's account in his bank at the moment of purchase. In this situation there would be little need to carry cash or to have a checking account. Bills would be paid by a simple subtraction of numbers. Similarly people would receive their income when employers or buyers of services credited or added the appropriate amount to a person's account.

Although such a procedure would characterize a cashless society, it would not imply a moneyless society. The numbers that would be added to or subtracted from accounts would still be given in terms of dollars. But the dollars would not be green pieces of paper or coins. Instead they would be just numbers in people's accounts, and these accounts would be found in the memory cores of computers employed by financial institutions. Thus the concept of money would still be used, although its form would change from tangible objects, i.e., paper and metal, to intangible numbers in people's accounts.

Whether we will experience a cashless society in our lifetime will depend upon the cost and convenience of such a monetary system. If some technical problems can be solved, particularly the problem of identifying people, we may see a gradual transition to this kind of monetary system. Thus the reason for this change is really no different than for changes in the past. The printing press made it possible for paper money to come into existence. A highly organized and coordinated banking system makes checking account money possible. And the computer may bring forth a cashless society. Of course, the use of coins and currency may still prove to be the best way to handle small, day-to-day purchases made through vending machines, drugstores, etc.

ALTERNATIVE MEASURES OF THE QUANTITY OF MONEY

Throughout the remainder of this chapter and the next several chapters we will refer often to the "quantity of money" in the economy. It is necessary, therefore, to define what is included in this quantity. In the context of macroeconomics there are two widely used definitions of the quantity of money. One, often called the narrow definition, includes currency and demand deposits. The other, known as the broad definition includes currency, demand deposits, and savings or time deposits.

Neither of these definitions can on face value be considered more correct than the other. The criterion for selecting one over the other is largely a matter of substitutability. When choosing the narrow definition, it is implied that time deposits are not close substitutes for currency or demand deposits. In some situations this may be a valid assumption. Using the broad definition implies that all three kinds of money are close substitutes for each other.

In Figure 5–1 we present the quantity of money in the United States from 1929 to 1969 inclusive, in terms of both the narrow and broad definitions. Although we observe a long-run upward trend in the quantity of money under both definitions, there have been rather noticeable fluctuations in this trend. Perhaps most significant is the absolute decline in the quantity of money during the early 1930s. Notice also the rapid increase

FIGURE 5–1.   Quantity of money in the United States, 1929–69

Source: 1929–47: Friedman and Schusitz, *A Monetary History of the United States, 1867–1960* (Princeton, N.J.: Princeton University Press, 1963), table A-1. 1948–69: *Economic Report of the President, 1970*, p. 236.

during the World War II years, the modest growth during the late 50s and early 60s. We will say more about these fluctuations in our discussion of monetary policy.

In the United States, currency (paper money plus coins) makes up a rather small share of the total quantity of money. Using the narrow definition (currency plus demand deposits), currency accounted for less than 25 percent of the total money as of December, 1969. Under the broad definition, currency made up slightly less than 12 percent of the money stock at this time.

We should point out too that the currency figure includes only dollars outside of banks, that is, dollars held by individuals and business firms. If dollars held by banks were included, we would be double counting bank deposits. For example, if currency inside banks were counted as part of the quantity of money, a $100 deposit of cash in a person's checking account would be counted once as demand deposits and secondly as the $100 in cash held by the bank.

VELOCITY OF MONEY

The velocity of money is a concept long used by economists, in fact it dates back to the 15th century. We tend to think of velocity as a measure of speed or motion. A similar meaning can be applied to the velocity of money. Here we are interested in the frequency or the number of times an average dollar changes hands during the period of a year. We know, of course, that most people do not hold all the dollars they receive as income for an entire year before spending this money. In fact, most of what we receive each month is spent within a short time for day-to-day purchases, rent, clothes, etc.

FIGURE 5–2. Velocity of money in the United States, 1929–69

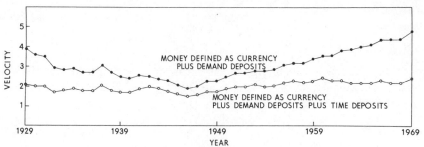

Source: Calculated from Figure 5–1 using GNP as the measure of income.

Two different ways of defining or measuring velocity have evolved.[1] One is known as transactions velocity; the other as income velocity. Transactions velocity is obtained by dividing the total value of all transactions or sales during a period of time (usually a year) by the quantity of money, as shown by formula (1):

$$V = \frac{P \times T}{M} \tag{1}$$

where V is velocity, P represents price or value of each transaction, T the number of transactions, and M the quantity of money in the economy. If for example, the value of annual transactions, i.e., $P \times T$, totaled $2,000 billion and there were $400 billion in circulation, the formula tells us that on the average each dollar changed hands five times during the year.

Income velocity is obtained by dividing a measure of national income or output such as GNP or NNP by the quantity of money, as shown by formula (2):

$$V = \frac{P \times Y}{M} \tag{2}$$

where P again represents prices and Y represents a measure of the physical output of final goods and services. The expression $P \times Y$, therefore, represents the money value of GNP, if this is the income measure being used.

Since measures of national income and the money stock are readily available, we can compute the income velocity for the United States. Of course, the velocity figure will be slightly larger using the narrow definition of money because the denominator is smaller. In Figure 5–2 we present the income velocity for the United States for each year, 1929 to 1969 inclusive, under both definitions of the money stock. We will be better

---

[1] See Irving Fisher, *The Purchasing Power of Money* (New York: Macmillan Co., 1913), chap. ii.

able to analyze the trends and fluctuations in the velocity figures a bit later in this chapter.

QUANTITY EQUATION OF EXCHANGE

From the formula defining velocity, it is an easy step to derive the so-called quantity equation of exchange. Multiplying both sides of the velocity formulas by M we obtain:

$$M \times V = P \times T \tag{1}$$
$$M \times V = P \times Y \tag{2}$$

The first expression is known as the transactions form of the equation of exchange and the second is known as the income form. We will be mainly concerned with the income form because it utilizes figures that are readily available.

The first thing to note about the equation of exchange is that it is purely a definitional concept, i.e., it is always true. This occurs because V always takes on the value that satisfies the equation. For example, if $M = 300$, $P = 1$, and $Y = 900$, then the velocity formula tells us that $V = 900/300 = 3$. Inserting the 3 into the equation of exchange we have $300 \times 3 = 1 \times 900$.

Even though the equation of exchange is purely a definitional concept, economists have used it as a tool for explaining or predicting major changes in prices and output in the economy as the result of changes in the quantity of money. Since the classical economists were mainly interested in explaining the level of prices, they utilized the quantity equation a great deal. A few examples will illustrate this point.

Consider first an increase in the quantity of money (M) with no change in real output (Y), or in V. In the initial situation below we utilize the example given above. Observe what happens when the quantity of money is doubled. If we assume no change in V or Y, there must be a doubling of the level of prices.

$$M \times V = P \times Y$$
Initial situation: $300 \times 3 = 1 \times 900$
Double M: $600 \times 3 = 2 \times 900$

On the other hand, a reduction by one half in the stock of money would reduce the value of money income by a half again assuming velocity does not change. In all likelihood part of the reduction in money income would be accounted for by a reduction in prices and part by a reduction in real output.

Of course, in reality the quantity of money is not likely to double or half over night. During "normal" times the government generally increases the quantity of money along with the growth of the economy. Thus even a slowing down in the growth of the quantity of money is noteworthy. Indeed nowadays it is considered a drastic move on the part of government to allow the quantity of money to decrease at all in absolute terms.

THE NEW QUANTITY THEORY OF MONEY

One of the major problems with using the simple quantity equation of exchange as a predictive device is the required assumption that velocity does not change. For example, a decrease in velocity can offset an increase in the quantity of money so that there may be no change in prices or output. The early classical economists tended to assume that velocity remained constant or at least changed relatively little from year to year. However it soon became apparent to most economists, particularly after the 1930's, that velocity did change from year to year, as we observed in Figure 5–2.

After the introduction of Keynesian economics in the early 1930's, the use of the simple quantity equation of exchange by economists diminished a great deal. In more recent years, however, there has been renewed interest in the so-called quantity theory of money, led perhaps by Professor Milton Friedman.[2] The new quantity theorists acknowledge the existence of year-to-year changes in velocity but maintain that velocity is determined by a few important variables. But before we discuss these variables, let us see how velocity is related to the amount of money people wish to hold, i.e., how it is related to the demand for money.

The old quantity equation of exchange provides a useful starting point. Recall that—

$$M \times V = P \times Y$$

Dividing both sides of the equation by V we obtain

$$M = 1/V \times P \times Y$$

If we let $1/V = K$, then we have

$$M = K \times P \times Y$$

where K is just the fraction of the nation's money income (or GNP) held as cash balances. For example, if $P \times Y$ is $1,000 billion and M is $250 billion, we see that K must be 1/4. In other words, people hold 1/4 the value of the nation's output as cash. Or we could say that people hold the equivalent of three months' income as cash. Keep in mind too that K is just the reciprocal of velocity. For example, if K is 1/4, velocity must be 4.

Notice also that if K increases, i.e., people hold a larger amount of money in relation to their income, then velocity decreases. Thus if we can

---

[2] See for example, Milton Friedman, "The Quantity Theory of Money: A Restatement," in Milton Friedman (ed.), *Studies in the Quantity Theory of Money*, The University of Chicago Press, 1956.

identify the major factors that influence the amount of money people wish to hold in relation to their income, we have at the same time identified the factors that influence velocity. With this in mind, let us turn to a discussion of the motives for holding money.

MOTIVES FOR HOLDING CASH BALANCES

First it is reasonable to expect that one motive for holding money is to make future purchases. By holding money people can spread their purchases out over a period of time from the date of their income. Naturally it would not be very convenient for people to make all of their purchases at one point in time, say right after payday. Instead most of us prefer to spread our purchases out over a period of time, and as a result we need to hold some cash in order to have money for these purchases.

A second major reason for holding cash is to have a reserve against future contingencies. We never know, for example, when a sudden toothache will necessitate an unplanned trip to the dentist or a flat tire on the car will require an unforeseen purchase at a service station. Hence, most of us like to have a few dollars set aside to avoid financial embarrassment in case of unforeseen situations. Also, it is desirable to have some money on hand to take advantage of exceptional bargains. If we knew in advance just how much we would spend in the coming year we would not have to hold as much in reserve.

Business firms also hold a certain amount of money either in the form of cash in their vaults or deposits in banks. From the standpoint of business firms, money or cash balances can be looked upon as a factor of production that saves on other services, particularly labor. For example, without a cash reserve, each payday someone in each firm would have to take the time to sell enough of the firm's assets, such as stocks or bonds, in order to acquire the necessary cash to pay its employees. Thus holding part of the firm's assets in cash or money also proves to be convenient for the business firm and increases its productivity from what it would otherwise be. Also firms, like individuals, may desire to have ready cash available either as a reserve against contingencies or to take advantage of exceptional bargains that come along.

COST OF HOLDING CASH BALANCES

So far we have seen that individuals and business firms hold a certain amount of their wealth or income in the form of money for two main reasons: (1) as a means of spreading out purchases or expenditures between their receipt of income and (2) as a reserve against unforeseen future expenditures. Next let us consider a major factor that determines what proportion of existing income people wish to hold in the form of money—the cost of holding money.

Offhand one might say that the cost of holding money is negligible because banks are very willing to guard our money for a very minor cost. But it is necessary to take into consideration how much monetary assets could earn if they were converted into so-called earning assets such as stocks, bonds, or consumer durables. Consider for example, the option of holding $1,000 in cash or in your checking account versus holding the $1,000 in bonds. The cash or checking account money earns zero interest. But the same amount of assets held in the form of bonds can be expected to earn interest, say 7 percent per year. Thus, in this example, the bonds would earn $70 per year in interest income. Hence the cost to the individual of holding wealth or assets in the form of money instead of earning assets is the interest income that could be earned on these assets. The higher interest on earning assets the more costly it becomes to hold money. Granted, time deposits earn a certain amount of interest. However, the interest return on time deposits may be lower than the interest return on other assets. If so, then the cost of holding assets in the form of time deposits is the difference between their return and the return on other assets such as stocks or bonds.

The existence of inflationary pressure in the economy also adds to the cost of holding money. For example, if the price level is rising at the rate of 6 percent per year, the purchasing power of each dollar held in the form of cash decreases by the same amount. Because inflation erodes the purchasing power of money, people may respond by decreasing their cash holdings during this period. In fact, during extreme inflations money becomes something of a "hot potato." For example, during the German "hyperinflation" of the early 1920's, people began to insist on being paid every day or even twice a day. Indeed, if one's wage depreciates by 10 to 20 percent from morning to evening, it pays to demand payment at noon in order to buy something that increases in value with the price level. And if inflation continues to increase the economy tends to revert to a barter system. In this case the government may have to scrap the old money and introduce a new monetary unit.

Granted, of course, during an inflation, the money rate of interest tends to rise, so to a certain extent the interest rate takes the cost of inflation into account. However, during extreme inflations the money rate of interest generally does not rise fast enough, or cannot rise enough because of usury laws, to fully compensate for the inflation. Hence inflation generally adds to the cost of holding cash over and above the increase in interest foregone.

The opposite would be true if the economy is experiencing a decrease in prices such as occurred in the United States during the Great Depression. Now money becomes more attractive to hold because its purchasing power is increasing as the price of goods and services decline. Again the likely decrease in the money rate of interest during such a period may reflect in part the decreased cost of holding cash.

A DEMAND CURVE FOR MONEY

Economists have found it useful to summarize the relationship between the rate of interest and the amount of money people wish to hold by means of a "demand" curve, sometimes called a "liquidity preference" curve. In a financial context liquid assets are assets consisting of cash, or assets that can be readily converted into cash. Therefore, the liquidity preference curve, or demand curve, represents the desire of people to hold liquid assets, i.e., monetary assets, in relation to the cost of holding these assets as reflected by the interest rate.

As shown in Figure 5–3, the money demand curve is represented by a downward sloping line. At high rates of interest the interest income of

FIGURE 5–3. A demand curve for money

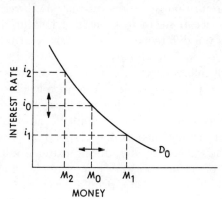

earning assets is high which means that the cost of holding monetary assets is relatively high. As a result it is assumed that people prefer to hold a smaller amount of money, other things equal. Similarly, at lower rates of interest, the cost of holding money declines, hence people prefer to hold a larger proportion of their wealth as cash or monetary assets.

More specifically, if the money rate of interest should rise from i_0 to i_2, the people in the country desire to decrease their holdings of money from M_0 to M_2. Similarly a decrease in interest to i_1 prompts people to increase their holding of money to M_1.

At the present time there is considerable disagreement among economists regarding the degree of responsiveness of money holders to changes in the rate of interest. Some economists maintain that people are relatively unresponsive to changes in the interest rate, i.e., the money demand curve is relatively "steep," at least in the normal range of interest rates, say from 3 to 10 percent. Other economists believe that changes in the rate of interest prompts people to change their cash holdings to a significant degree. This latter group would be especially prone to argue that the money demand becomes horizontal or close to horizontal at very low rates of interests, perhaps at 1 percent or less. We will see after we develop the more complete Keynesian model that the degree of responsiveness of money demand to interest rate changes has an important implication for monetary policy.

SHIFTS IN THE DEMAND FOR MONEY

Most economists probably would agree, however, that there can be significant shifts in the demand for money. If, for example, people change their preferences and desire to hold more money at any given level of interest, there would be a shift upward and to the right of the demand curve as shown by D_1 in Figure 5–4. Note that at a given interest rate, i_0, the increase in money demand from D_0 to D_1 means that people wish to increase their holding of monetary assets from M_0 to M_1. Similarly a

FIGURE 5–4.   Shifts in the demand curve for money

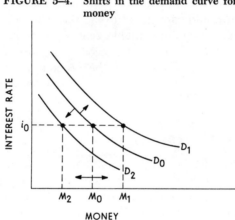

decrease or shift to the left of the liquidity preference curve reflects a decreased desire of people for monetary assets vis-a-vis earning assets. This is illustrated by D_2 in Figure 5–4. Thus at any given interest rate, say i_0, money demand curve D_2 tells us that people desire to decrease their holding of money from M_0 to M_2.

FACTORS SHIFTING THE DEMAND FOR MONEY

Perhaps the main factor shifting the money demand curve is a change in money income. In general as incomes rise people tend to increase their holdings of money or monetary assets. From our own personal experience we know that as a child our holdings of monetary assets were relatively small because our money income and expenditures were small. As a child we may have held only a few dollars in a "piggy bank" mainly for use as spending money or to save up for some special purchase or occasion. Then as young adults attending high school and college, perhaps holding a part-time job, our income and expenditures increased somewhat. Along with this increase in income, most of us increased the amount of monetary assets we held. Much the same is true for income growth of the entire economy. As expected, when operating on a larger scale with higher incomes people find it convenient to hold a larger amount of money for the purposes of spacing purchases or keeping something in reserve for contingencies. Thus D_1 in Figure 5-4 would correspond to a higher level of money income than D_0. By the same token D_0 would correspond to a higher income than D_2.

In addition the money demand curve can shift because of expected changes in future economic conditions. For example, suppose people expect a recession in the near future. Because of the increased possibility of being laid off, it is reasonable to expect that many people will attempt to set aside a bit more money to tide them over the recessionary period. This situation also would correspond to the shift from D_0 to D_1 in Figure 5-4. Of course, just the opposite might occur if people expect a high level of economic activity for several years to come. With less concern over the future, the money demand curve for the economy then might shift to the left as people try to convert monetary assets into nonmonetary types.

RELATIONSHIP BETWEEN VELOCITY
AND THE DEMAND FOR MONEY

In our discussion of the quantity equation of exchange we pointed out that velocity is not likely to be a fixed number. Then proceeding to the new quantity theory we saw that $1/V$ is simply the proportion of income held as cash balances. Now in our discussion of the demand for money we considered three major factors influencing the desired amount of monetary assets held by people. These are (1) the cost of holding money as reflected mainly by the interest rate, (2) the level of money income, and (3) the expected future economic conditions of the economy. The first is reflected in the downward sloping nature of the curve; the other two are reflected by shifts in the curve.

A change in the demand for money, either because of a movement along the curve or because of a shift in the curve that is greater than a change in income, implies that people desire to hold a different amount of money in relation to their income, i.e., there is a change in "K." But recall that $K = 1/V$. Thus a change in "K" also implies a change in velocity.

We might ask at this point, how does a change in the desired stock of money affect the velocity of money? It is important, first of all, to distinguish between the individual and society. If the individual wishes to increase his holdings of cash balances, he can sell part of his other assets or reduce spending in order to build up his cash reserves. But when we consider all individuals as a group, i.e., the entire society, we must remember that when one person increases his cash holdings someone else must decrease his, assuming that the total stock of money in society does not change. In other words, as a group it is impossible for society to increase its actual nominal cash balances even though it might desire to do so.

Nevertheless, according to the quantity theorists, the desire to increase cash balances can have an affect on the economy and on velocity. For if nearly everyone attempts to increase his cash balances by selling assets or decreasing spending, there will be a tendency for prices and output to decline which is to say that the money value of GNP declines. Hence if we divide the same nominal stock of money into a reduced level of money GNP, velocity will decrease.

The quantity theorists also point out that even though the actual nominal stock of money might remain unchanged, people are able to satisfy their desire for increased real cash holdings because of the decline in the price level. That is, the reduction in prices makes each dollar worth more, so in the final analysis people are able to achieve their goal of increasing the value of the cash they hold. Economists would refer to this as an increase in the real cash balances held by the public.

A similar line of reasoning can be employed to explain what happens when people try to decrease their holdings of cash balances. In this case people attempt to buy assets in exchange for cash or increase their rate of spending in order to draw down their cash balances. This increased spending might then lead to inflationary pressure, which in turn would give rise to a higher money value of GNP. And when we divide the same nominal amount of money into a higher money GNP, we obtain an increase in velocity. By the same token, it is argued that when prices increase, the desire for decreased cash balances is satisfied because the real value of society's nominal cash balance has been decreased.

We should point out too that many economists argue that the major disturbances in the monetary sector has come mainly on the supply side. In other words, they believe that the demand for cash balances is rather stable, except for a gradual shifting to the right over time in response to a rise in income. However, they point to rather excessive year to year fluctuations in the growth of the supply of money. We shall study this contention in more detail in the chapter on monetary policy.

CHANGES IN VELOCITY

Now that we have some idea of the relationship between the demand for money and velocity, we are in a better position to at least speculate on the reasons for the observed changes in velocity over the past four decades as shown in Figure 5–2. We should caution, however, that this is an area of considerable controversy in economics and that much remains to be learned regarding the factors that influence velocity as well as the manner in which velocity is influenced.

Looking first at the early 1930's, the era of the Great Depression, we observe in Figure 5–2 a rather sharp decline in velocity particularly in reference the narrow definition of money. Most quantity theorists probably would agree that the depressed state of economic activity contributed to the increased desire to hold cash balances, i.e., the decrease in velocity. With unemployment growing, many people undoubtedly wished to build up their cash reserves in case they might be laid off. Indeed, there is a good possibility that an attempt to increase cash balances itself contributed to the depression as people reduced their spending in order to build up their cash reserves. Thus it can be argued that there was something of a "snowball" effect in operation. The initial increase in unemployment probably contributed to expectations that led to a decrease in velocity which in turn contributed to more unemployment.

Of course, most quantity theorists probably would attribute the depression to the drastic reduction in the supply of money during this time, not the increased desire to hold cash balances. We will be better able to assess this argument after we have developed the more complete Keynesian model in a following chapter.

It is interesting to note that velocity continued to decline during the World War II years. But as we know this period was just opposite in character to the Great Depression—rising prices and full employment instead of deflation and high unemployment. On the surface, at least, it might appear that we must look to other reasons for the increased desire to hold cash balances during World War II.

It has been argued by some economists, however, that the same basic reason that brought forth a decrease in velocity during the 1930's continued to affect peoples' behavior during the 1940's—namely, economic instability. It must be admitted that during World War II many people expected the economy to "hit bottom" again once hostilities ceased. Consequently it seems reasonable to believe that there might have been a continued attempt to increase the amount of cash held by people relative to their incomes.

The post–World War II years brought a reversal to the downward trend in velocity and in fact brought rather a sharp increase in velocity at least from the standpoint of the narrow definition of money. Several explanations have been offered for this phenomonon. First it is pointed out that in spite of the Korean War, the 1958 recession, and Vietnam, the United States has enjoyed a certain amount of economic stability, at least in comparison to the Great Depression and World War II. Thus, if people feel somewhat more secure economically, they may wish to reduce their cash balances in relation to their income.

It has been suggested too that the upward trend in interest rates since World War II, especially during the 1960's, has made it more expensive to hold cash relative to other assets. As a result there would be somewhat of an incentive to "economize" on holding cash. It is not all certain, however, whether interest rates have risen enough to noticeably affect peoples' decisions to hold cash vis-a-vis other assets. At the same time, we do observe that people have been holding more and more of their money (broadly defined) in the form of time deposits, particularly during the 1960's. It is tempting to argue that recent increases in the interest rates paid on time deposits may have had something to do with this.

A third possible explanation for the recent increase in velocity is the increased use of the credit card. By being able to charge a greater share of our purchases, it may be possible to reduce our cash balances. In other words, we can make our outflow of cash more nearly coincide with paydays. Then in between paydays we need not hold as much cash on hand for day-to-day purchases.

MAIN POINTS OF CHAPTER 5

1. The demand for money in the context of this chapter refers to the fraction of a person's total assets that he wishes to hold in the form of money.

2. Throughout history man has utilized a variety of different objects as money. What was used depended mainly on the technology and resources available at the time. Money should be relatively cheap to produce, reasonably durable, and hard to duplicate.

3. From the standpoint of total society money has three main functions: (1) it serves as a medium of exchange, (2) a standard of value, and (3) a store of value. Money can be thought of as a tool that enhances the total output of society. Without money people would be required to spend a large share of their time "shopping" rather than producing.

4. Even though paper money has no value as a commodity, it can be used as a medium of exchange if the majority of people in society are willing to accept it in payment for goods and services.

5. In years to come we may experience a trend towards a cashless society where income and expenditures will be characterized by bookkeeping entries rather than an exchange of paper or metal. This does not mean, however, that we will have a moneyless society. The monetary unit will continue to be used but will change in form from tangible paper or metal to intangible numbers in the memory cores of computers.

6. Narrowly defined, the quantity of money includes currency plus demand deposits. Under the broad definition the quantity of money includes currency, demand deposits, and time deposits.

7. The velocity of circulation of money is a measure of how many times a year the average dollar changes hands. Transactions velocity is obtained by dividing the value of all transactions during the year by the quantity of money. Income velocity is obtained by dividing some measure of net income or value added (such as GNP) by the quantity of money.

8. By multiplying both sides of the velocity formula by M, we obtain the quantity equation of exchange. The transactions form is equal to $M \times V = P \times T$. The income form is equal to $M \times V = P \times Y$.

9. According to the quantity equation, an increase in the quantity of money must result in an increase in prices unless offset by a proportionate decline in velocity or increase in real output. Similarly a decrease in the quantity of money must result in a fall in prices and/or output, unless offset by an increase in velocity.

10. A major criticism of the simple quantity equation of exchange is that velocity is continually changing so that predictions based on a constant velocity may prove erroneous.

11. The proponents of the new quantity theory of money argue that although velocity may not remain constant from year to year, it is possible to explain or predict changes in velocity by a limited number of other factors.

12. By dividing both sides of the quantity equation of exchange by V we obtain the equation $M = 1/V \times P \times Y$ or $M = K \times P \times Y$ where K is equal to $1/V$. Another way to interpret K is that it is the fraction of money income held as cash balances. The new quantity theory is concerned with explaining and predicting changes in K, or velocity.

13. Individuals desire to hold a certain fraction of their assets in the form of cash in order to make purchases at times other than at the receipt of income. Also people desire to hold a certain amount of cash for unforeseen purchases.

14. The cost of holding money is the income or services foregone by not holding this wealth in the form of earning assets.

15. The demand curve for money represents the relationship between the cost of holding money, denoted by the money rate of interest, and the amount that people wish to hold. It is a downward sloping line implying that as the cost of holding cash diminishes people will be willing to hold larger quantities.

16. Shifts in the demand for money may occur as the result of changes in income or changes in expected economic conditions. For example, as

incomes rise, the money demand curve tends to shift to the right, meaning that people wish to hold a larger amount of money at a given interest rate. Also if people expect "hard times" in the future they tend to increase their holdings of money in anticipation of reduced future income.

17. An increase or shift to the right of the money demand curve over and above any increase in income implies that people wish to hold a larger amount of cash balances relative to their income. This is equivalent to an increase in K or a decrease in velocity.

QUESTIONS FOR THOUGHT AND DISCUSSION

1. Suppose you find yourself as a Peace Corps worker among a primitive Indian tribe in the Andes mountains. Assume that the tribe has virtually no contact with the outside world. Also suppose that all exchange transactions between the members of the tribe take place by barter, i.e., the tribe has never used money.

   a)   If you wished to persuade the tribe to adopt the use of money, what arguments could you use? Would it be sufficient just to convince the tribal leaders?

   b)   What objects would you suggest as possible monies? Why?

   c)   Would there be a need for different denominations?

   d)   Who, if anyone, should control the quantity to be used? Why should it be controlled?

2. "Since the love of money is the root of all evil, society would be better off without money." Comment.

3. Explain the difference between a "cashless" society and a "moneyless" society.

4. Explain the meaning of velocity of circulation. Also explain the difference between transactions velocity and income velocity.

5. What is the relationship between the velocity formula and the quantity equation of exchange?

6. According to the equation of exchange, what happens in an economy if the quantity of money is increased more rapidly than the growth in real output? What assumptions did you make about the components of the equation of exchange to make this prediction? Is there any evidence in U.S. history to support this prediction?

7. What happens in an economy if the quantity of money is reduced in absolute terms? What must you assume about the quantity equation to make this prediction? Is there any evidence in recent history to support this prediction?

8. "The quantity equation can be criticized because the two sides of the equation may not always be equal." Comment.

9. What was your annual money income last year? How much money on the average did you hold as currency, demand deposits, and time deposits?

What was your income velocity? How does this compare to the overall U.S. average?

10. Have you increased the average amount of cash balances you hold during the year since you graduated from high school? Is your present income velocity different than what it was during your high school years? If so can you explain why?

11. *a)* What does the money demand curve show?
    b) What is the meaning of a shift in this curve?
    c) What factors tend to shift the curve?

13. Explain the relationship between shifts in the money demand curve and changes in velocity.

CHAPTER 6

THE SUPPLY OF MONEY

In Chapter 5 we were concerned mainly with the amount of money people wish to hold given certain conditions such as prevailing interest rates, incomes, and expectations of future economic activity. In this chapter we will be concerned mainly with the actual supply of money in the economy and how this supply is changed. We will see that the commercial banking system is the primary vehicle for changing the quantity of money. And we will see also that the Federal Reserve System has the power to influence the actions of commercial banks.

Because commercial banks and the Federal Reserve System play such vital roles in determining the money supply, it will be useful to become better acquainted with their structures and functions. However, in our study of the banking system we will utilize the balance sheet a great deal. So before we undertake our discussion of banking let us first review this important accounting tool.

THE BALANCE SHEET

Basically the balance sheet itemizes the assets, liabilities, and net worth of a person, firm, or institution as of a particular point in time. Assets can be defined as anything of value. A person's assets typically would include clothes, car, real estate, appliances, cash, stocks, bonds, etc. A business firm's balance sheet would include mainly the real estate and capital equipment that the firm has under its control, together with its monetary assets such as cash and bank deposits. A commercial bank's assets include many of the same items found in an ordinary business firm. There are some special items among a bank's assets, however, that will come to our attention later.

We should be aware, though, that the asset value of a particular item does not tell us anything about who has ultimate claim on the item. For example, if you "own" a $1,000 automobile but have $500 yet to pay on it, you have a $500 claim on the auto and the lender has a $500 claim. The balance sheet would carry the auto as a $1,000 asset regardless of how much you still owed on it. For this reason it is necessary to know the amount of liabilities and net worth also.

The liability figures in a balance sheet indicate the amount owed to creditors. Sometimes the balance sheet will separate "short-term" from long-term liabilities to indicate how soon the debts will have to be paid. For our purposes it will be sufficient to know just that liabilities are debts that will have to be paid sometime in the future. Net worth represents the amount of the assets owned free and clear by the individual(s) controlling the assets. Essentially we can view liabilities as the creditors claim to the assets in a balance sheet and net worth as the "owners" claim to these assets.

As its name implies the balance sheet must always balance, that is, the total value of assets must always equal the total claim on these assets. We are assured that assets always equal liabilities plus net worth because the net worth figure is obtained as a residual by subtracting liabilities from assets. These relationships are summarized below:

Assets   = Liabilities + Net Worth
Net Worth = Assets − Liabilities

A convenient method of presenting the balance sheet is in the form of a T-account. With this format assets are listed on the left-hand side of the vertical line and liabilities and net worth on the right-hand side. The following example illustrates the format of a T-account balance sheet and some typical entries for a college student. Notice that the balance sheet is drawn up at a particular point in time. Typically business firms or institutions compute their balances at the end of the calendar year or end of their fiscal year. The asset figures should reflect the current market value of the items listed, $1,500 in this example. The unpaid balances of two loans outstanding represent the liabilities of the student, $500 in this example. The $1,000 net worth figure is found by subtracting the $500 in liabilities from the $1,500 assets total.

**Balance sheet of a college student
as of a point in time**

ASSETS		LIABILITIES + NET WORTH	
Automobile	$1,000	Bank loan	$ 300
Typewriter	100	Loan from parents	200
Clothes	400	Net worth	1,000
	$1,500		$1,500

EVOLUTION OF BANKING

Equipped with this knowledge of the balance sheet, we now are ready to take a closer look at banks and banking. Of course, banks, as most of our institutions, did not suddenly appear in their present form. Therefore, let us consider briefly how the early banks probably came into existence.

During the early period of civilization, gold and silver were the predominate forms of money. Those who were fortunate enough to accumulate a sizable amount of these metals were confronted with the problem of keeping it safe from those who were bent on redistributing the wealth of the land, i.e., thieves and robbers. It should not be surprising then that the ancient goldsmith emerged as the person best able to store money for safekeeping. Since the basic raw material used in his business had to be closely guarded anyway, the goldsmith, no doubt, found it profitable to take in other people's gold for safekeeping in return for a fee. Of course, at the time of deposit the customer was given a receipt indicating the date and amount of deposit. Understandably this receipt had to be presented when the depositor wished to reclaim his gold.

In providing a storage service the goldsmith's place of business became, in effect, a warehouse for gold. It also became the forerunner of the modern bank. The goldsmiths accepted deposits of money and paid it out again on demand. But this describes in large part the activities of a modern bank. However, present-day banks also make loans. Let us see how this activity might have emerged.

It probably didn't take long for the more preceptive goldsmiths to discover that during any one day the gold withdrawn was in large part offset by the gold deposited. During some days withdrawals may have exceeded deposits by a small amount, or vice versa. But on any given day, the goldsmith was not likely to have all his gold withdrawn, unless his reputation suddenly became suspect. We know too that gold is a completely homogenous commodity, that is, an ounce of gold is an ounce of gold no matter who deposits it. Hence the actual gold that was withdrawn during any one day probably was the same gold that had come in through deposits on that very day or the day before. After all, because gold is homogeneous there would be no need for the goldsmith to dig to the bottom or to the back of his vault to locate gold deposited months or years before. At any rate, the perceptive goldsmith undoubtedly noticed that a relatively large share of his gold deposits was lying in his vault gathering dust.

Let us say, for example, that only about 20 percent of his gold was actively used to pay withdrawals on days when deposits were unusually low. For all practical purposes the remaining 80 percent of the gold was never used. In fact it no doubt was considered a hindrance since it required more space and provided a greater temptation for would-be robbers.

There always have been people who were in need of loans for various and sundry purposes. Without people or institutions that specialized in making loans, borrowers had to prevail upon friends or relatives. For the very poor who had only poor friends and poor relatives there wasn't much chance of obtaining credit. It took people awhile to get used to the idea of paying interest, however. And without interest to compensate for waiting and for the risk involved, there isn't much incentive to lend money.

Once the payment of interest, in one form or another, became socially acceptable, the goldsmiths discovered a grand opportunity to benefit both themselves and their customers. By lending out some of this unused gold they provided a source of credit for people who wanted to make a fairly large purchase, such as a house or a cart. These people were certainly helped because the loans, no doubt, enabled many of them to purchase resources that increased their earning power and standard of living, just as is true today. The goldsmith benefited because of the interest income that he earned from his loans. Finally, his depositors benefited because they could now be paid for depositing gold rather than having to pay for the storage service.

So far we have followed the evaluation of banking through two steps. First, institutions evolved to satisfy the demand for storage services by people who had accumulated money. Secondly, these institutions, goldsmiths in the main, discovered that daily deposits and withdrawals normally came close to canceling each other out. Thus goldsmiths could lend out part of their deposits, keeping only a part on reserve. Today we refer to this procedure as fractional reserve banking.

It will be helpful to represent each of these steps on a balance sheet. To simplify the procedure we will ignore the items not directly connected with the transactions we are interested in, such as the assets representing physical facilities and net worth. The balance sheet on the left below represents the deposit of $1,000 in gold. (In ancient times, of course, the dollar had not been conceived, but we will use it in our example because it is the monetary unit most familiar to us.) The physical commodity gold becomes an asset to the goldsmith because it is now under his control. On the right-hand side of the T-account we must represent the claims to this gold. Since the gold was owned entirely by the depositors, the entire claim to the gold is represented by the receipts given out by the goldsmith. These receipts, therefore, were liabilities to the goldsmith because he eventually was called upon to pay out this amount in gold.

The right-hand balance sheet illustrates the lending out of part of the gold on deposit. In this example we show a $500 loan. The IOU, promissory note, or whatever the borrower gave the goldsmith at the time the loan was made, becomes an asset to the goldsmith. This is offset on the asset side by a $500 reduction in the gold item because it is taken out by the borrower. Note that total assets remain unchanged at $1,000, just the form is changed. The liabilities side remains unchanged in both form and total.

Deposit of $1,000 in gold		Lending $500 of the original $1,000 deposit	
ASSETS	LIABILITIES + NET WORTH	ASSETS	LIABILITIES + NET WORTH
Gold $1,000	Receipts $1,000	Gold $ 500	Receipts $1,000
		IOUs 500	
		$1,000	$1,000

An additional step towards banking as we know it today was taken when depositors began to use their deposit receipts as money. It is fairly easy to see how this practice came into being. Visualize yourself as living in that time with say $50 of gold on deposit at the local goldsmith. Suppose that you decided to trade in your old chariot for the latest model. Suppose also that the new chariot cost you $50 in gold plus your trade-in. You could, of course, make a trip to the goldsmith to draw out your $50 in gold. But the chariot dealer would just have to return to the goldsmith the same day with the same gold for redeposit. Both you and the chariot dealer could save a trip to the goldsmith if you just endorsed your deposit receipt over to the chariot dealer instructing the goldsmith to pay him the $50 on demand.

The practice of exchanging deposit receipts instead of gold resembles a well-known practice in use today—namely that of exchanging checks instead of the actual currency on deposit in banks. Thus the deposit receipt was the forerunner of the present-day check. Of course, the check is a bit more convenient because it can be made out in any denomination. Eventually people discovered this, and as a result deposit receipts were made more flexible. Also with more widespread use, receipts or checks became a widely accepted form of money.

So far we have taken the goldsmith up to the point where it is just one step removed from the modern bank. The evolutionary process became complete when goldsmiths began to give out deposit receipts instead of gold when making loans. It is easy to visualize how this practice got started. Suppose in the $500 loan example that the people who took out these loans turned around and immediately redeposited the gold in the goldsmith's vault. The goldsmith then would have to give these people deposit receipts. After all we would not expect borrowers to want to carry gold around any more than the people who originally deposited it. Moreover, as deposit receipts became a commonly accepted form of money it would be foolish to risk losing the gold that had been borrowed when pieces of paper would serve the same purpose.

Of course, for borrowers who did not want to take the gold with them, it was natural that the physical removal and immediate redeposit of gold at the time loans were transacted should be eliminated. Now all the goldsmith had to do was fill out a deposit receipt that borrowers could take with them. Notice, however, that this procedure results in a somewhat different balance sheet than resulted in the more primitive loan transaction shown earlier where the borrower took the gold with him. The following balance sheet illustrates the case where $500 of the original $1,000 deposit was loaned out but instead of physically removing the gold borrowers accepted deposit receipts instead.

Lending out $500 of the original $1,000 deposit
and issuing deposit receipts to the borrowers

ASSETS		LIABILITIES + NET WORTH	
Gold	$1,000	Receipts to depositors	$1,000
IOUs	500	Receipts to borrowers	500
	$1,500		$1,500

Notice here that if receipts to borrowers are considered money, then the goldsmith, or lending institution, in fact creates money by making loans and issuing these receipts. We will discuss this phenomenon in more detail just a bit later when we look at the transactions of a modern commercial bank.

We have now taken the goldsmith up to the point where he was doing essentially the same things as the modern commercial bank. First, he took in deposits, second he made loans, and third he issued and honored deposit receipts that in effect became money. In order to complete the evolutionary process from the goldsmith to the modern commercial bank, we must next consider the central banking system called the Federal Reserve System in the United States. All of the principal nations of the world have a central banking system. Some examples include the Bank of England, the Bank of France, and the Bank of Canada, each serving its respective nation.

THE FEDERAL RESERVE SYSTEM

Throughout the 19th and early 20th centuries the United States economy suffered from rather large and frequent ups and downs in economic activity. Following the panic of 1907, Congress became convinced that a major cause of the country's financial woes came from the country's decentralized banking system. At the time the banking system was comprised of thousands of private commercial banks each operating as a business, namely to make a profit.

It became evident that rational, profit-maximizing behavior of each commercial bank operating on its own was not conducive to stability of the total economy. For example, during expansionary periods banks faced a strong demand for their loans. As a result banks obliged by increasing loans. But as we will see shortly, this action increased the money supply which augmented the boom and ensuing inflation. On the other hand, during recessionary periods, banks along with businessmen became pessimistic about the future, and as a result reduced their loans outstanding. This in turn reduced the money supply which contributed to a still further reduction in economic activity.

Also during certain periods within the year the banking community experienced shortages and surpluses of money. For example, during the Christmas shopping season the volume of business activity tends to rise substantially. Recall from the preceding chapter that an increase in income or GNP shifts the demand for money to the right reflecting the increased volume of transactions. Unless there is a corresponding increase in its supply, money becomes "scarce" and interest rates rise. As a result there may be an unnecessary curtailment of economic activity. Similarly during slack periods of the year, mainly during the first quarter, the supply of money that would fulfill the demand without a rise in interest rates during the peak season would be too large resulting in unnecessary instability in the money market.

Because of these seasonal fluctuations in the demand for money, it became clear that the country also needed an agency that could provide an "elastic" currency, that is, a money supply that could expand and contract with the seasonal fluctuations in the economy. Thus the need for a central bank became evident because of the "perverse elasticity" of money that accentuated booms and recessions, and also because of the need for a greater elasticity of the money supply during peak and slack periods within the year.

Thus on December 23, 1913, President Woodrow Wilson signed the Federal Reserve Act which brought into being the Federal Reserve System. Understandably there was a great deal of reluctance on the part of bankers to create a strong, centralized banking authority located in Washington or New York. Yet the inadequacy of a completely decentralized banking system was evident. As a result the Federal Reserve System was set up as somewhat of a compromise between a powerful government bank such as the Bank of England or Bank of France and a totally private banking system.[1]

To maintain some form of decentralization, the country was divided into 12 Federal Reserve districts each having a Federal Reserve Bank.

---

[1]For a detailed description of the Federal Reserve System and its functions, see Board of Governors of the Federal Reserve System, *The Federal Reserve System: Purposes and Functions.*

Several of the Federal Reserve banks have one or more branches located in other cities of the district. The Federal Reserve System is supervised by a seven-member Board of Governors located in Washington, D.C. The Board of Governors are assisted by a Federal Advisory Council and a Federal Open-Market Committee. As the name implies the Advisory Council advises the Board of Governors on monetary policy. The Open Market Committee buys and sells securities which as we will see later in the chapter affects the quantity of money in the economy.

Federal Reserve banks are sometimes called "quasi-public" banks because they are owned by private commercial banks but controlled by the Board of Governors. The Board of Governors is really a government agency because the members are appointed by the President of the United States. The present Chairman of the Board is Arthur Burns.

Federal Reserve banks also have been called "bankers banks" because they perform essentially the same functions for commercial banks as commercial banks do for private individuals. You and I, for example, cannot walk in to a Federal Reserve Bank and make a deposit or negotiate a loan. But these services are available to commercial banks who happen to be members of the Federal Reserve System. We will see later why a commercial bank might be in need of a loan. The United States Treasury also maintains a deposit in the Federal Reserve System so in a sense the "Fed," as it is often called, serves as the bank for the federal government.

We can obtain a better idea of economic characteristics of the Federal Reserve System by looking at the balance sheet for the entire system, as shown below:

Consolidated balance sheet of the Federal Reserve System, as of March 31, 1970 (billion $)

ASSETS		LIABILITIES AND NET WORTH	
Cash	$ 0.2	Reserves of member banks	$22.4
Gold certificates	11.0	Treasury deposits	1.2
Securities	55.8	Federal reserve notes	46.2
Loans to banks	0.6	Other liabilities and net worth	9.6
Other assets	11.8		
Total Assets	$79.4	Total Liabilities + Net Worth	$79.4

Source: *Federal Reserve Bulletin*, April, 1970.

On the asset side, the largest item is securities. Mainly these are U.S. Government Bonds issued by the Treasury. The Open Market Committee is continually buying and selling securities which we will see has an important bearing on the quantity of money in the economy. Gold Certificates represent the stock of gold held by the U.S. government. The loans item represents short-term credit extended to commercial banks that are members of the Federal Reserve System for the purpose of bolstering their reserves.

On the right-hand side of the balance sheet the three items listed all represent liabilities of the Federal Reserve. Commercial banks that are members of the Federal Reserve System are required to keep a certain fraction of their deposit liabilities on reserve either in their respective Federal Reserve banks or as vault cash in their respective banks. Member bank reserves represent liabilities of the Federal Reserve System because these funds are in a sense held in trust for the commercial banks and may be relinquished at any time. Treasury deposits represent the checking account money that the federal government has no deposit for the purpose of paying its bills. Federal reserve notes, the largest single liability item, is the official name of the paper currency in use today in the United States.

COMMERCIAL BANKS

Before we discuss the major kinds of transactions that take place in the banking community, let us take a brief look at the structure of the commercial banking system. By commercial banks we have in mind those institutions that provide checking account services for their customers. We will want to distinguish commercial banks from those that just accept deposits and make loans such as mutual savings banks and savings and loan associations, which have come to be known as financial intermediaries.

As of December 31, 1969, there were 13,662 commercial banks in the United States. Those that have received their charter from the federal government are called national banks, and those operating under a state charter are known as state banks. At the end of 1969 there were 4,669 national banks and 8,993 state banks in the United States. All of the national banks are required to hold membership in the Federal Reserve System, that is, they must buy stock in the system. Each state bank is free to choose whether or not it wishes to be a member of the Federal Reserve System. Of the 8,993 state banks, only 1,202 are members. At the same time, we should point out that most of the larger state banks are members so the major share of the deposits in the country come under the jurisdiction of the Federal Reserve System.

All "member banks" are required to hold a certain fraction of their deposit liabilities on reserve as cash in their vaults or on reserve in the Federal Reserve bank in their district. This fraction, often called the reserve ratio, varies between demand and time deposits and also between size of bank, as shown in Table 6–1.

The 16½ percent figure, for example, means that reserve city banks must maintain at least $16½ on reserve either in their own vaults or in their Federal Reserve banks for each $100 of demand deposits they have on their books. The other figures have a similar meaning. The Federal

TABLE 6–1. Required reserve ratios for member banks

	Demand Deposits	Time Deposits
Reserve city banks...........	16½ percent	3 percent
"Country" banks............	12 percent	3 percent

Reserve Board of Governors has the authority to change these reserve ratios over a fairly broad range, although this power is seldom used. We should point out too that nonmember state banks must maintain reserves against their deposits. These reserves are kept in the reserve city banks which tend to be located in the financial districts of large cities. In a sense, these large reserve city banks act as Federal Reserve banks for the smaller "country" banks.

It is generally assumed that legal reserve requirements were set up to protect depositors. No doubt they have this effect. But an equally valid reason for having legal reserve requirements is to provide a means for the Fed to have some control over the maximum amount of bank loans and thus over the maximum quantity of money in the economy. We will see shortly that in the process of making loans, commercial banks actually create money.

COMMERCIAL BANK TRANSACTIONS

In order to understand how the banking system can alter the quantity of money in the economy, it is first necessary to understand the nature of transactions that take place within the banking community. We already have caught a glimpse of the banking world in our discussion of the goldsmith at the beginning of the chapter. As we proceed you will probably note a strong resemblance between the modern commercial bank and the ancient goldsmith that we discussed earlier. It will be easier to understand banking transactions if we start with the most basic, the deposit of cash by a customer, and then move on from there.

1. *Deposit of $10,000 cash by a customer.* Suppose, to make the example more meaningful, that you decide to open up a bank. After receiving your charter you rent some facilities and obtain some of the basic equipment used by a bank which among other things might include a vault and some conservative clothing. On your first day of operation a local businessman brings in $10,000 in cash and wishes to establish a checking account in your bank.

Our main interest at this point is how this transaction affects your balance sheet. The $10,000 in cash that has come under your control becomes an asset of your bank. In the balance sheet below we refer to this cash deposit as total reserves. Of course, we know a balance sheet must balance so at the same time there is a corresponding increase on the liabilities side. This is accomplished by increasing the demand deposit item by $10,000. Bear in mind that demand deposits represent a liability to you because you may be required to pay this amount to your customer at any time. To simplify the arithmetic assume the required reserve ratio is 0.20, or 20 percent, so that along with the $10,000 increase in demand deposits your required reserves increase by $2,000 (0.20 × $10,000). Thus out of the $10,000 deposit of cash, $2,000 is taken up by required reserves and the remaining $8,000 are excess reserves. In the balance sheets to follow we show only the changes that take place in order to concentrate on the particular transaction at hand.

Deposit of $10,000 in cash by a customer

ASSETS	LIABILITIES + NET WORTH
Total reserves (cash) + $10,000 Required reserves + 2,000 Excess reserves + 8,000	Demand deposits + $10,000

Notice in this transaction that you have not yet created any money. The cash that has come into your bank is now removed from the money supply (recall that only cash outside of banks is considered part of the quantity of money) but this has been offset by the increase in demand deposits. The quantity of money in the economy has changed in composition from cash to demand deposits but not in total amount.

2. *Deposit of required reserves in Federal Reserve Bank.* Assume you are a member of the Federal Reserve System and decide to deposit the entire amount of required reserves in the Federal Reserve bank in your district. In this transaction only the Federal Reserve balance sheet is affected in total because your reserves remain the same. You still have $10,000 in total reserves: $2,000 in the Federal Reserve bank and $8,000 in your vault.

Federal Reserve balance sheet
deposit of $2,000 required reserves
in the Federal Reserve bank

ASSETS		LIABILITIES + NET WORTH	
Cash	+ $2,000	Member bank reserves	+ $2,000

3. *A $1,000 check is drawn on your bank.* It is reasonable to suppose that your depositor will begin to write checks against his account. Suppose he buys $1,000 worth of supplies and pays for the purchase by writ-

ing a check. Naturally the supplier will soon after deposit this check in his account, which we will assume is in some other bank, call it Bank B. We will see that this transaction effects the balance sheet of three banks: your bank, call it Bank A, the Federal Reserve, and Bank B.

Your depositor, of course, must have his checking account balance reduced by the amount of the check. But how will you know he has written a check? The procedure followed is for Bank B to first add $1,000 to the supplier's checking account and to offset this by adding $1,000 to the reserve entry in his balance sheet. Then the check goes to the Federal Reserve Bank where the Fed adds or credits Bank B's reserves by $1,000 and subtracts or debits your reserves (Bank A) by a like amount. This service that the Fed provides for its members is often referred to as a "clearing house" function. The Fed then sends the canceled check back to you, which informs you that your depositor should have his checking account reduced by $1,000 and that your reserves in the Federal Reserve are reduced by the same amount. Lastly you would send the canceled check back to your depositor so he would know his account has been reduced. The entire transaction is summarized by the balance sheets below:

Effects of a $1,000 check drawn on Bank A

Bank A

ASSETS		LIABILITIES + NET WORTH	
Reserves	−$1,000	Demand deposits	−$1,000

Federal Reserve

ASSETS		LIABILITIES + NET WORTH	
		Bank A reserves	−$1,000
		Bank B reserves	+$1,000

Bank B

ASSETS		LIABILITIES + NET WORTH	
Reserves	+$1,000	Demand deposits	+$1,000

Note that all three balance sheets continue to balance after the transaction is complete. In fact it is always a good idea to represent commercial bank transactions by balance sheets because they provide a good check on one's accuracy. If the balance sheets do not balance after working through the transaction, you can be sure you have made an error. Unfortunately the converse is not true; erroneous balance sheets can still balance.

Assuming that the original $10,000 depositor is the only person who has put money into your bank, the $1,000 check has reduced your total demand deposits and reserves to $9,000. With a 20 percent reserve ratio, this means that your required reserves drop slightly to $1,800 and that your excess reserves are reduced to $7,200 ($9,000 − $1,800). Of course, it is reasonable to believe that before long your depositor also would bring checks into your bank that were drawn on other banks. These checks would tend to replenish your reserves at the Fed and increase your bank's demand deposits.

So far we have not created any new money. The practice of writing checks just transfers demand deposits from one bank to another. In the above example, your bank lost $1,000 in demand deposits but Bank B gained a like amount.

MONEY CREATION

Being a banker, naturally you are eager to make loans, because the interest return on money lent out is a prime source of income for most banks. The first question is, how much can you loan out. Let us suppose that checks coming into your bank have offset checks going out as discussed in transaction three above. Thus, your balance sheet shows $10,000 in demand deposit liabilities and $10,000 in total reserves as illustrated in the top balance sheet below. The required reserve ratio of 0.20 tells you that 20 percent or $2,000, of the $10,000 demand deposits must be kept on reserve either in your vault or at the Federal Reserve Bank. Thus, the remaining 80 percent or $8,000 may be loaned out.

Consider next what happens when a likely prospect comes along in need of an $8,000 loan, say to build an addition to his home. He signs a promissory note agreeing to pay you certain specified interest and payments on the principal. In return you set up a checking account for him. The moment you set up this checking account, you, in effect, create $8,000 in additional money. After all, demand deposits are money. Thus, banks create money by making loans.

So far you have added $8,000 to the demand deposit item in your balance sheet. Now you have a total of $18,000 in demand deposits in your bank, "backed up" by $10,000 in reserves. This situation is depicted in the middle balance sheet below. But notice at this point you still have excess reserves. Under the 0.20 reserve ratio you are required to have only $3,600 in reserves, but you still have $10,000. What happened, did we make a mistake?

The answer is no because as soon as this $8,000 loan is spent, i.e., checks written against it, you must expect that these checks will be deposited in some other bank. And you recall from the check-writing transaction of the previous section, a check drawn against your bank reduces your reserves at the Fed by the amount of the check. Suppose then that the entire loan is spent by writing a single check, say in payment to a contractor. If the contractor deposits this check in his bank, say Bank B, the Fed reduces your reserves by $8,000 (you better be sure you have $8,000 at the Fed) and increases the reserves of Bank B. The end result as it affects your bank is shown on the bottom balance sheet.

The process of making a loan; balance sheet of Bank A
Initial Situation

ASSETS			LIABILITIES + NET WORTH	
Reserves		$10,000	Demand deposits	$10,000
Required reserves	$2,000			
Excess reserves	8,000			

Loan Is Made

ASSETS			LIABILITIES + NET WORTH	
Reserves		$10,000	Demand deposits	$18,000
Required reserves	$3,600			
Excess reserves	6,400			
Note		8,000		
		$18,000		$18,000

Loan Is Spent

ASSETS			LIABILITIES + NET WORTH	
Reserves		$ 2,000	Demand deposits	$10,000
Required reserves	$2,000			
Excess reserves	—0—			
Note		8,000		
		$10,000		$10,000

In this example, we assumed that the demand deposits were created at the time of the loan. We could have assumed instead that the borrower took his money in cash, say 80 crisp $100 bills. You still would have created $8,000 in additional money because cash inside banks is not considered part of the money supply, whereas cash outside banks is a part of the money supply. Eventually, of course, the contractor that received the $8,000 would take it to his bank for deposit, thus exchanging cash for demand deposits. So we end up at the same place regardless of whether we assume the loan goes out as a check or as cash.

MULTIPLE EXPANSION

But the story of your loan doesn't end when the $8,000 check is cleared against your bank. Let us now go to Bank B, the contractor's bank. When the check is cleared, the Fed increases Bank B's reserves by $8,000 and at the same time Bank B's demand deposit item is increased by the same amount. But if Bank B receives $8,000 in new demand deposits and reserves, we know part of this $8,000 will be excess reserves. Operating under a reserve ratio of 0.20, then 20 percent of the $8,000 or $1,600 represents required reserves. The remainder, $6,400 in this example, are excess reserves available to be loaned out.

In order to focus entirely on the $6,400 loan that Bank B can make let us omit the other items on its balance sheet. The top balance sheet below represents the influx of new reserves into Bank B because of the $8,000 check. The middle or intermediate balance sheet shows the immediate effect of making the loan, and the one on the bottom shows the end result after the loan is spent. Notice in this case that Bank B has created $6,400 in new demand deposits by making the loan.

Second round of the multiple expansion process; balance sheet of Bank B
Receipt of $8,000 Check

ASSETS			LIABILITIES + NET WORTH	
Reserves		$ 8,000	Demand deposits	$ 8,000
Required reserves	$1,600			
Excess reserves	6,400			
		$8,000		$ 8,000

Loan Is Made

ASSETS			LIABILITIES + NET WORTH	
Reserves		$ 8,000	Demand deposits	$14,400
Required reserves	$2,880			
Excess reserves	5,120			
Note		6,400		
		$14,400		$14,400

Loan Is Spent

ASSETS			LIABILITIES + NET WORTH	
Reserves		$ 1,600	Demand deposits	$ 8,000
Required reserves	$1,600			
Excess reserves	–0–			
Note		6,400		
		$ 8,000		$8,000

So far in these first two rounds of the multiple expansion process a total of $14,400 in new money has been created—$8,000 with your original loan and $6,400 with Bank B's loan. There is no reason why the multiple expansion process has to stop here. We could carry it on to Bank C and then round after round to infinity. But by now you probably see what is going on. When a loan check comes into a bank, it acquires some excess reserves which enable the bank to increase its loans. Of course, the amount of the loan and demand deposits created become smaller and smaller the further the process is carried. The multiple expansion process is summarized in Table 6–2.

You probably noticed a similarity between the multiple expansion process and the multiplier discussed in Chapter 4. Rather than carrying the

TABLE 6–2.   Summary of the multiple expansion process

	New Total Reserves	Excess Reserves, Loans Made, Dollars Created
Bank A..............	$10,000	$ 8,000 = 1 × $8,000
Bank B............	8,000	6,400 = 0.80 × 8,000
Bank C............	6,400	5,120 = (0.80)² × 8,000
	.	.
	.	.
	.	.
To infinity..........	.	.
		$40,000

process out to infinity, which becomes a bit tedious before long, we can employ a simple formula to determine how much the money supply will eventually increase. Recall from Chapter 4, the following expression:

$$1 + x + x^2 + x^3 + \cdots + x^n = 1/1 - x$$

In this case

$$x = 1 - \text{the reserve ratio}$$

Thus

$$1/1 - x = 1/1 - (1 - R)$$

where R is the reserve ratio. But

$$1/1 - (1 - R) = 1/1 - 1 + R = 1/R$$

because the 1's cancel out

Therefore, to find the ultimate expansion of the money supply stemming from an influx of new excess reserves, we multiply the original increase in excess reserves by 1/reserve ratio. In our example $R = 0.20$, so the "money multiplier" is 1/0.20 or 5. Thus the sum of the right-hand column in Table 6–2 is equal to $1/0.20 \times \$8,000$ or $40,000.

We should at the same time remember that the multiple expansion process can work in reverse, that is, a decrease in excess reserves can bring about a multiple contraction of the money supply. For example, suppose the contractor (no pun intended) pays back the $8,000 loan. In so doing you decrease his checking account by $8,000 and tear up his note. Now you have "destroyed" $8,000. If you do not relend the $8,000, the total money supply in the country will decline by $1/R \times \$8,000$. This happens because Banks B, C, D, etc., lose reserves as checks are drawn against them for payment to your contractor friend. In the process they lose reserves and must contract their loans outstanding also. Lest you receive the impression, however, that the entire banking system revolves around your bank, remember that any commercial bank in the country has the same option of renewing or not renewing loans.

It is necessary to mention also that the full multiple expansion or contraction takes place only if the participating banks are "fully loaned up" at all times, that is, they keep no excess reserves. In reality, though, most banks try to retain some excess reserves rather than operating right at the margin so to speak. Generally if banks face a strong demand for loans and high interest rates can be obtained, they tend to operate with less excess reserves than when the loan business is "sluggish" and interest rates are low. If a bank happens to find itself with less than the legal reserves, it can in an emergency borrow from its Federal Reserve Bank, although the Fed tends to discourage habitual borrowers.

Bear in mind too that the multiple expansion or contraction process is not likely to approach an infinite number of rounds. However, the major change in the money supply comes during the first few rounds. In the example above the first three rounds alone created $19,520 or almost half of the ultimate expansion. At any rate, the multiplier of $1/R$ provides an upper bound to how much the money supply will expand or contract for a given change in excess reserves.

BOND PURCHASES

A commercial bank with excess reserves on its books may choose to purchase bonds rather than make direct loans to individuals or businessmen. Most banks in fact like to diversify their portfolios and purchase a variety of earning assets with their excess reserves. Government bonds, either federal, state, or municipal, are a popular "investment" for banks. The bonds may be purchased directly from the issuing agency or from a second party who happens to be holding them. Either way the purchase of a bond by a bank has the same effect as making a loan, that is, it creates money.

This will be easiest to see if we go back to our original example before your bank made the $8,000 loan. Instead suppose you had purchased $8,000 in bonds held by a wealthy widow who wanted to use the money for a new Cadillac. Once you have the bonds, you either pay her the cash, give her a certified check, or create a checking account in her name. In any case, you have created $8,000 in new money. As soon as the lady spends the $8,000, another bank is likely to experience an increase in its deposits and excess reserves and off we go again on the same multiple expansion process.

AN IMPLICATION OF FRACTIONAL RESERVE BANKING

By now you probably realize that a bank does not hold in "cold storage," so to speak, all the money that has been brought in for deposit. A certain fraction, the required reserves, must be held; but the remainder, or excess reserves, can be used to make loans or purchase bonds. As we pointed out at the beginning of the chapter, a bank is able to operate with fractional reserves because on any one day deposits and withdrawals tend to cancel out. During a normal day the difference between deposits and withdrawals may not exceed 2 or 3 percent of a bank's total deposits. Hence, if a bank has 15 to 20 percent of its deposits on reserve there generally is no danger of running out of cash.

There have been times, however, when depositors became fearful that their banks would close and they would lose their "hard-earned" cash. In the early 1930's, for example, when a rumor would start in town that the bank was about to close, depositors rushed in to draw their money out. When this happened it was inevitable that the bank should close. If enough of a bank's depositors became convinced that a bank was going to fail, it failed.

After the financial crisis of the early 1930s the Federal Deposit Insurance Corporation (FDIC) was set up. Nowadays all deposits are insured up to $15,000 so there is no need for most people to fear losing their deposits. From time to time we still hear of people keeping their money in a mattress or some such hiding place because they distrust banks. No doubt a good share of this distrust was built up during the Great Depression.

FEDERAL RESERVE TRANSACTIONS

In our discussion of the Federal Reserve System we noted that the Open Market Committee is continually buying and selling securities in the market. We will now see that these transactions are an important determinant of the supply of money in the economy.

First let us consider the sale of a $1,000 bond to an individual. To pay for the bond the person writes out a $1,000 check against his account in a commercial bank. When the check is cleared the Fed deducts $1,000 from the bank's reserve account and in turn the bank deducts this amount from the person's checking account. The initial transaction is illustrated below:

Initial result of a Federal Reserve purchase of a $1,000 bond from an individual

Commercial Bank		Federal Reserve Bank	
ASSETS	LIABILITIES + NET WORTH	ASSETS	LIABILITIES + NET WORTH
Reserves —$1,000	Demand deposits —$1,000	Securities —$1,000	Bank reserves —$1,000

Notice first that the bond sale by the Fed immediately reduces the money supply by $1,000, that is, demand deposits are reduced by this amount. But we should be aware too that commercial bank reserves also are reduced. If the reserve ratio is 0.20, required reserves decline by $200 and excess reserves go down by $800. From our discussion of the multiple expansion and contraction process, we know that this $800 decline in excess reserves will result in an ultimate contraction of $1/0.20 \times \$800$ or $4,000 in the economy in addition to the initial $1,000 decline making a total decrease in money of $5,000.

The opposite happens, of course, when the Fed purchases bonds in the open market. Here a $1,000 purchase immediately increases commercial bank reserves and demand deposits by $1,000. Then after the multiple expansion process has run its course the initial $800 increase in excess reserves allows the money supply to increase by another $4,000 making a total increase of $5,000.

The Fed also buys from and sells bonds to commercial banks. The final outcomes of these transactions are the same as those where the Fed dealt directly with an individual, although the initial effect is slightly different. Now a bond sale by the Fed to a commercial bank will be paid for by subtracting commercial bank reserves on the Fed's balance sheet. Hence there is no immediate decline in demand deposits, but the $1,000 reduction in excess reserves eventually can result in a $1/0.20 \times \$1,000 = \$5,000$ reduction in the money supply. The same reasoning applies to a bond purchase from a commercial bank by the Fed except now there would be a multiple expansion of money.

The main point to keep in mind here is that a Federal Reserve sale of a bond reduces the money supply and a purchase tends to increase money. Intuitively these transactions make sense. An open-market sale injects bonds into the private economy but in exchange pulls money and reserves out. Conversely an open-market purchase pulls bonds out and in exchange injects money or reserves into the economy.

Whether or not the full multiple expansion or contraction process takes place depends a great deal on the action of banks and the general public. This is especially true on the expansion side. For example, suppose the Fed wants to increase the money supply through an open-market purchase. But if banks are reluctant to make loans or if people are reluctant to borrow, the money supply may expand relatively little.

MAIN POINTS OF CHAPTER 6

1. The balance sheet itemizes the assets, liabilities, and net worth of a person, firm, or institution. Assets include anything of value. Liabilities represent the claims of creditors against the assets and net worth represents the "owner's" claim to the assets. Assets always equal liabilities plus net worth because net worth is computed as the difference between assets and liabilities. Thus Assets = Liabilities + Net Worth because Net Worth = Assets − Liabilities.

2. Goldsmiths who provided places of safekeeping for money emerged as the forerunners of modern banks. Because deposits came close to offsetting withdrawals on any given day and because gold or money is a homogeneous commodity, only a small fraction of the total gold deposits actually changed hands during a day's business. Hence, goldsmiths found that part of their gold deposits could be loaned out. This was the beginning of fractional reserve banking.

3. To avoid carrying gold, people soon began to exchange deposit receipts in place of gold. This was the beginning of checking account money or demand deposits.

4. We can identify three steps in the evolution of banking: first, the deposit of money or gold for safekeeping with people called goldsmiths; second, the lending out of gold because only a small fraction was actively in use; and third, the gradual acceptance of deposit receipts as money.

5. The Federal Reserve System was established in 1913 to prevent unwanted expansions and contractions of money and credit during boom and recession periods respectively, and also to provide for an "elastic" currency because of seasonal fluctuations in business activity within the year.

6. The Federal Reserve System consists of 12 Federal Reserve banks, one in each of the 12 districts, and a number of branch banks. The system is controlled by seven-member Board of Governors appointed by the President of the United States.

7. As of December 31, 1969, there were 13,662 commercial banks in the United States. Of this total, 4,669 were national banks and 8,993 were state banks. Although a majority of the state banks are not members of the Federal Reserve System, the largest ones do belong so the largest share of the deposits in the country are under the jurisdiction of the Fed.

8. Each commercial bank is required to hold a certain percent of its deposits on reserve as cash either in its own vault, in the Federal Reserve Bank of its district, or in a reserve city bank. The percent of deposits that must be held as reserves is known as the reserve ratio. These reserves are intended to protect depositers but perhaps more important they provide a control for the Fed over the maximum amount of loans that can be made by commercial banks.

9. A deposit of cash by a customer in exchange for demand deposits does not change the total quantity of money in the economy, it only changes the form in which money is held from cash to demand deposits.

10. When a check is drawn on Bank A and deposited in Bank B, the demand deposits and total reserves in Bank A are drawn down by the

amount of the check, but these items are increased by the same amount in Bank B. Thus there is no change in total bank reserves or in demand deposits outstanding.

11. Commercial banks create money by making loans because the borrower receives demand deposits or cash that he can later spend. When the loan is spent and deposited in another bank, this amount adds to the second bank's demand deposits and total reserves. Part of these reserves become excess reserves on which the second bank can make loans, etc. The maximum multiple expansion that can take place is equal to $1/R$ times the initial increase in excess reserves. The same formula applies to a multiple contraction brought on by a reduction in excess reserves.

12. The purchase of a bond by a bank has the same effect as making a loan. Money is created in exchange for the bond. Also the same multiple expansion process takes place.

13. One implication of fractional reserve banking is that only a small proportion of a bank's total deposits are available for withdrawal on a given day.

14. The sale of bonds by the Federal Reserve to individuals or commercial banks has the effect of pulling money out of the private economy and reducing reserves. Hence there is a multiple contraction of the money supply. On the other hand the purchase of bonds by the Federal Reserve either from banks or individuals serves to inject additional money and reserves into the economy thereby allowing a multiple expansion of the money supply.

QUESTIONS FOR THOUGHT AND DISCUSSION

1. Construct a balance sheet for yourself showing only your major assets and liabilities along with your net worth.

2. Commercial banks sometimes have been called "warehouses for money." In what ways are commercial banks similar to conventional warehouses, such as places to store fur coats? And in what ways do banks differ from ordinary warehouses? Also what is the main difference in the commodity stored?

3. Explain why banks are able to loan out a substantial share of the money they receive as deposits.

4. Suppose the government decided that banks could no longer loan out part of the money deposited with them. Think through some of the consequences of this decision. If the government did not wish that loans be decreased, what could it do to allow banks to continue loaning as much as before?

5. Trace out the major steps that took place in the evolution of the banking system.

6. Explain what happens in the banking system when you write a check in payment for your tuition. Use balance sheets.

7. Suppose you are discussing banking with a friend who works in a bank. You point out that banks actually create money. But your friend says nonsense, the bank only lends out a fraction of its deposits. Thus how can it create money? How would you explain what happens?

8. Your banker friend in Question 7 really "breaks up" when you say that banks can create $5 in new money for every one dollar of new cash that comes into the banking system. Try to explain this.

9. It has been said that checks are nothing more than warehouse receipts. Is there an element of truth to this statement? Explain.

10. How is a bond purchase by a commercial bank similar to a loan by the bank.

11. What would happen to the bank you have your checking or savings account in if every depositor wanted his money on the same day?

12. "If the Federal Reserve wants to increase the money supply it should purchase government bonds." True or false and explain.

13. Will your answer to Question 12 be different if the Fed buys bonds from banks or from individuals? Explain.

CHAPTER
7
THE KEYNESIAN MODEL WITH MONEY

In Chapter 4, you recall, we developed the simplest Keynesian model of an economy. Then in Chapters 5 and 6, we turned our attention to money, looking first at the demand for cash balances and secondly at the banking system. Our task in this chapter is to integrate money into the simple Keynesian model in order to build a somewhat more complete model of the economy. With this more complete model, which we shall call the Keynesian model with money, we will be better able to explain the causes of unemployment and inflation and to analyze policies that might to taken to ease these problems.

EQUILIBRIUM IN THE GOODS AND SERVICES SECTOR

The equilibrium NNP that we obtained in the Keynesian model without money presented in Chapter 4 can be thought of as an equilibrium of the goods and services sector of the economy. Recall that equilibrium NNP in the context of this model occurs where aggregate demand is equal to aggregate supply. At this point you recall the desired aggregate demand of consumers, investors, and the government is equal to the desired output of goods and services by the business community. Thus at equilibrium there is neither an unintended accumulation or drawing down of inventories. And as a result there is no "pressure" on the economy for a change in output or income. To refresh your memory, the simple Keynesian model without money is shown in Figure 7–1.

INTEREST AND INVESTMENT

In our discussion of the investment component of aggregate demand, recall too that the interest rate was a major determinant of the level of

FIGURE 7–1. The Keynesian model without money
illustrating equilibrium NNP

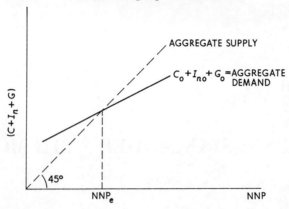

annual investment. When the interest rate rises the level of investment
tends to decline because the higher interest payment reduces the expected
level of profits. Also with a high interest rate and a "tight" credit situation, loans tend to be more difficult to obtain which also discourages investment. The opposite is true, of course, for a decline in the rate of
interest which tends to stimulate investment. Of course, any change in interest which changes the investment component of aggregate demand will
in turn change the level of aggregate demand. Hence a rise in the interest
rate tends to shift the aggregate demand line downward and reduce equilibrium NNP. By the same token, a lower rate of interest is associated with
a higher aggregate demand line and a high level of equilibrium NNP.

It will be useful to represent the relationship between interest and investment on a separate diagram. Economists would say there is an inverse
relationship between interest and investment. And in graphing such a relationship we obtain a downward sloping line as in Figure 7–2. At the
relatively high interest rate of i_0, the annual level of net investment is
equal to I_0. But at a lower rate of interest, say i_1, investment increases to
I_1, and at the still lower rate of i_2 investment increases to I_2. Let us refer
to the line that traces out the relationship between interest and investment
as the investment line.

At this point it will not be necessary to concern ourselves with the exact relationship between interest and investment, that is, we will not specify whether investment changes a great deal for a 1 percentage point
change in interest or whether there is only a slight change in investment.
Later on in the chapter we will see, however, that the responsiveness of
investment to the interest rate is of considerable importance. Bear in mind
too that we have no way of determining from our discussion so far what

FIGURE 7–2.   Relationship between interest and investment—the investment line

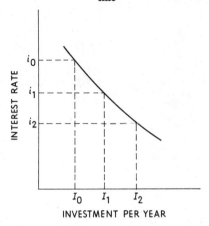

INVESTMENT PER YEAR

rate of interest and investment will prevail in an economy. All we have done is to trace out a relationship between the two.

INTEREST AND EQUILIBRIUM NNP

If we pull together the discussion so far, it becomes apparent that the interest rate has an important bearing on the equilibrium level of NNP. The chain of causation can be summarized as follows:

Interest → Investment → Aggregate demand → Equilibrium NNP

Thus if we choose an interest rate such as i_1 in Figure 7–2, we can determine from the investment line that the annual level of net investment will be I_1. Then if we add this amount of investment to consumption and government expenditures, we can determine the aggregate demand line. And once we know aggregate demand we can immediately determine equilibrium NNP, or equilibrium in the goods and services sector as economists sometimes refer to it.

We present in Figure 7–3 the three aggregate demand lines that correspond to the three rates of interest and investment shown in Figure 7–2. Note that aggregate demand is held down by a high rate of interest because investment is relatively small. Then as the interest rate declines, investment increases and aggregate demand also increases. Furthermore, the upward shifts in aggregate demand give rise to higher equilibrium levels of NNP. The interest rate in the parentheses after each aggregate

FIGURE 7–3. Relationship between the interest
rate and aggregate demand

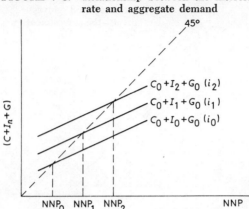

demand line correspond to those in Figure 7–2 and serve as a reminder
that each aggregate demand line corresponds to a particular level of interest and investment.

THE EXPENDITURES EQUILIBRIUM LINE

Economists have found it convenient to summarize the relationship between the interest rate and equilibrium NNP by a line, much like we did
in Figure 7–2 for the relationship between interest and investment. Again
in this case we observe an inverse relationship between the two variables.
At high rates of interest equilibrium NNP is relatively low, but as interest declines and aggregate demand shifts up the equilibrium level of NNP
increases.

The three combinations of interest and equilibrium NNP presented in
Figure 7–4 correspond to those shown in Figure 7–3. All we have done is
to rearrange the diagram somewhat, placing the interest rate on the vertical axis but keeping NNP on the horizontal axis. To simplify the presenta-
tion, we have utilized only three different interest rates and equilbrium
levels of NNP. There is no reason, of course, why we could not have
chosen hundreds of arbitrarily small changes in interest and then plot the
hundreds of corresponding equilibrium NNP levels. But three combinations are sufficient to convey the idea that a relationship exists between
the interest rate and equilibrium NNP.

We can refer to the line that is traced out in Figure 7–4 as the expenditures equilibrium line (EE) because every point on the line represents
an equilibrium level of NNP for the corresponding interest rate. But you
recall that equilibrium NNP is that level of NNP at which the desired
expenditures of consumers, investors, and the government is equal to the

FIGURE 7-4.   Relationship between the
interest rate and equilib-
rium NNP—the expendi-
tures equilibrium line

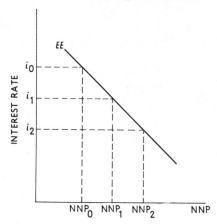

desired output of goods and services so that there is neither a drawing
down or building up of inventories. In other words, points on the EE
line represent alternative equilibrium levels of expenditure in the goods
and services sector of the economy.

If you reflect back for a moment to Chapter 4, you may remember that
the model we developed then implied there was only one equilibrium
level in the goods and services sector. But now we see that there is an
entire range of possible equilibrium points as shown by the EE line in
Figure 7-4. However, the information that we have at our disposal at
this point does not allow us to determine which of these many possible
equilibrium values of NNP will actually prevail in an economy, mainly
because we do not know what interest rate will prevail. All we have done
so far is to trace out a relationship between many possible interest rates
and their corresponding levels of equilibrium NNP.

So far all we know about the EE line is that it is downward sloping
in nature, i.e., there is an inverse relationship between the interest rate
and equilibrium NNP. But we will see in the next two chapters that the
exact slope of the EE line will be an important determinant of the appropriate government policies to reduce unemployment or inflation. Thus it
it necessary to understand what determines the slope of the EE line, that
is, what will make the line slope downward very steeply or what will
cause it to have a very gentle slope?

The slope of the EE line is determined mainly by the slope of the investment line. If the investment line is very steep, as I in Figure 7-5 (A),
then the corresponding EE line will also be very steep as shown by EE
line in Figure 7-5 (B). A very steep investment line reflects the idea that

investment is not very responsive to changes in the interest rate. For example, an interest rate decline from i_0 to i_1 in Figure 7-5 (A) does not bring forth much of an increase in investment. As a result there is a relatively small upward shift in the aggregate demand line, which in turn means that equilibrium NNP will not change by very much. On the other hand, an investment line that is relatively flat as I' above implies that in-

FIGURE 7-5.   Relationship between the slope of the investment line and the EE line

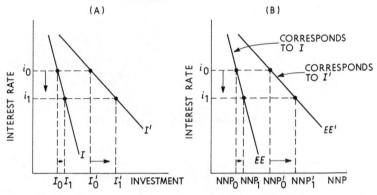

vestment changes a relatively large amount for a given change in interest. And the large change in investment brings forth a relatively large change in aggregate demand and NNP.

EQUILIBRIUM IN THE MONETARY SECTOR

In constructing the EE line we have shown that many possible equilibrium levels of NNP are possible in the so-called goods and services sector of the economy. But we have no way of determining at this time which equilibrium level of NNP will actually prevail at a point in time. This can be done only after we have determined equilibrium in the so-called monetary sector.

To determine equilibrium in the monetary sector we must utilize the concepts of the demand for and the supply of money. In Chapter 5 you will recall we constructed a demand curve for money. This was a line showing how much of their assets people choose to hold as cash at various interest rates. We assumed that at high interest rates people tend to reduce their desired holdings of cash in favor of other assets because of the increased interest income that can be obtained from the nonmoney assets. And at low interest rates relatively little income is foregone by holding assets as cash so it may be argued that people choose to hold a larger share of their assets in this form because of the convenience and security that money provides. The wishes of people to hold cash are summarized by a downward sloping line, as in Figure 7–6 (A).

In Chapter 6 we discussed the supply of money. Here we saw that the Federal Reserve can have powerful influence on the quantity of money that is put out into the economy through purchase or sale of securities. We will discuss the Fed's influence on the money supply more thoroughly in Chapter 9. It will be useful at this point, however, to represent the supply of money by a line much as we did for the demand for money. Only in this case the line will be nearly vertical or at least will be steeply upward sloping when graphed against the interest rate. A vertical supply of money line means that the Fed supplies the same amount of money regardless of the interest rate. An upward sloping line, however, implies that the Fed allows the money supply to increase slightly when the rate of interest increases. An upward sloping supply line is a plausible assumption, however, because when there is a strong demand for loans and the interest rate is high, banks tend to increase their loans outstanding which as you know results in more demand deposits. Thus in our future discussion of the supply of money we will represent it by a steeply upward sloping line as in Figure 7–6 (B).

FIGURE 7–6. Representing the demand for and supply of money

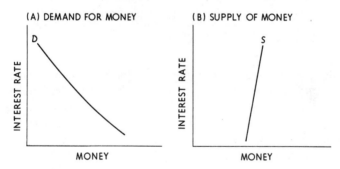

Our next task is to combine the above demand and supply diagrams into one to determine equilibrium in the monetary sector. Notice that both diagrams have interest on the vertical axis and money on the horizontal axis. Thus we can just superimpose one diagram on the other to obtain Figure 7–7. This diagram will allow us to determine the so-called equilibrium in the monetary sector.

Perhaps the easiest way to explain the meaning of equilibrium in the monetary sector is to begin at an interest rate that does not represent equilibrium and then see what happens. Suppose by accident the interest rate happens to be i_0. At this relatively high rate the public wishes to hold only M_{d0} as cash balances whereas the Federal Reserve and the banking system are supplying M_{s0}. Keep in mind now that someone must be holding at all times all of the money that is supplied, M_{s0} in Figure 7–7. So at interest rate i_0 people are actually holding more cash than they wish to hold. As you might expect, then, people might try to loan out some of their "excess" money and as a result additional funds appear on the loan market. With the additional funds available, borrowers are able to press for lower interest loans. Soon competition in the loan market drives the interest rate down.

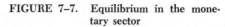

FIGURE 7–7.   Equilibrium in the monetary sector

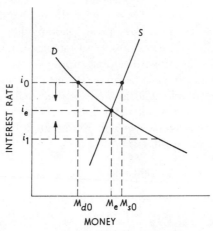

On the other hand, if the interest rate happens to be relatively low, say at i_1, people desire to hold more cash than is being supplied to the economy. Then as people try to sell "earning assets" such as stocks and bonds in exchange for cash, there is a reduction of funds in the money market which serves to drive the interest rate upwards.

Notice that in both of these disequilibrium situations the change in the interest rate, either a rise or fall, changes the preference of people for holding their assets as cash. As the interest rate declines, the amount of money people wish to hold comes closer and closer to the amount actually supplied. Similarly as the interest rate increases, people desire to hold less and less of their wealth as cash until the amount they desire to hold exactly coincides with the amount actually supplied. Thus the interest rate serves as the mechanism for equilibrating the desired holdings of cash (money demand) with the actual holdings of cash (money supply).

By now you probably recognize that unless the interest rate corresponds to the intersection of the demand and supply curves for money, there will always be a pressure on it to change. Thus the interest rate that corresponds to this intersection, such as i_e in Figure 7–9, is referred to as the equilibrium rate of interest in the monetary sector.

THE MONETARY EQUILIBRIUM LINE

Perhaps you recall from Chapter 5 that a major factor shifting the demand for money is the income or output of the economy. As the income of people increases, they tend to hold larger amounts of money for any given interest rate. Thus it is necessary to bear in mind that any time we see a demand curve for money, such as shown in Figure 7–7, we must also remember that it is drawn for a given income level of society. A higher income level would imply a higher demand for money, that is, a demand that lies further to the right than the one shown in Figure 7–7.

So far, then, we have just derived one possible equilibrium rate of interest for the economy. But as soon as we speak of many possible equilibrium levels of NNP, as shown by the expenditures equilibrium line, we must also speak of many possible equilibrium rates of interest. We can follow a procedure very similar to that used in constructing the *EE* line and construct a so-called monetary equilibrium (*ME*) line. Only now we will choose various possible levels of NNP to obtain a series of possible equilibrium values of the interest rate.

In constructing the *ME* line we will assume a constant supply of money to the economy. Each of the demand curves for money shown in Figure 7–8 (A) corresponds to a given level of NNP. At relatively low levels of income, denoted by NNP_0, the demand for money also is relatively low, as illustrated by D_0. Then at higher levels of NNP, as denoted by NNP_1 and NNP_2, the corresponding demand curves for money are higher. Of course, the equilibrium rates of interest also increase along with the increases in the demand for money.

All we have done to obtain the *ME* line in Figure 7–9 (B) is to plot the interest rates obtained in Figure 7–9 (A) against their corresponding levels

FIGURE 7–8.   Relationship between NNP and the equilibrium rate of interest—the monetary equilibrium line

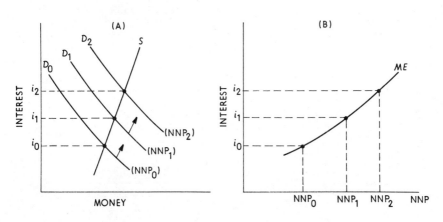

of NNP. The *ME* line, therefore, traces out a series of many possible equilibrium rates of interest for many possible levels of NNP, given a constant supply of money. Notice also that the *ME* line slopes upward. This tells us that higher levels of NNP will result in higher rates of interest, given the supply of money.

So far all we know about the *ME* line is that it slopes upward. But it will become important in the next two chapters to know what affects the slope of this line. The slope of the *ME* line depends to a large extent on the slope of the demand curve for money. If the demand curve for money is relatively steep, meaning that changes in the interest rate have relatively little effect on the amount of money people wish to hold, the *ME* line also will be steep, as in Figure 7–9 (B). Here you will note that a given shift to the right of the demand for money because of an increase in NNP raises the interest rate a relatively large amount, making for a steep *ME* line. On the other hand, if people are quite responsive to the interest rate in deciding on the money they wish to hold, the money demand curve will be relatively flat. Here a given shift in the money demand curve will not raise the interest rate in the monetary sector very much, making for a flat *ME* line. The horizontal shift in the demand for money is the same in both diagrams (A) and (B) below, although this may not appear to be the case at first glance. It will be useful to prove to yourself the relationship between the slope of the demand curve for money and the *ME* line by deriving the *ME* lines that go along with Figures 7–9 (A) and (B).

To summarize briefly, so far in this chapter we have derived the *EE* and the *ME* lines. The former was obtained by choosing alternative rates of interest and observing what happens to the equilibrium NNP. We found that with lower rates of interest, investment increases which shifts

FIGURE 7–9. Relationship between the slope of the demand for money and the slope of the *ME* line

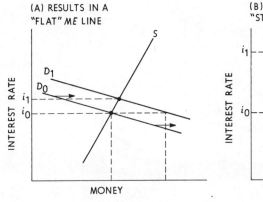

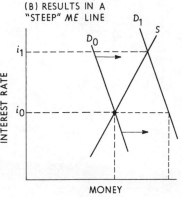

the aggregate demand line upward, giving us a higher equilibrium NNP. The relationship between the interest rate and the resulting equilibrium level of NNP is summarized by the *EE* line. The *EE* line slopes downward because lower rates of interest correspond to higher levels of equilibrium NNP. Also the slope of the *EE* line depends on the responsiveness of investment to changes in the rate of interest.

The *ME* line was obtained by choosing alternative levels of NNP and observing what happens to the equilibrium interest rate in the economy. At higher levels of NNP, the demand for money increases which results in a higher equilibrium rate of interest. The relationship between the level of NNP and the interest rate is summarized by the *ME* line. The *ME* line slopes upward because higher levels of NNP result in higher equilibrium interest rates. Also the slope of the *ME* depends on the responsiveness of the demand for money to changes in the interest rate.

OVERALL EQUILIBRIUM

We know now that there are many possible equilibrium levels of NNP and many possible equilibrium levels of the interest rate in the economy, as shown by the *EE* and *ME* lines. Our next step, then, is to determine which of these possible equilibria will actually prevail. Suppose we pick an interest rate and find its corresponding level of NNP from the *EE* line. But if this interest rate is either too high or too low to be the equilibrium rate in the monetary sector for this level of NNP, pressures will exist in the money market to change the interest rate. And as soon as the interest rate changes, there is a change in the equilibrium level of NNP which forces us to start the entire trial-and-error process over again. It is easy to see how this little game would soon drive an ordinary person "up the wall," perhaps even an economist would find it frustrating.

A much easier way of determining overall equilibrium in the economy is to superimpose the *EE* and *ME* lines on the same diagram and observe where they intersect. This is shown in Figure 7–10. Notice here that there is one interest rate and one level of NNP, i_e, and NNP_e, respectively, that results in a simultaneous equilibrium in both the expenditures and monetary sectors of the economy. By choosing i_e we find that the corresponding equilibrium level of NNP in the expenditures sector would be NNP_e. But it also turns out that NNP_e is the level of income that results in an equilibrium interest rate of i_e in the monetary sector. Now the economy is in a complete or overall equilibrium. There are no pressures in either sector to cause a change in either the interest rate or NNP.

Although Keynes presented all the ingredients and the rationale for this more complete model of the economy in his book, it took another English economist, J. R. Hicks, to formulate it in terms of the diagram in

FIGURE 7–10.   Overall equilibrium

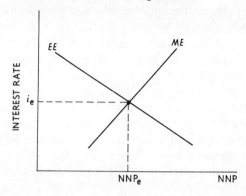

Figure 7–10.[1] Hicks' notation and that followed in many other textbooks is somewhat different than what we have used here so it might prove useful to translate our set of notations into the others. Our *EE* line was originally called the *IS* line by Hicks and many later writers. It is called *IS* because it turns out that at any given level of equilibrium NNP the desired level of investment by the business community is exactly equal to the desired level of savings by households, hence the notation $I = S$ or just *IS* for short. The *ME* line in this chapter was originally labeled *LL* by Hicks and other authors because it is derived from the liquidity preference curve which we have called the demand curve for money.

The notation used in this chapter to construct the more complete model of the economy follows to a certain extent that used by Martin J. Bailey in his book *National Income and the Price Level* (New York: McGraw-Hill Book Co., Inc., 1962). A significant addition to the basic Hicksian model was made by Bailey in that he was able to incorporate the price level as an explicit variable in the model. Let us see how this was done.

INCORPORATING THE PRICE LEVEL

Looking first at the expenditures sector of the economy, Bailey argues in his book that decisions by consumers, investors, or the government to spend on *real* consumption or investment goods and services are made on the basis of *real* income not money income. Or looking at it from another point of view, as prices and incomes increase with a rise in the price level, people increase their consumption expenditures by the same proportion. For example, suppose that at a certain price level which we might label as 100 on the Consumer Price Index, a family with an income of $10,000 spends $8,000 per year on consumption goods. Now if prices should dou-

[1] J. R. Hicks, "Mr. Keynes and the "Classics": A Suggested Interpretation," *Econometrica*, Vol V (1937), pp. 147–59.

ble and then stabilize for a time, Bailey would argue that the family whose money income is assumed also to double would increase its monetary expenditures on consumption goods and services to $16,000 per year. Or if prices and money income should fall by one half, the family would reduce the money value of consumption to $4,000 per year. Since the money value of consumption changes in direct proportion to changes in the price level, there is no change in the real value of goods and services consumed because of changes in the price level. Economists refer to this assumption as an absence of a "money illusion." If both prices and incomes double, for example, it is assumed people do not feel richer just because they carry around twice as many pieces of paper called dollars.

The same assumption is made for business and government expenditures on investment goods and services. Thus all of the components of aggregate demand and of the *EE* line remain the same in real terms with changes in the price level. As a result we can write the *EE* line in real terms by dividing all of the variables by an index of the price level. Whatever the price level happens to be the *EE* line stays in the same place. This is illustrated in Figure 7–11 where we have labeled the expenditures equilibrium line *EE/P*. Also note that we now label the horizontal axis of the diagram by NNP/P. Essentially we are saying that the money value of expenditures and equilibrium NNP changes in the same proportion as the price level so there is no change in the real value of expenditures and NNP. We still label the vertical axis by the money rate of interest, however, because we can only deal with different levels of prices and not movements of prices. Recall that it is the percentage change in prices that causes the money rate of interest to differ from the real rate.

Let us turn next to the monetary sector and the demand for money. Here Bailey assumes that in deciding how much money to hold, people take into account both their money incomes and the price level, just as they did in regard to consumption and investment. For example, if a family desires to hold $3,000 in money when its money income is $8,000, it is assumed that the family will desire to hold $6,000 if prices double and its money income rises to $16,000. In other words, it is assumed that changes in the price level do not alter the "real cash balances" a family desires to hold.

With regard to the other half of the monetary sector, the supply of money, Bailey assumes that the monetary authority (Federal Reserve or the government) does not react to changes in the price level. For example, if the monetary authority is supplying $300 billion in money to the economy, an increase in the price level will not prompt it to supply more dollars. Recall from our discussion of the quantity equation of exchange that an increase in the quantity of money supplied to the economy over and above the increase in real output will result in a price level increase providing that velocity does not decrease. Thus it is assumed that the mone-

FIGURE 7-11.   Incorporating the price level
in the complete model

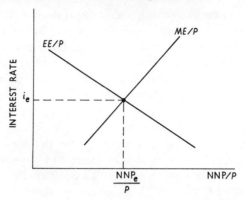

tary authority can alter the level of prices by changing the money supply but that a change in prices will not by itself prompt a change in the money supply. We will discuss the significance of the assumption that the money supply is not changed by a change in the price level just a bit later in the chapter. To serve as a reminder that the price level also is incorporated into the monetary sector, we label the ME line as ME/P in Figure 7-11.

ADJUSTMENTS THROUGH PRICE AND INTEREST CHANGES

In our discussion of the simple Keynesian model without money in Chapter 4, we saw that an economy can come to rest at an equilibrium that does not correspond to full employment without inflation. If equilibrium NNP happens to be less than full employment, the model tells us that the economy will experience persistent unemployment. On the other hand, if equilibrium NNP is greater than full-employment NNP the model implies that the economy will experience inflationary pressure.

In the more complete model with money, it is also possible for equilibrium NNP to occur at a point that does not correspond to full-employment without inflation. This is illustrated by the FE lines in Figures 7-12 (A) and (B). In diagram (A) the FE line falls to the right of the overall equilibrium which represents an unemployment situation. Diagram (B) represents an inflationary situation because full employment occurs at a lower level of real NNP than equilibrium.

According to the simple model of Chapter 4, there is no way for an economy to automatically adjust from a situation of unemployment to one of full employment. The only way that full-employment equilibrium can be reached in this case is for aggregate demand to shift as a result of a shift in the spending patterns of consumers, investors, or the government. However, we will now see that according to the more complete model which incorporates the price level, it is possible for an economy to adjust to an unemployment situation more or less by itself, i.e., no basic shift in the expenditure patterns of consumers, investors, or the government. By the same token, the more complete model will allow us to be a bit more explicit in showing the results of a situation where equilibrium NNP is greater than full-employment NNP, i.e., an inflationary situation.

Let us consider the unemployment case first. In the event of prolonged unemployment and an unintended buildup of unsold goods and services, it is expected that there will be a downward pressure on prices and wages. Recall from our previous discussion it is assumed in the more complete model that even though prices and wages decline, the monetary authority still holds the nominal supply of money in the economy at a fixed level. However, as prices decline, the real value of the fixed nominal money supply begins to increase. In other words, a fall in prices means that the same number of dollars has a greater "purchasing power." It is as though the government actively supplied more money to the economy under a stable price level.

But now comes the rub. If people were holding a desired amount of real cash balances before the price fall, as an equilibrium situation implies, then an increase in the amount of real cash balances that has occurred because of the price reduction, throws people out of equilibrium. In other words, at the given rate of interest people will be holding more real cash balances than they desire. As a result we might expect people to try to reduce their holdings of cash by offering a greater amount in the loan market. This in turn has the effect of lowering the rate of interest as more dollars become available to borrowers. As a next step, the decline in the interest rate prompts the business community to step up investment spending providing the investment line is downward sloping as in Figure 7–2. The increase in investment spending in turn leads to an increase in real output and income as shown by the movement to the right down along the EE/P line in Figure 7–12 (A).

The line of causation in this unemployment adjustment process can be summarized as follows:

> Decrease in prices → Increase in real cash balances → Increase of funds in the money market → Decrease in the interest rate → Increase in investment → Increase in real income and output of the economy

Some economists also would argue that consumption can be affected by the increase in real cash balances and decrease in interest. That is, if real cash balances increase, people may feel richer and thus increase their rate of consumption spending. Economists have referred to this as the "real balance" effect. Similarly, a decline in the interest rate and "easier money" also may prompt consumers to step up their spending, especially on consumer durables. If so, the increase in consumer spending would augment the increase in investment spending to bring forth the increase in real output in the economy.

The adjustment of an inflationary situation illustrated by Figure 7–12 (B) would be similar, although opposite in character. Here the increase in prices brought about by shortages and a drawing down of inventories would have the effect of reducing real cash balances, given a constant supply of money. As people attempt to replenish their cash reserves, funds are withdrawn from the money market which in turn increases the rate of interest. In this case investment, and possibly consumption, declines resulting in a decline in real output. As the overall equilibrum approaches the full-employment level of output, the inflationary pressure diminishes and the leftward shift in the ME/P line ceases. Of course, in this case, we have to assume that there was some chance for real output to increase beyond the so-called full-employment level of the economy.

From the standpoint of the mechanics of the model, it is the change in prices that shifts the ME/P line. In the unemployment, or deflationary case, the supply of real dollars increases with a fall in prices. In other words, the supply of money line can be looked upon as shifting to the right. If you refer back to Figure 7–8 (A) you can see that an increase or shift to the right of the money supply line will result in lower equilibrium rates of interest for each level of NNP. Then if you plot these new lower equilibrium rates of interest over on Figure 7–8 (B), you will notice that the ME line shifts to the right, or increases. Thus a fall in the price level has the effect of shifting the monetary equilibrium curve to the right and lowers the overall equilibrium rate of interest, as shown in Figure 7–12 (A). The direction of shift in the ME/P curve is fairly easy to remember

FIGURE 7–12. Adjustments through price changes

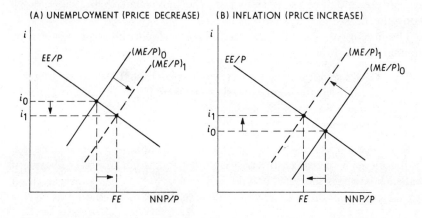

(A) UNEMPLOYMENT (PRICE DECREASE)   (B) INFLATION (PRICE INCREASE)

if you visualize the numerator (ME) as remaining constant with the decline in the denominator (P). Hence there is an increase in the entire fraction which means that the ME/P curve shifts to the right.

Similar reasoning can be applied to a situation where equilibrium NNP/P is greater than full-employment NNP/P. Only now there is an upward pressure on prices. As prices rise with the supply of nominal dollars held constant, there is in effect a decrease in the real supply of money. It is as though the government decreased the money supply under a stable price level. Referring back to Figure 7–8 (A) we see that a reduction in the money supply, i.e., a shift to the left of the money supply line, would raise the equilibrium rate of interest at each level of NNP/P. Thus the series of new, higher interest rates would trace out a new, higher ME/P line. The direction of shift of ME/P because of a change in the price level is easy to remember if you visualize ME or the numerator as remaining constant with an increase in P, the denominator. As a result the whole fraction is reduced in value, i.e., there is a decrease in the ME/P line.

THE ROLE OF GOVERNMENT

The fact that an economy as represented by this more complete model is able to adjust from an unemployment situation towards full employment by means of a decrease in prices and interest is not meant to imply that the government is no longer needed to help the economy maintain a high level of employment. Although the economy may be capable of adjusting to unemployment on its own, the time required to regain a level of full employment may be too long to be acceptable to the general public. For during the process of adjustment, millions of people can find themselves out of work for several months or even years.

In the following two chapters we will consider what the government can do to help the economy avoid prolonged periods of unemployment. Also we will see that inflation is not inevitable. However, we will see as well that the government can itself be a strong destabilizing force in the economy that may lead to increased unemployment or inflation.

MAIN POINTS OF CHAPTER 7

1. The point of intersection between aggregate demand and aggregate supply can be thought of as equilbrium in the goods and services or expenditures sector of the economy.

2. The relationship between the interest rate and the level of annual investment in the economy can be represented by a downward sloping line. The lower the interest rate, the larger the level of investment.

3. As the interest rate declines and investment increases, there are corresponding upward shifts in the aggregate demand line which in turn results in higher levels of equilibrium NNP in the goods and services sector.

4. The expenditures equilibrium (EE) line is obtained by plotting alternative interest rates against its corresponding level of equilibrium NNP. The EE line is downward sloping because lower rates of interest correspond to higher equilibrium levels of NNP in the goods and services sector.

5. The slope of the EE line is determined mainly from the slope of the investment line. If the investment line slopes down very steeply, meaning that investment is not very responsive to changes in the interest rate, the EE line also will be relatively steep.

6. Equilibrium in the monetary sector corresponds to the intersection of the demand for and supply of money curves. At rates of interest higher than the equilibrium people do not desire to hold as much money as the monetary authority is supplying. As people try to reduce their money holdings by attempting to lend, the rate of interest declines until the point is reached where the demand for money is equal to the supply.

7. The monetary equilibrium (ME) line is obtained by plotting the equilibrium interest rates that are obtained from alternative levels of NNP. At higher levels of NNP the demand for money is increased resulting in a higher point of intersection between the demand and supply of money. Thus the ME line slopes up meaning that higher levels of NNP correspond to higher equilibrium rates of interest in the monetary sector.

8. The slope of the ME line depends upon the slope of the demand curve for money. If the money demand curve is relatively steep the ME curve also will be relatively steep, and vice versa.

9. Overall equilibrium in the economy occurs at the intersection of the EE and ME lines. At the overall equilibrium the interest rate and NNP are perfectly matched; NNP_e corresponds to i_e in the monetary sector, and i_e corresponds to NNP_e in the goods and services sector.

10. Following the technique of Martin Bailey, the price level is incorporated into the goods and services and monetary sectors. It is assumed in this model that public and private consumption and investment expenditures change in direct proportion to changes in the price level so there is no change in their real magnitudes.

11. Regarding prices and the monetary sector, it is assumed that people change their desired holdings of money in direct proportion to the price level so there is no change in the demand for real cash balances from a change in prices. However, it is assumed that the government

does not change the supply of money in response to a change in prices so the real supply of money does change with price level changes.

12. A decrease in the general price level which can occur during a period of prolonged unemployment has the effect of increasing the real cash balances held by people. If holders of real cash balances were originally in equilibrium with respect to the interest rate, an increase in real cash balances brought about by the decrease in prices throws them out of equilibrium. Then as they attempt to reduce their holdings of cash, interest is forced down, hence investment and possibly consumption is stimulated.

13. Although an economy may be capable of adjusting to an unemployment situation, the adjustment process might be long and painful, involving a prolonged period of unemployment.

QUESTIONS FOR THOUGHT AND DISCUSSION

1. Define "equilibrium NNP" in the context of the simple Keynesian model without money. Is it possible from this model to determine the price level and the interest rate? Explain.

2. Explain the relationship between the interest rate and aggregate demand in the simple Keynesian model.

3. Illustrate using diagrams how to derive the expenditures equilibrium (*EE*) line. Why does it slope down?

4. Illustrate how the slope of the investment line determines the slope of the *EE* line.

5. From your knowledge of the *EE* line, can you determine which level of NNP and the interest rate will actually prevail in an economy? Explain why or why not.

6. What do we mean by "equilibrium" in the monetary sector?

7. With a given demand for money and a supply of money, can we determine the interest rate that will prevail in the economy? Why or why not?

8. Using diagrams, illustrate how to derive the monetary equilibrium (*ME*) line.

9. What determines the slope of the *ME* line?

10. Suppose two of your friends are having an argument. One argues that the rate of interest is more important in the complete model because it determines the level of aggregate demand and thus equilibrium NNP. The other argues that NNP is most important because it determines the demand for money and thus the interest rate. How would you settle this argument?

11. What is meant by the absence of a "money illusion"? Do you think people have a "money illusion"? Why or why not?

12. Suppose the economy is experiencing unemployment. Illustrate using the complete model with money and prices how an economy adjusts towards a full-employment position. Why does the *ME/P* line shift?

CHAPTER
8
FISCAL POLICY

Although "fiscal policy" has become somewhat of a household phrase, it will be useful nevertheless to define its meaning in rather precise terms. We can think of fiscal policy as the conscious attempt by government to promote full employment without inflation through its spending and taxing powers. Throughout this chapter, then, we will be primarily concerned with the effects of government spending and taxation on the level of output and employment in the economy.

BUILT-IN STABILIZERS

Before we turn to a discussion of the deliberate changes in taxes and spending that can be undertaken by the government to promote full employment without inflation, it is necessary to call attention to fiscal policy measures that have been "built-in" to our economic system. These policies specify that government spending or tax changes will take place automatically in response to upturns or downturns in economic activity.

Two important automatic spending measures are unemployment compensation and the various welfare programs. These programs, you will note, are designed to "feed" money into the economy during recessionary periods. For example, as unemployment rises and family incomes fall, the influx of money through unemployment compensation prevents a more drastic decline in economic activity. Then as the economy recovers and people return to their jobs there is a reduction in unemployment compensation which helps to hold down inflationary pressure in the future period. Thus unemployment compensation is in effect an automatic or built-in stabilizer for the economy. Welfare programs have a similar effect, although these are perhaps more important as a long-term means of livelihood for persons outside the labor force and the long-term unemployed.

The U.S. progressive income tax also can be thought of as somewhat of a built-in stabilizer. By a progressive income tax we mean a tax in which the rate of tax increases with higher incomes. Thus in recessionary periods the government taxes the income of the economy at a lower rate than during inflationary times. In a sense, then, the progressive income tax is a built-in stabilizer because it leaves proportionately more "purchasing power" in the economy during recessions and pulls proportionately more out during inflationary times.

Built-in or automatic stabilizers often are referred to as nondiscretionary fiscal policy because they operate without specific congressional edict. Granted, of course, the built-in stabilizers were originally created by an act of Congress, but once they are instituted Congress does not have to pass further legislation in order for the stabilizers to "do their thing."

Most of our discussion in this chapter will dwell on so-called discretionary fiscal policy. Here we have in mind tax or spending policies designed to deal with specific problems during specific periods of time. A good example of such a policy is the income tax surcharge of recent years. By adding an additional, temporary tax, the government hoped to pull purchasing power out of the economy to reduce the inflationary tendencies. Other examples of discretionary fiscal policies include the public works projects of the 1930's and the start of the super highway construction program of the late 1950's. Both of these policies were aimed at stimulating business activity so as to reduce unemployment during these periods, although the highway program was sold in part at least by citing its military significance.

In our discussion of discretionary fiscal policy, we will utilize the Keynesian models that we developed in Chapters 4 and 7. Indeed the major reason for developing these models is to provide a framework for analyzing government policies.

FISCAL POLICY IN THE CONTEXT OF
THE SIMPLE KEYNESIAN MODEL

In discussing the simple Keynesian model in Chapter 4 and again in regard to the complete model of Chapter 7, we mentioned that the equilibrium level of NNP may not coincide with full-employment NNP. If equilibrium occurs at a lower level of NNP than is necessary for full employment, an unemployment situation will develop. Conversely, if equilibrium NNP is greater than the level that corresponds to full employment, inflation will appear.

The problems of unemployment and inflation are illustrated in the context of the simple Keynesian model in Figure 8–1 (A) and (B). Notice in diagram (A) that full employment can be obtained only if there is an upward shift in aggregate demand. This can be accomplished either through an increase in government spending, a tax cut, or some combination of the two. As you recall from Chapter 4, an increase in government spending adds to the aggregate demand for goods and services and as a result adds to the total output and income of the economy.

Of course, it is necessary to assume in this case that the increase in government spending does not result in a decrease in private consumption or investment. For example, if the government decides to build a number of atomic powered electric generating plants, private companies might well decide to reduce their construction of a like number of these plants. Hence the decrease in private investment might simply cancel the increase in public investment. If the government is interested in shifting aggregate demand upwards, it should, therefore, purchase goods or services that are not readily substituted for private goods and services. There is less likelihood of offsetting reductions in private expenditure if the increased government spending concentrates primarily on public goods such as public education, sewage disposal facilities, highways, public parks, and yes, even on the military or the space program. Of course, the government should not spend for the sake of spending but rather should spend on goods and services that maximize the welfare of the public.

The manner of financing the increased government spending also is of extreme importance. If the government should happen to have a surplus in the treasury at the time of the increased spending, there is no problem. However, if the treasury is "bare," which is most likely to be the case if the economy is in a downturn and tax receipts are down, the government must obtain additional funds from somewhere. A number of alternatives are available. First the government can increase taxes. But this would be a rather unwise alternative if the objective is to stimulate economic activity because higher taxes draw "purchasing power" out of the economy and dampen economic activity.

It is reasonable to expect, therefore, that the government most likely will engage in deficit spending during a recession. In other words, it will spend more than it receives in taxes. In this situation the government still has two alternatives: (1) it can borrow from the public by selling government bonds or (2) it can print money. We will be better able to evaluate the outcome of these two alternatives in the following chapter on monetary policy, but an intuitive explanation at this point will call attention to the problems involved. Let us consider first, the sale of government bonds. Recall from Chapter 6 that the sale of government bonds to commercial banks or the public reduces the money supply. But in reducing the money supply, the government can increase interest rates and consequently dampen economic activity. Thus the undesired outcome of financing the increased government spending could in this case at least partially offset the desired effect of the the increased spending. Of course, the Federal

Reserve may choose to make an open-market purchase of bonds at this same time which, you recall, tends to increase the money supply.

The difference between government spending and tax revenue also can be made up by printing additional currency. Then as these dollars are used to purchase the additional goods and services, the money supply is increased. We will see in the following chapter that an increase in the money supply serves as an additional stimulant to the economy. Hence the increase in government spending will not have to be as great to achieve full employment as the simple model illustrated in Figure 8–1 (A) might imply. Although, again in this case, the Federal Reserve has the power to offset the influx of newly printed cash by selling government securities in the open market.

Perhaps the main point to be made here is that the manner of financing additional government spending can have important side effects that either work to offset the impact of the additional spending or make it more potent than might be anticipated.

FIGURE 8–1. Fiscal policy in the context of the simple Keynesian model without money

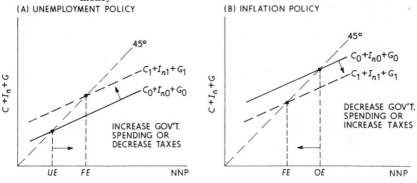

During a recessionary period as depicted by Figure 8–1 (A), as an alternative to increasing its spending, the government could decrease taxes. This action also would stimulate the economy by leaving more dollars in the hands of households and business and in so doing allow the private sector to increase its spending. However, many of the same financing problems discussed above arise in regard to a tax cut. Presumably the government would not wish to decrease its spending during a recession, so the decrease in taxes again leaves the government with a budget deficit. The same alternatives as we discussed in regard to an increase in government spending are available. In order to hold government spending at its previous level the loss of revenue because of the tax cut can be made up by selling bonds to the public, i.e., borrowing, printing money, or some combination of the two. And as we saw, the resulting changes in the nation's money supply accordingly will tend to offset or augment the effect of the tax cut unless the Federal Reserve chooses to take action to hold the money supply constant.

Although the options of an increase in government spending versus a tax cut have similar economic consequences, there are some other considerations that the government may wish to take into account. For one thing, it is rather difficult for the government to use the increased spending tool swiftly because new projects or programs generally take time to conceive and set in motion. This is especially true for large investment projects such as roads, land reclamation, etc.

Political considerations are important also. An additional problem with increased government spending is that it tends to be distasteful to the more conservative members of society. For an administration that must draw on bipartisan support, as all do, the combination of high unemployment and increased government intervention in the economy may be more than a political party wants to bear. On the other hand a tax reduction during a recessionary period can be instituted rather quickly and at the same time Congress can demonstrate to the folks back home that it is doing something about the high unemployment. Much "political hay" was made out of the tax cut that was instituted during the Kennedy administration. A like amount of increased government spending might have gone by largely unnoticed.

The problem of excess demand and inflationary pressure on the economy is illustrated in Figure 8–1 (B). Here the problem is just the opposite of what we have been just discussing. The relatively high level of aggregate demand has pulled the equilibrium level of NNP past the point of full employment. Hence the increased money value of NNP that occurs as the economy moves past the full-employment (FE) point is due largely to higher prices rather than increased output. In this situation the appropriate action by the government would be to decrease or shift down the level of aggregate demand, assuming that it wants to reduce the inflationary pressure on the economy.

As you would expect from the previous discussion, the government, in this case, should decrease government spending, increase taxes, or some combination of the two. Either or both of these measures serve to draw purchasing power out of the economy and relieve the pressure of private demand against the available supply of goods and services. From the standpoint of government finance, there is much less of a problem here than we encountered in the unemployment case. The budget surplus that the government might acquire because of its reduced spending or increased taxation can easily be held until needed at some later date.

Perhaps the most troublesome problem stemming from any decrease in government spending is the rise in unemployment brought on by the loss of government contracts. Firms that produce goods and services for the government have little alternative but to lay off employees when this market "dries up." And markets for new products and new jobs for these released employees do not emerge in a "twinkling of an eye." It takes time for business firms to retool to new markets and for unemployed people to search out new jobs. If the government spending cut is severe, as is generally the case following a war, the adjustment period may take several years. Hence we might expect to observe an increase in unemployment following a significant reduction in government spending. Moreover, if the inflation has built up a momentum, the immediate consequences of a government spending cut may be rising unemployment with continued inflation, as occurred during the greater part of 1970.

A tax increase, the other fiscal policy alternative open to the government during an inflation, is subject to a different kind of problem, namely that of political expedience. Few members of Congress like to go on record as favoring higher taxes especially before an upcoming election. As a result there is likely to be considerable "foot-dragging" and debate over tax bills that really should be enacted quickly if they are to have their desired effect. A good example of this problem occurred during the latter part of the Johnson administration where Congress debated the proposed tax increase for about two years before passing it.

THE SIMPLE KEYNESIAN MODEL
AS A PREDICTIVE DEVICE

One advantage of the simple Keynesian model is that it is possible to specify to the dollar how much the government should change its spending or taxes in order to bring the economy to a full-employment equilibrium without inflation. Of course, we must specify where the full-employment equilibrium is in relation to the current NNP, and also we must know the nation's marginal propensity to consume (MPC). Assuming that this information is possible to obtain, let us see how this little predictive device works.

Recall from our discussion of the multiplier process in Chapter 4 that a dollar of new or additional spending will bring forth several additional dollars of spending. This occurs because spending by one person is income to another, and when people receive income they generally spend part of it. The fraction of an additional dollar of income that is spent is defined as the marginal propensity to consume. Also recall from Chapter 4 that the government spending multiplier is equal to $1/1 - $ MPC, assuming there is not an offsetting change in the private sector to a change in government spending or that the financing problems do not cause a change in the money supply. Therefore, if MPC is 0.75, as we have assumed, an additional dollar of government spending ultimately will bring forth $4 of new spending in the economy $(1/1 - 0.75 = 4)$.

Referring back to Figure 8–1 (A), suppose the economy is "stuck" in an unemployment equilibrium as denoted by *UE* on the horizontal axis. To provide some plausible numbers for our problem, let us assume that the full-employment NNP is equal to $936 billion and the unemployment equilibrium (*UE*) is $900 billion. Thus the economy should be "nudged" ahead by $36 billion to attain full employment. In terms of the diagram, we can view a $1 billion increase in government spending as shifting the aggregate demand line upwards by $1 billion. Now we know that with a multiplier of 4, a $1 billion increase in government spending increases NNP by $4 billion. Thus it is not very difficult to figure out that government spending should increase by $9 billion to push the economy ahead by $36 billion. A convenient formula[1] that can be used to determine how much government spending should be changed to obtain the desired change in NNP is:

$$\Delta G = \Delta NNP/M_g$$

where ΔG is the calculated change in government spending or shift in the aggregate demand line, Δ NNP is the desired change in NNP, and M_g is the government spending multiplier.

This formula can be applied, of course, to either an upward shift in aggregate demand to remedy unemployment or a downward shift to ease inflationary pressure. If, for example, the economy is experiencing inflation, as depicted by Figure 8–1 (B), all we would have to do is estimate the difference between *OE*, the "overemployment" equilibrium, and *FE*, and then insert this number into the above formula. For example, if *FE* is $936 billion and *OE* is $952 billion, the desired decrease in equilibrium NNP would be $16 billion ($952 − $936). Inserting $16 billion into the above formula, we can determine that the government could remedy the inflationary situation by reducing its spending by $4 billion.

Offhand we might guess that the government could achieve the same effects through comparable changes in taxes as through the changes in spending we have just discussed. But this is not quite right. A $1 billion tax change will not have as large an impact on the economy as $1 billion change in government spending. In other words, a $1 billion tax decrease, for example, will not shift the aggregate demand line up by the full $1 billion. Why? To understand this phenomenon, it is first necessary to be aware that people do not change their spending by the full amount of the tax change. The MPC tells us that. For example, if the government reduces taxes by $1 billion, the people will have an additional $1 billion that can be considered as additional disposable income. But it is not likely

---

[1] From our definition of the multiplier we know that $\Delta G \times M_g = \Delta NNP$. Dividing both sides of this equation by M_g, we obtain the formula above.

they will spend the entire $1 billion; they will spend part and save part. If their MPC is 0.75 the people will spend $0.75 billion and save the remaining $0.25 billion. Thus a tax decrease of $1 billion will shift the aggregate demand line upwards by only $0.75 billion if the MPC is 0.75.

The fact that people increase or decrease their saving as well as their spending in response to a tax change is the reason why the tax multiplier is less than the government spending multiplier. With just a little extra effort we can determine how much less the tax multiplier will be. Perhaps the easiest way to approach this is to compare the multiplier process of a government spending change with a comparable tax change. In Table 8–1 we compare the first three rounds of the multiplier process for a $1 billion government spending increase with a $1 billion tax decrease. Notice that on the first round in the government spending column, the entire $1 billion is spent. But in the tax column the first round only shows $0.75 billion being spent. The remain $0.25 billion is saved. And in all subsequent rounds the numbers in the tax column are smaller.

TABLE 8–1. Comparing the multiplier process of a government spending change with a tax change

	$1 Billion Increase in Government Spending	$1 Billion Decrease in Taxes
Round 1	$1 billion	$0.75 billion
Round 2	0.75	0.56
Round 3	0.56	0.42
	.	.
	.	.
To infinity	.	.
	$4 billion	$ 3 billion

Using the multiplier formula developed in Chapter 4, we see that the total increase in spending in the economy will increase by $4 billion because of the $1 billion initial increase in government spending. However, in the case of the $1 billion tax decrease, total spending only increases by $3 billion. Hence the government spending multiplier is 4 in this case and the tax multiplier is 3, or one less. The amazing thing about this is that under the assumptions of the simple model, the tax multiplier always will be one less than the government spending multiplier for a "lump-sum" tax such as we have assumed. If we let MPC be 0.80, for example, M_g would be 5 and M_t (the tax multiplier) would be 4. The fact that the tax multiplier is one less than the government spending multiplier can be proven algebraically but this is best left to the intermediate level macro course.

Now that we know that the tax multiplier is always one less than the government spending multiplier, we can modify the formula that we developed in regard to a government spending change so it can be used also to predict a tax change. Now we have:

$$\Delta T = \Delta \text{NNP}/M_t$$

where ΔT is the computed change in taxes, Δ NNP is the desired change in NNP, and M_t is the tax multiplier. Also keep in mind that $M_t = M_g - 1$.

Using this little formula, we can compute the tax changes that will bring the economy to the desired full-employment equilibrium. Faced with a similar unemployment situation discussed in regard to a government spending change where FE was \$936 billion and UE was \$900 billion, the necessary \$36 billion increase in NNP could be achieved by a \$12 billion tax decrease ($\Delta T = 36/3 = 12$). Or in the inflationary situation where NNP needed to be reduced from \$952 to \$936 billion, the job could be accomplished by a \$5⅓ billion tax increase ($\Delta T = 16/3 = 5⅓$).

Keep in mind, though, that even though the needed tax changes are larger than the government spending changes, the tax changes shift aggregate demand by the same amount as the government spending changes. It just takes a larger tax change to do the same job as a given government spending change. If we want to determine how much a tax change shifts aggregate demand, we can use the formula $\Delta D = \Delta T \times \text{MPC}$, where ΔD is the shift in aggregate demand and ΔT is the tax change.

THE BALANCED BUDGET MULTIPLIER

It is interesting to note as well that increasing government spending and taxes by a given amount will increase the equilibrium level of NNP by this very same amount. For example, suppose the government increases its spending by \$1 billion and at the same time increases taxes by \$1 billion so as to maintain a balanced budget, at least for this change in spending. If the MPC is 0.75, the government spending multiplier tells us that the government spending increases by itself will increase equilibrium NNP by \$4 billion. But because M_t is one less than M_g, the tax increase will not completely offset the government spending increase.

Viewing this process as a sequence, the \$1 billion government spending increase shifts aggregate upwards by \$1 billion and increases equilibrium NNP by \$4 billion after the multiplier process has run its course. Now applying the tax increase to this new, higher aggregate demand line, we know from our previous discussion that initial spending will decline by \$0.75 billion so that aggregate demand shifts down by \$0.75 billion. Or we can apply the tax multiplier to the \$1 billion increase in taxes to determine that equilibrium NNP declines by \$3 billion. Thus the government spending increase pushes NNP up by \$4 billion but the tax increase pulls it back by \$3 billion, leaving a \$1 billion net increase.

If we would have increased government spending and taxes by $10 billion, the net increase in NNP would have been $10 billion. Moreover, this would be true regardless of the size of the MPC. It will be helpful to prove this to yourself by choosing different changes in G and T and working out the outcome under different values of MPC. You will find that the value of MPC does not alter the fact that comparable changes in G and T always change equilibrium NNP by this exact same amount. Economists refer to this phenomenon as the balanced budget multiplier. The value of this multiplier is always one because equilibrium NNP always changes by one times the initial change in G and T.

IMPLICIT ASSUMPTIONS OF THE SIMPLE MODEL

Because the simple Keynesian model seemingly gives such exact and simple answers to complex problems, it may leave the impression that we know more than we really do about combating unemployment or inflation. We ought to review, therefore, some of the basic assumptions that we have made in using the model. As we pointed out earlier, it is assumed that changes in government spending are not offset by opposite changes in private spending. Also we have assumed that government spending changes have not affected the money supply.

In our discussion of taxes and the tax multiplier we have implicitly assumed that taxes are of a "lump-sum" variety. In other words, taxes are assumed not to change with a change in income. Thus the tax multiplier for an income tax can be expected to be somewhat different. About all we need to say here is that the tax multiplier for an income tax will be somewhat smaller than the lump-sum tax multiplier we have discussed in this chapter. This is proven algebraically in more advanced macro courses but we can at least present the economic rationale behind the difference here. Under an income tax, a tax decrease, for example, means that the various tax rates are reduced. But as the economy is stimulated and NNP increases, more people are caught in the higher tax brackets which tends to offset somewhat the initial tax reduction. Hence tax revenue does not decline as much as under a lump-sum tax so NNP does not increase as much. Thus the tax multiplier is somewhat smaller for the income tax.

A very crucial assumption of the simple model is that either the interest rate does not change with changes in aggregate demand, or if the interest rate does change it does not affect the level of consumption or investment to a significant degree. There is a great deal of disagreement among economists as to how important the interest rate is to consumption or investment. Those who argue that the interest rate is not very important in determining investment, i.e., the line graphing the interest rate against investment is nearly vertical, would in turn argue that the simple model is a fairly accurate predictor of the effects of fiscal policy on the economy. In other words, they would say that the multipliers discussed in this chapter provide a fairly accurate picture of the changes that would actually occur with changes in government spending or taxation.

On the other hand, those economists who maintain that the interest rate changes significantly with shifts in aggregate demand and that these changes have a significant affect on investment or consumption, tend to place relatively less faith in the simple model as a predictive device. Given their assumptions, the economic rationale of their arguments is quite plausible. An increase in government spending, for example, and the subsequent increase in aggregate demand increase the rate of interest because of the increased demand for loans to finance much of the additional investment and consumption. The increase in the rate of interest, however, tends to dampen or hold back investment and consumption so that equilibrium NNP does not increase as much as would be predicted by the government spending multiplier. The complete Keynesian model with money provides a better framework for analyzing this argument, however, so let us now consider fiscal policy in the context of this model.

FISCAL POLICY IN THE CONTEXT OF
THE KEYNESIAN MODEL WITH MONEY

Fiscal policy, as you know, relates to changes in government spending and taxation to obtain full employment without inflation. We also know that changes in government spending and taxation affect aggregate demand in the context of the simple model. Thus in terms of the complete model we would have to say that fiscal policy affects the expenditures equilibrium line because this line is derived from the aggregate demand line.

Our first task, then, is to see how changes in government spending or taxation affect the EE/P line. To begin, we know that an increase in government spending shifts aggregate demand upwards. Recall that the aggregate demand line is drawn for a given interest rate. Thus we obtain a higher level of equilibrium NNP for a given interest rate. But this implies that the EE/P line shifts upwards and to the right. In other words, we now obtain a larger NNP for a given interest rate. It will be helpful if you check this for yourself by drawing an aggregate demand line for a given interest rate, shift it upwards because of the increase in government spending, and then plot the two equilibrium values of NNP on the EE/P diagram. Your diagram should look something like Figure 8–2 (A). Thus an increase in government spending shifts the EE/P line upwards and to the right because aggregate demand is shifted upwards. A decrease in taxes, which also shifts aggregate demand upwards, would, as expected, shift the EE/P line upwards and to the right as well.

Figure 8–2 (A), therefore, represents a situation where the economy initially is suffering from unemployment, as denoted by the intersection of EE/P and ME/P. In other words, the equilibrium level of NNP/P is less than the level that corresponds to full employment. As we saw in Chapter 7, full employment eventually could be obtained in this case if the price level declined so as to shift the ME/P line downwards and to the right. But as we mentioned, this process might take years to complete and in the meantime the economy might suffer from a high rate of unemployment. The problem could be taken care of quite handily, then, by the government increasing its spending or cutting taxes. Of course, the problems of a possible reduction in private spending when the government increases its spending or of financing a deficit without altering the money supply still confront us in this model as in the simple model.

FIGURE 8–2. Fiscal policy in the context of the complete model

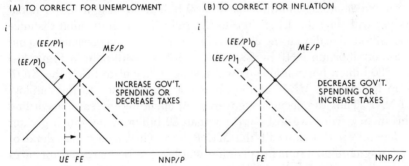

The problem of an inflationary economy is depicted in Figure 8–2 (B). In this situation the intersection of the EE/P and ME/P lines falls to the right of full-employment NNP. Unless the government takes action to shift either the EE/P line or the ME/P line to the left, the price level will rise until the ME/P line shifts left far enough on its own to intersect EE/P at the level of real NNP that corresponds to full employment. If the government wants to use fiscal policy to accomplish the objective of full employment without inflation, it should decrease its spending and/or increase taxes so as to shift the EE/P line to the left until it intersects the ME/P line at the point that corresponds to full employment.

We should be reminded again of the problems involved in such a policy. A decrease in government spending may eventually reduce inflationary pressure, but the adjustment period when laid-off workers search for new jobs and business retools for the private market may be long and painful. As we mentioned in regard to the simple model, when the "brakes are put on" there will likely be a period when inflation, if it has built up momentum, keeps rolling along while unemployment is rising.

THE MULTIPLIERS IN THE CONTEXT
OF THE COMPLETE MODEL

In our use of the simple model, we were able to predict in rather precise terms the exact amount government spending or taxes should be changed to achieve full employment without inflation. In this more complete model, however, we cannot be as precise. It is not that the complete model is less adequate; indeed it is more adequate because it takes the monetary sector into account. The reason we cannot use the multipliers to predict full-employment NNP in the model is because changes in the interest rate either hold back or augment the spending or tax changes.

Consider the unemployment situation depicted in Figure 8–3. Choosing the same numbers as we used in the unemployment example for the simple model illustrated in Figure 8–1 (A), let full-employment NNP be $936 billion and the unemployment equilibrium (UE) be $900 billion. If the government spending multiplier is 4, a $9 billion increase in government spending will shift the EE/P line to the right by the horizontal distance of $36 billion. Recall that the $9 billion upward shift in aggregate demand increase equilibrium NNP by $36 billion. But you will note in Figue 8–3 that a $36 billion horizontal shift will not be sufficient to bring the EE/P line up to intersect ME/P at the point that corresponds to full-employment NNP. Thus the necessary government spending increase, according to this model, will have to be greater than $9 billion. How much greater will depend on the slope of the ME/P line. The steeper the slope of ME/P, the more government spending will have to be increased (or taxes decreased) in order for the EE/P line to intersect ME/P at the point corresponding to full-employment NNP. Thus fiscal policy is a rather ineffective device if the ME/P line is relatively steep. Recall from Chapter 7

FIGURE 8–3.   Fiscal policy and the dampening
effect of a higher interest rate

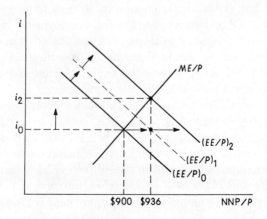

that the steeper the demand curve for money, the steeper is the ME/P line.

In the situation illustrated in Figure 8–3 the $9 billion increase in government spending shifts the expenditures line from $(EE/P)_0$ to $(EE/P)_1$. But as you can see this represents less than half the needed shift to reach the position of $(EE/P)_2$. Hence we can infer that government spending would have to be increased by at least $18 billion to obtain the desired $36 billion increase in NNP. In other words, it appears that the multiplier would be closer to 2 than to 4.

The economic explanation for the reduction in the multiplier is that the increase in the interest rate from i_0 to i_2 in Figure 8–3 dampens or discourages investment and possibly consumption. If people become more reluctant to invest or buy consumer durables with higher interest rates, the government must push harder and harder to stimulate the economy, and this implies a smaller multiplier.

We should point out, however, that the slope of the EE/P line also is important. If EE/P is nearly vertical then the slope of the ME/P line does not have much bearing on the size of the multiplier. You might verify this for yourself by superimposing a vertical EE/P line on Figure 8–3 and observing that a $36 billion horizontal shift now brings the vertical EE/P line over the desired distance to intersect with ME/P at the full-employment level of NNP/P. A vertical EE/P line you recall from Chapter 7 means that investment exhibits absolutely no response to changes in the rate of interest. In other words, the investment line is vertical when graphed against interest on the vertical axis.

Those economists who are "pro-fiscal-policy" will tend to argue that the investment line is nearly vertical which implies a nearly vertical EE/P line. Economists who are more skeptical of fiscal policy, on the other hand, stress the importance of the interest rate on investment and the resulting slope of the EE/P line. The more responsive investment is to changes in the interest rate, the less steep the EE/P line will be and the harder it is for fiscal policy to have much effect on the economy.

FLUCTUATIONS IN ECONOMIC ACTIVITY

Ideally we would like to see the economy exhibit a stable growth trend in the output goods and services, thereby avoiding excessive recessionary or inflationary tendencies. But in reality, most, if not all growing economies, experience considerable fluctuation in economic activity. Fiscal policy, as we mentioned, is one means of smoothing out these economic fluctuations.

Figures 8–4 and 8–5 might prove helpful in gauging the extent of economic instability in the United States economy over the past four decades as well as providing some insight into the possible causes of the instability.

Here we present the year-to-year percentage changes of the major components of gross national product. A percentage change of a component that is above the zero axis, i.e., positive, implies growth during that particular year. The higher the line, the larger the percentage growth. Conversely, if the line falls below the zero axis into the negative region, it is an indication that the particular item declined in absolute amount during the year. We present all items in real terms, i.e., deflated by a change in the price level, to more clearly identify basic shifts in the expenditure pattern of the economy.

Perhaps the first impression received from Figure 8–4 is the relatively large fluctuations in gross investment compared to personal consumption expenditures. In the United States, at least, investment seems to be a very volatile component of GNP. Notice that investment took a number of wild swings during the 1930s, plummeting sharply during the early part of the decade, recovering briefly in the mid 30s, only to take another noticeable decline during 1938. The two sharp swings of investment during the 1940s were, of course, a result of World War II. At the outbreak of the war investment was curtailed to devote all possible resources to war production. Then after the war, investment bounced back to rebuild our aging productive capacity.

The post–World War II era brought somewhat less severe fluctuations in investment, although we can observe nine different years when it de-

FIGURE 8–4. Annual percentage changes in U.S. personal consumption and gross domestic investment spending, 1930–69 (1958 prices)

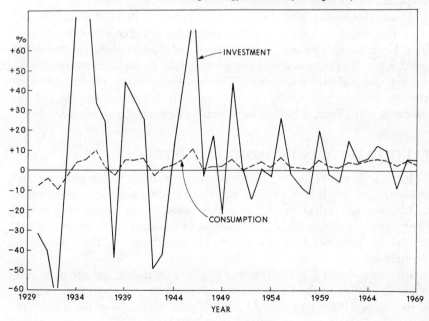

clined in absolute terms. The variation in real personal consumption expenditure has been on a much more moderate scale. Granted, consumption did decline in absolute terms during the early 1930's, but not the percentage decline observed for investment. Similar to investment behavior, the post–World War II years also brought a moderation in consumer expenditure variation. In fact, the major portion of the 1960's brought a relative stability in consumption, at least more stability than the economy had experienced during the previous three decades.

Turning next to Figure 8–5, we observe a comparable degree of fluctuation in government spending, particularly at the federal level. This is not to imply, however, that fluctuations in government spending are necessarily undesirable. Indeed, according to our previous discussion, the government should step in during recessionary times to bolster spending in the economy. A good example of this occurred in the 1930's. The increased public expenditure on public works projects and the like was designed to pull the economy out of the depths of the Great Depression.

Of course, the major changes in federal government spending came during and immediately following war periods. The largest relative changes occurred in connection with World War II, first to mobilize the economy from a peacetime to a wartime basis, then to cut back on the huge military expenditure after the war. It is not difficult, either, to identify the Korean and Vietnam military build-ups on Figure 8–5, although

FIGURE 8–5. Annual percentage changes in federal government and state and local government expenditures, 1930–69 (1958 prices)

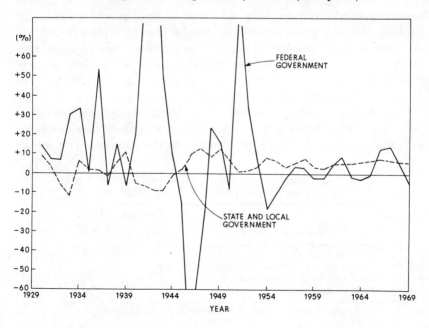

these were not of the relative magnitude of World War II. The expenditures of the state and local governments, although exhibiting some fluctuation during the 30's and 40's, have since then been one of the more stable components of the economy.

In the context of the Keynesian model with money, we can look upon an absolute decrease in consumption or investment spending as contributing to a shift to the left in the EE/P line. Unless offset by comparable increases in government spending, the end result is a decrease in equilibrium NNP/P and an increase in unemployment. By the same token, rapid increases in consumption or investment can be represented by a significant shift to the right of the EE/P line, thereby contributing to inflationary pressure in the economy.

It should also be kept in mind that substantial fluctuations in government spending, unless to offset changes in private spending, also can contribute to rather severe fluctuations in overall economic activity. Such fluctuations have come about mainly as a result of wars, either to build up the military or to reduce it. The recent space and military cutbacks during 1969 and 1970 provide a current example of this problem. As a result there seems to be increasing concern over the destabilizing effects that the federal government can have on the economy. More and more people are urging the government to exercise greater care in letting the economy down somewhat more gently and also to help the economy adjust to large federal spending reductions.

The degree of influence over the total economy by any one component of GNP will depend also on its relative size. For example, annual consumption expenditures are about 4.5 times as large as gross investment spending. Hence a given percentage change in consumption likely will have a much larger absolute impact on the economy than an equal percentage change in investment. The figures in Table 8–2 provide an indication of the relative importance of each component of GNP and how the relative importance of each has changed over the years.

Notice that personal consumption is by far the largest component of GNP. Thus, rather small percentage changes in consumption can bring substantial absolute changes total spending in the economy. The second

Table 8–2.   Relative size of the major components of U.S. gross national product 1929 and 1969

	Percentage of GNP	
Component	1929	1969
Personal consumption	69	64
Gross domestic investment	20	16
State and local government	9	10
Federal government	2	10

Source: Economic Report of the President, 1970, pp. 178–79.

major point of interest in Table 8–2 is the substantial increase in the role of the federal government in the economy. Federal spending has now become a substantially larger "fish" in the "economic pond," and as a result sharp changes in direction of federal spending can create some rather large "waves" in economic activity.

TIMING OF FISCAL POLICY

In our discussion of fiscal policy, we started out with the simple Keynesian model which provided us with simple and exact answers. But then we began to get a hint of complications when we looked at financing problems and the effect of government spending reductions on the level of employment. Still more complications were brought in when we graduated to the more complete model. Here we saw that the simple multipliers may not be correct after all, so that we cannot be as precise in saying how much the government should change its taxes or spending to correct an unemployment or inflationary situation.

The preceding complications are relatively minor, however, compared to the ones we will now discuss. There are two major sets of complications or problems that arise in the implementation of fiscal policy; both relate to timing. The first is the problem of when to undertake needed changes in government spending and taxation in order to stabilize the economy. The second is the lag between the decision to undertake spending or tax changes and their effects on the economy.

The first problem is really a matter of identifying when the economy is headed for a recession or a runaway inflation. As we saw in the previous section, the economy tends to fluctuate from year to year in a rather uneven and unpredictable fashion. The difficulty, then, is to decide whether an upturn or downturn is just a minor fluctuation, or whether it is the beginning of something big. If the government takes rather drastic measures to curb a recession, for example, at the hint of a slight downturn in economic activity, the result might well be a forthcoming inflationary spiral. Theoretically, then, the government should take anti-recessionary measures, a spending increase or a tax cut, when the economy is just beginning to enter a downturn in economic activity as illustrated by time T_0 in Figure 8–6. By the same token, anti-inflationary measures should be reserved for a time such as T_1. The object is to smooth out the "booms" and "busts" as shown by the even dotted line starting at T_0 in Figure 8–6.

If the government is successful in identifying critical turning points in the economy, such as T_0 and T_1, there is still the question of doing something soon enough to have the desired effect. Suppose, for example, that the time span between T_0 and T_1 is three years. If it takes the government two years to push a tax cut through Congress or a similar period to decide on new government projects, the actual effect may be just the opposite of what is desired. If the anti-recessionary measures do not begin to be felt until around T_1, the result may well be to stimulate the economy in the forthcoming boom period following T_1. As a result the inflation following T_1 could be even worse than it would have been had no action been taken at all. This is illustrated by the dotted line beginning at T_2.

FIGURE 8–6.   Illustrating the problem of the correct timing of fiscal policy

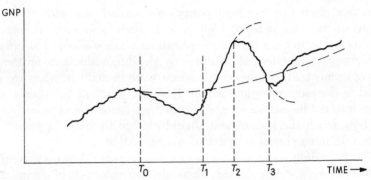

As a further problem, it is not very feasible to shut down government projects that have been initiated during a recession even when an inflationary period looms on the horizon. Hence these additional projects serve to accentuate the forthcoming inflation.

The exact same problems of timing and effect confront the government when inflation threatens such as at T_1. Again a tax increase or a spending reduction may require one or two years to pass Congress, especially the tax increase if there is an upcoming election. As a result the anti-inflationary policy may become a pro-recessionary policy and pull the economy into a more severe state of unemployment as illustrated by the downard sloping dotted line beginning at T_3.

If these problems aren't bad enough, there is also the problem of predicting when actual government spending or tax changes will have their major effect on the economy. We have implicitly assumed in our previous discussion that the desired effect of policy takes place immediately after action is taken. But this need not be the case. The major problem is that relatively little is known about the duration of lags between government action and its effect. Indeed the lag may change from one year to the next.

Another difficulty of implementing fiscal policy is that the government may have higher priorities than maintaining a economically stable economy. One of the major priorities appears to be the waging of war. Although the federal government may be fully aware of the destabilizing effects of a huge military build-up or cutback, it may still choose to implement these policies. This is not to pass judgment on the rightness or wrongness of such decisions; each instance must, of course, be evaluated separately. The main point is that the federal government may be faced with conflicting goals, and the goal of economic stability may not always come out on top.

By now you probably realize that fiscal policy is not nearly as simple as it might have first appeared in the context of the simple model. The more complete model brings out some of the hidden problems and controversies, but even this is a crude tool when we consider the timing aspects and other goals of the government. The more economists learn about the economy, the more they are impressed with its complexity and how much more there still is to learn.

THE NATIONAL DEBT

A discussion of fiscal policy would not be complete without bringing in the national debt, or the public debt as it is often called. The national debt can be defined as the amount of money the government owes the people. The government borrows from the people by issuing and selling government bonds. In recent decades many people have expressed concern about the size of the national debt. We hear phrases such as "the country going bankrupt" or "fiscal irresponsibility" in relation to the government increasing the public debt.

Is the public debt really something to be concerned about? It is important first to keep in mind that the public debt is debt which the government owes to the people. However, because the people "own" the government, it is debt which the people owe to themselves. If the government decided to pay off say $100 billion of the public debt, it would increase taxes by $100 billion and immediately pay this amount back to the people. As you can see, this $100 billion dollar payment would not make the nation any "poorer" because the people would still have the $100 billion. Granted, there may be some redistribution of wealth towards former bondholders, but the total wealth of the nation would remain unchanged. Of course, it is not likely the government ever would want to pay off such a large amount of the debt in a short period of time because it would likely have a destabilizing effect on the economy.

A helpful analogy is to consider the public debt as you would consider debt owed by your right hand to your left. When the debt is paid, your right hand has less money but your left hand has more, so in net you are neither richer or poorer. The public debt would be another matter, however, if the government had borrowed from another nation. For example, if the United States owed $100 billion to the Canadian government, paying off the debt would leave the United States with $100 billion less in goods and services. But because the U.S. public debt is owed mainly to U.S. citizens, its existence should not be a cause for concern.

The figures in Table 8–3 permit us to take a brief look at the growth and magnitude of the public debt. In the interest of clarity the debt of the federal government is separated from the debt of state and local governments. Also, for the sake of comparison, figures on private debt are provided. All debt figures are presented in constant 1969 prices to facilitate comparison over time.

TABLE 8–3.   Public and private debt in the United States, selected years (1969 prices)

Year	Public Debt (Billion $) Federal	Public Debt (Billion $) State & Local	(Billion $) Private Debt	Federal Debt Per Person	Federal Debt % of GNP
1929	$ 35	$ 29	$ 346	$ 287	16%
1939	112	43	327	801	47
1945	515	27	286	3,681	119
1949	335	29	321	2,245	85
1959	304	73	665	1,710	50
1968	311	137	1,198	1,546	34

Source: *Economic Report of the President, 1970.* Deflated by Consumers Price Index, 1969 = 100.

Notice first that the debt of the federal government increased very rapidly from 1929 to 1945. During the 1930's, the federal debt increased about threefold, mainly because of the Great Depression and the attempt of the federal government to stimulate the economy by increasing its spending. The public works projects of the 1930's bear evidence of this increased spending. As the country moved into the 1940's the World War II period brought even greater increases in the federal debt. During this period the cost of goods and services purchased by the federal government far exceeded its tax revenue even though taxes were increased. The excess of government purchases over tax revenue was made up in part by borrowing from the people, i.e., selling government bonds, and in part by printing money.

In view of the large and rapid mobilization from a peacetime to a war economy, these policies probably were the most expedient that the government could have taken. Taxing for the full cost of the war, no doubt, would have dampened work incentives during a time when the country needed a 100 percent effort from all its citizens. Except for a brief period during the Korean War, the federal government has been able to decrease its debt somewhat since World War II, at least up until the Vietnam War. Note, however, that the federal debt again increased during the 1960's.

The upward trend in state and local government debt folowed a somewhat different pattern. There was some increase in this debt during the depression years but not to the extent of the federal debt. And during World War II state and local government debt declined, taking into account the increase in the price level. Since the end of World War II, however, state and local debt has increased about fivefold. The "baby boom" following World War II, bringing the increased demand for school facilities, no doubt, is a major factor contributing to this increase. Also the highway building program of the late 1950's and 1960's necessitated further borrowing by state governments.

Except during World War II and the immediate postwar period the private debt—debt between individuals and between business firms—has been larger than the public debt. Moreover, the increase in private debt has been especially rapid during the 1960's, reflecting perhaps a general feeling of optimism on the part of consumers and investors.

Although many individuals and politicians have expressed concern over the growth and size of the federal debt, it must be admitted that relative to the size of the economy, the federal debt has decreased substantially since World War II. On a per capita basis, the federal debt has declined in real terms by almost one half since the end of World War II. And as a percent of GNP, the federal debt has declined by about 70 percent. It should be kept in mind that the debt figures presented in Table 8–2 have been inflated to 1969 prices to facilitate comparison over time. Thus the actual debt that prevailed in years past was substantially smaller than is shown by the table. For example, the federal debt in 1929 was only $16.5 billion in 1929 prices.

Adjusting the debt figures by the CPI does not alter the fact that debt which is incurred during inflation is paid back with inflated dollars. Thus the lenders, which are the people who have purchased government bonds in the case of public debt, suffer a loss because of inflation. For example, $1,000 "invested" in a 25-year government bond in 1944 was worth only about $500 in real purchasing power when the bond matured in 1969 because of the doubling of the price level over the intervening period. Thus the people who purchased war bonds during the 1940's in effect paid a "tax" that they probably didn't count on at the time the bonds were purchased.

WHO PAYS THE ECONOMIC COST OF WAR?

It is evident that the major share of the federal debt existing today was incurred to finance wars, mainly World War II and to a lesser extent Korea and Vietnam. The fact that the government chose not to finance the entire cost of wars through increased taxes has prompted some people to argue that borrowing to finance part of the cost of war passes this portion of its cost on to future generations. Is this a valid argument?

Perhaps the best way to look at the economic cost of war is in terms of what is given up. During a war the people living at the time must forego consumer goods and services in order to produce more war goods. This is true regardless of whether the government taxes, borrows, or prints money to finance the war. In both cases of taxing or borrowing, the government removes purchasing power from the private sector. This reduces the purchase of nonmilitary goods and services by the public while increasing the wherewithal of the government to buy military goods and services.

Printing money has the same effect. The extra money is used by the government to purchase military goods and services and the resulting price increase reduces the purchasing power of money and other assets of a fixed money value such as bonds. In a sense, then, printing money is the same as levying a tax—it is a tax on people who hold assets that do not rise in value with the price level.

Young men drafted into military duty during a war, or for any other time for that matter, also bear a disproportionately high economic cost of the military. This happens because the military pay for most young men is substantially less than what they could earn in civilian life, even taking into account food, clothing, and lodging that is provided. We can say, therefore, that war is too "cheap" because its dollar cost does not reflect the full value of nonmilitary goods and services given up.

We must conclude, therefore, that the economic cost of war, as well as the cost of human life, is borne by the people living during a war. The fact that future generations "inherit" the public debt does not alter this fact. Because we must also remember that the government bonds inherited by future generations are assets that offset this debt. Even the interest to service the debt, which amounts to about 6 percent of the federal budget, cannot be considered a burden because this money goes back to the public.

There is one sense in which future generations bear the economic cost of war, and that is through the reduction of investment during wartime. For example, during the height of World War II, the relatively small amount of gross investment was not large enough to offset the depreciation of capital equipment, so there was a net decline in the nation's capital stock. As a result the nation's productive capacity is somewhat smaller today than it might have been without the war. This effect is, of course, much greater for countries that are ravaged by war.

IS THE UNITED STATES A WAR ECONOMY?

In our discussion of unemployment and inflation in Chaper 2 we noted that wars have brought decreased unemployment and prosperity, while a return to a peacetime economy has brought increased unemployment. This observation has prompted some people to argue that the United States is a war economy, meaning that war is necessary to provide full employment.

But as we mentioned, it is not reasonable to expect an economy to adjust immediately back to a peacetime economy when war is ended. The laying off of millions of people from the production of military goods and the release of millions of men from military service amounts to a drastic "shock" to the economy. It may take several years for the economy to completely adjust.

But after the adjustment period is over, can we expect the economy to "absorb" all the people who want to work? Those who argue that unemployment will always plague a peacetime, free market economy imply by their argument that society has all the goods and services it desires; everyone is in a state of being completely satiated. Of course, this is not likely to be true. Very few people, if any, can truthfully say that they have everything they desire. Hence as long as there are people who long for goods and services they do not have, which includes, by the way, a pleasant environment, there is no reason why everyone in society who wants a job at the prevailing wage should not be working. Thus it is by no means clear that the existence of a large military establishment is needed to provide full employment.

MAIN POINTS OF CHAPTER 8

1. Fiscal policy can be defined as the conscious attempt by government to promote full employment without inflation through its spending and taxing powers.

2. Built-in stabilizers are fiscal policy measures that go into effect automatically in response to changes in economic activity. They are designed to counteract or smooth out cyclical changes in the economy. Some examples include unemployment compensation and the progressive income tax.

3. In the context of the simple Keynesian model, an increase in government spending and/or a decrease in taxes shifts aggregate demand upwards, thereby increasing equilibrium NNP and reducing unemployment. Conversely, to combat inflation the aggregate demand line can be shifted down by means of a decrease in government spending and/or an increase in taxes.

4. Some problems of undertaking fiscal policy as described by the simple Keynesian model include the possibility of offsetting changes in spending by the private sector and the problem of financing a deficit so as not to induce offsetting changes in aggregate demand. There is also the problem of Congress acting too slowly to obtain the desired results. In addition, a decrease in government spending during inflation will likely bring increased unemployment.

5. Knowing the nation's MPC and the desired change in NNP, it is possible to use the simple Keynesian model to predict the needed change in government spending or taxes to alleviate unemployment

or inflation. The formula that can be used to specify a government spending change is $\Delta G = \Delta NNP/M_g$. The formula for specifying a needed tax change is $\Delta T = \Delta NNP/M_t$.

6. Under the assumption of a "lump-sum" tax, the tax multiplier in the simple model is one less than the government spending multiplier. This occurs because the entire change in government spending shows up on the first round of the multiplier process, but in the case of a tax change the first round of the multiplier process is equal to MPC times the tax change.

7. The balanced budget multiplier is one, meaning that an equal change in G and T will change equilibrium NNP by one times this change in G and T.

8. An important implicit assumption of the simple Keynesian model is that changes in the interest rate caused by changes in aggregate demand do not in turn cause offsetting changes in investment or consumption.

9. In the context of the complete model with money, an increase in government spending and/or a decrease in taxes shifts the EE/P line up and to the right thereby increasing equilibrium NNP/P and decreasing unemployment. Conversely, to combat inflation, the EE/P line can be shifted down and to the left by means of a decrease in government spending and/or an increase in taxes.

10. The slope of the EE/P and ME/P lines have an important bearing on the effectiveness of fiscal policy. If EE/P is downward sloping but not vertical and ME/P is upward sloping, fiscal policy is less effective than is implied by the simple Keynesian model.

11. The most volatile component of United States GNP appears to be investment spending, although the federal government has contributed to rather large fluctuations because of wartime spending and postwar adjustments. However, some moderation in fluctuations of economic activity can be observed since World War II.

12. Another complication of fiscal policy that plagues both the simple model and the complete model is the matter of timing. For example, anti-recessionary policy that is implemented too late or takes effect later than anticipated can contribute to future inflationary pressures and have a destabilizing effect. Similarly, anti-inflationary measures that mistakenly take effect during a recession make the recessions worse than if the government had done nothing.

13. The public debt is debt which the government owes to the people and is incurred by the sale of government bonds to the people. However, because the people "own" the government it is debt which the people owe to themselves. Thus paying off the debt does not involve a loss of wealth or purchasing power to the nation as a whole.

14. The economic cost of a war is borne by the people living during the war period because they must give up consumer goods and services in order for the nation to produce more military goods. This will be true regardless of whether the government borrows from the people by selling them bonds, prints money, or tax them for the full cost of the war.

15. Young men drafted into military service in a sense pay a "tax" to support a war because their pay is substantially less than they could earn in civilian life, even taking into account the food, clothing, and lodging they are provided.

16. The adjustment from a war to a peacetime economy can be expected to bring increased unemployment. However, as long as there are people who would like to consume more goods or services than they now do, there is no reason why everyone who wants to work at the prevailing wage rate should not be working. Thus the existence of a large military establishment should not be needed to provide full employment.

QUESTIONS FOR THOUGHT AND DISCUSSION

1. Illustrate, using the simple Keynesian model, how an unemployment situation could arise. What would be the appropriate fiscal policy to combat this unemployment? Illustrate the consequences of this action on your diagram.

2. Do the same as in Question 1 for an inflationary situation.

3. Suppose in some distant future year, you find yourself a member of the President's Council of Economic Advisors. Suppose also that the country is experiencing increased unemployment. The President has heard of the simple Keynesian model and wants to use it to predict necessary government policy. What cautions might you pass on to the President in using this model?

4. A friend points out to you that decreases in government spending lead to increases in unemployment. Therefore he argues that increased government spending is necessary to insure full employment. Would you agree? Explain.

5. "In reducing unemployment, a $100 million government spending increase is equivalent to a $100 million tax decrease." Do you agree? Explain.

6. Compare the effect of the government spending multiplier as depicted by the simple model with this multiplier in the more complete model. Will the multiplier likely be larger or smaller in the complete model? Specify your assumptions.

7. If full-employment NNP is $100 million greater than the current equilibrium NNP, how much should the government increase its spending to promote full employment in the context of the simple model? Assume the

MPC is 0.80. Would this increase in government spending be large enough in the context of the complete model? Explain.

8. Referring back to Question 7, how much should taxes be decreased to reach full employment? Would your answer be the same for the complete model? Explain.

9. Suppose the government wants to increase spending by $10 billion because of necessary government programs. In order to not cause any inflationary pressure on the economy, how much should the government increase taxes? (Assume the simple "lump-sum" tax.)

10. How might fiscal policy have a destabilizing effect on the economy?

11. "Paying off the public debt would drive the country over the edge of bankruptcy." Do you agree? Explain.

12. "By borrowing from the people to finance a war, the government is able to pass a 'major' portion of the cost of the war on to future generations." Do you agree? Explain.

13. Strictly from an economic standpoint, do you think that government bonds are a good "investment" for a person during wartime? Explain.

14. "Young men in the military pay a disproportionately high economic cost of fighting a war." Do you agree? Explain.

CHAPTER

9

MONETARY POLICY

We now come to the second major tool of the government to promote full employment without inflation—monetary policy. We can define monetary policy as the deliberate action of the government or monetary authority to manage the supply of money and the interest rate with the goal of achieving and maintaining full employment without inflation. In the United States the monetary authority is the Board of Governors of the Federal Reserve System.

MONEY VERSUS THE INTEREST RATE

As you might have gathered from the preceding chapters, the effect of money and the interest rate on the economy has been subject to a great deal of controversy among economists and government policymakers, extending from the Great Depression up to the present. One major point of contention has been the appropriate indicator for monetary policy. In deciding on the correct monetary policy to follow, should the major indicator be the interest rate or should it be the quantity of money? During much of the history of monetary policy in the United States, it appears that the interest rate has served as the prime guideline for action, and perhaps still does.

It is not difficult to understand how this came about when we remember that the Federal Reserve Board of Governors has been comprised mainly of commercial bankers. In the world of commercial banking, the interest rate is of vital importance. Bankers, of course, are aware that a relatively high interest rate tends to reduce the amount of borrowing from what it would otherwise be, while a low interest rate stimulates borrowing and spending. With this experience, it is understandable that the monetary authority should place considerable emphasis on the interest rate as a means of influencing economic activity. But undue emphasis on the interest rate creates some problems.

First, it might appear that the maintenance of a stable interest rate would promote a stable economy. The problem with this idea is that there are many factors contributing to changes in economic activity other than the interest rate. Suppose, for example, that businessmen become pessimistic about the future, expecting a slowdown in economic activity and a subsequent accumulation of unsold goods. Naturally they will tend to reduce their rate of investment at the former rate of interest they had been paying. In this case the decreased demand for loans will by itself tend to reduce the rate of interest somewhat. But if the monetary authority wishes to restore the former rate of investment and economic activity, it should decrease the interest rate even more to offset the pessimistic attitude of businessmen. If the monetary authority attempted to keep the interest rate up at its initial level, it would just contribute to the recession because this would reduce investment even more.

Taking another example, this one from more recent U.S. experience, suppose the government decided to increase its spending by a large amount to wage war. If the country is at or near full employment already, the increased demand for goods and services pressing on the available supply can be expected to drive prices up unless private spending is reduced. In this case the monetary authority should drive the interest rate up even further in order to reduce private investment and to a certain extent reduce private consumption. Trying to maintain a stable interest rate in these situations would just add to the inflationary pressure in the economy.

The Fed's preoccupation with the money rate of interest has caused a great deal of confusion about the appropriate monetary policy and at times might have led to a perverse policy. During the Great Depression, for example, the monetary authority was able to point to the decline in the money rate of interest as evidence that the appropriate policy was being followed. In retrospect, it appears now that the Fed in fact followed an extremely pro-recessionary policy in allowing the money supply to decline by a third from 1929 to 1933. The observed decline in the money rate of interest during this time appears to have been just a "straw in the wind" as far as having much effect on the economy. Indeed, some economists argue that if the Fed would have even maintained the money supply at the 1929 level, the Great Depression likely would have turned out to be a mild recession, thereby making a drastic reduction in the interest rate unnecessary. Although, in the event of a continued rise in unemployment, the interest rate then should have been pushed down to lower and lower levels until spending began to pick up. Thus the maintenance of a stable interest rate in the face of recession or inflation will involve a perverse monetary policy, while allowing the interest rate to seek its own level generally implies a very "weak" monetary policy or no policy at all.

Confusing the interest rate, which might be considered the price of money, with ordinary prices of goods and services also leads one to erroneous policy recommendations. For example, during the inflationary spiral of the late 1960's, it was not uncommon to hear proposals coming from Congress calling for a reduction in the interest rate so that the price of money would not add to the inflation of the economy. The problem, however, is that such action would have added to the inflationary pressure in the economy rather than reducing it. Inflation tends to result in a high money rate of interest, but it does not follow that by reducing the rate of interest, inflation will be curbed. Indeed, as we will see later in the chapter, just the opposite will likely happen.

PRIMARY TOOLS OF MONETARY POLICY

As mentioned, the Federal Reserve System is the monetary authority in the United States. Since monetary policy is largely a matter of regulating the money supply, let us explore next the tools available to the Fed to carry out this task. Essentially the Fed has three primary tools which it can use to regulate the supply of money. These include (1) open-market operations, (2) changes in the required reserve ratio of commercial banks, and (3) changes in the "discount" rate that commercial banks pay to borrow from the Federal Reserve.

We already have discussed the effect of open-market operations in Chapter 6, but perhaps just a bit of review will prove helpful. Recall that the Fed is continually buying and selling government securities in the bond market. For example, an open-market purchase of a bond from a bank, institution, or individual leads to an increase in the money supply. In this case the Fed receives the bond, which is not money, and in exchange the seller receives a check (or cash) which is money. Thus the quantity of money in the economy increases as the result of the open-market purchase. In the case of purchasing a bond from a bank, the initial change occurs as an increase in bank reserves, but ultimately new money is created when the banking system makes loans against these reserves. Keep in mind too that the money supply is likely to change by some multiple of the initial bond purchase because of the multiple expansion effect. And, you recall, a similar line of reasoning applies to the open-market sale of a bond by the Fed. Here the Fed receives money, the seller receives the bond, and as a result the money supply will likely decline by a multiple of the bond purchase. Open-market purchases and sales of bonds is the major tool that the Federal Reserve uses to change the quantity of money in the economy.

We might reasonably ask at this point, how can the Fed be sure that it will always be able to buy or sell the desired amount of bonds? After all, people are not forced to do business with the Fed. The answer is that when buying bonds, the Fed must offer a price that is competitive in the market else prospective sellers will sell to other buyers. If the bond purchase is extremely large, the Fed may have to increase its bid price in order to induce more sellers to part with their bonds. Similarly when the Fed sells bonds, it may have to reduce their price to a point that makes the offering attractive to prospective buyers.

We should point out too that the price of a bond and the interest rate are inversely related. For example, suppose the government sells a $1,000 bond and as specified on the bond agrees to pay 6 percent annual interest to the holder, or $60 per year. Even if the market price of the bond should decline to $500, the $60 annual interest still continues to be paid by the government. Only now the holder of the bond receives a 12 percent return on his money—$60 per year from $500 invested. Thus a decrease in the market price of bonds implies that their interest return rises. Thus if bonds become cheap enough, the interest return eventually becomes attractive enough for buyers to take the bonds off the hands of the Fed. Of course, the Fed may suffer a capital loss in the process, but it is not in business to make profits anyway. The Federal Reserve System exists to regulate the money supply and in so doing stabilizes the economy at a level that represents full employment without inflation. On the other hand, an increase in the price of bonds implies that their interest return decreases.

The second major tool that can be used by the Fed to regulate the supply of money is the legal reserve ratio. Recall from the discussion of banking in Chapter 6 that commercial banks are required to hold a certain fraction of their deposits on reserve, either as cash in their own vaults or as money in a reserve account in their Federal Reserve bank (if the bank is a member of the Federal Reserve System). By changing the legal reserve ratio, the Fed can change the amount of bank loans and thus change the amount of money in the economy. Remember that banks create money by making loans.

In our examples in Chapter 6, we assumed for convenience of computation, a required reserve ratio of 0.20, meaning that commercial banks are required to keep 20 cents on reserve against each dollar of demand deposits. Thus $1,000 of total reserves in the banking system can "support" $5,000 in demand deposits $(1/R \times \$1,000)$, assuming the multiple expansion process had run its course and banks are fully loaned up. Now if the Fed should reduce the required reserve ratio to say 0.10, this same $1,000 in total reserves could support $10,000 in total deposits. Banks could in this case increase loans and thus increase demand deposits. On the other hand, an increase in the reserve ratio would require banks to contract their deposits for a given amount of reserves.

Notice, if you will, the basic difference between open-market operations and a change in the reserve ratio. The former is a device to change the total reserves in the banking system while the latter is a means of changing the amount of deposits that can be supported from a given amount of total reserves. However, the Federal Reserve seldom uses its power to change the legal reserve ratio, mainly because it is almost too powerful a tool. Even a very small change in the reserve ratio has rather drastic effects on the banking community and causes large and abrupt changes in the money supply.

The third major tool or device that the Fed can use to change the money supply is a change in the "discount rate." The discount rate is the rate of interest that the Fed charges member banks when these banks obtain loans from the Fed to bolster their reserves. Occasionally a commercial bank will find itself dangerously close to the upper limit of its loans given its reserves, or actually over the limit especially during peak lending periods. In this situation the commercial bank can temporarily increase its reserves by borrowing reserves from the Fed.

The Fed generally changes the discount rate in conjunction with a large open-market transaction. Suppose there is inflationary pressure in the economy which prompts the Fed to make a large open-market sale in order to reduce reserves and the money supply. But the resulting "tight money" situation and high interest rates provide banks with an incentive to borrow from the Fed in order to maintain reserves so that loans need not be reduced greatly. This is just good business. But to make it less profitable for banks to borrow for reserves, the Fed will raise the discount rate along with the open-market sale. Similarly when the Fed wants to stimulate bank lending it can reduce the discount rate to make it more profitable for banks to borrow to obtain reserves.

SECONDARY TOOLS OF MONETARY POLICY

The three items discussed in the previous section are the three main tools the Federal Reserve can use to regulate the supply of money in the economy and thus to influence economic activity. The Fed also has a number of other means to influence economic activity that we might mention briefly. First there is the idea of "moral suasion," sometimes called "jawbone control." These terms describe attempts by the Fed to influence commercial bank lending by persuasive means. For example, during inflationary times the Fed might frown on excessive borrowing by a bank that tries to expand its reserves. Similarly during recessionary times the Fed might extol the virtues of a vigorous lending policy on the part of banks. Perhaps the main drawback of moral suasion is that it doesn't work very well. When it comes to making a choice between bowing to the wishes of the Fed versus maximizing profits, most self-respecting bankers choose the latter.

The Fed also can influence economic activity by what is known as selective credit controls. For example, the Fed regulates the length of the repayment period on instalment loans. If people are required to repay a new car loan in, say, 24 months as opposed to 36 months, fewer people tend to buy new cars. Another device is the regulation of "margin requirements" on stocks. If, for example, the margin requirement is 60 percent, a person need only pay 60 percent of the price of the stock from his own money and is allowed to borrow the remaining 40 percent.

MONETARY POLICY IN THE CONTEXT
OF THE SIMPLE MODEL

The fact that the simple model contains no information on the monetary sector of the economy limits its usefulness as a device to analyze the effects of monetary policy. However, it is possible to present an intuitive idea of how monetary policy affects the economy in the context of this model.

It is easiest to trace the effects of a change in the money supply in the simple model if we view the process as sort of a chain of causation. To begin, suppose the Fed makes a large open-market purchase. From our past discussion we know that this action increases money and bank reserves. With increased reserves banks can undertake to expand their loans. After all, banks earn a large share of their income from loans so it would be foolish to hold the extra reserves in "cold storage."

However, in order for banks to induce individuals and businesses to borrow more, they will likely have to lower their interest charge. And a reduction in the interest rate provides an incentive for business firms to borrow for new investment projects such as buildings, machines, equipment, etc. Also lower interest rates provide an incentive for consumers to save a bit less and spend a bit more, particularly on consumer durables such as autos and appliances. In the simple model this increase in spending would be represented by an upward shift in aggregate demand. Finally our knowledge of the multiplier process tells us that new spending will increase by some multiple of the initial increase in consumption and investment and give rise to an increase in equilibrium NNP. We can summarize the chain of causation as follows:

Increase in $M \rightarrow$ Decrease in $i \rightarrow$ Increase in I and $C \rightarrow$ Increase in aggregate demand $\rightarrow$ Increase in equilibrium NNP

Of course, just the opposite would be expected to occur in the case of an open-market sale of bonds. The resulting decrease in money and reserves leads to an increase in the interest rate, other things equal. Then as investment and possibly consumption decline, aggregate demand shifts down resulting in a decrease in equilibrium NNP.

The effect of monetary policy also can be illustrated on the familiar aggregate demand and supply diagram as shown by Figure 8–1 of the previous chapter. Diagram (A) of Figure 8–1, if you check back, represents an unemployment situation. Here the appropriate monetary policy would be to increase the money supply so that the interest rate declines and shifts aggregate demand upwards. In the case of an inflationary situation illustrated by Figure 8–1 (B), the appropriate monetary policy would be to reduce the supply of money thereby increasing the interest rate and shifting aggregate demand downward and reducing equilibrium NNP.

We cannot be as precise in predicting the ultimate effects of monetary policy, however, as we were able to do with fiscal policy. Recall that by using the multiplier, we were able to predict to the exact dollar how much of a tax or government spending change was needed to match equilibrium NNP with the full-employment level. In order to make such precise predictions for monetary policy we would need two additional pieces of information. First we would have to know how much an open-market purchase or sale of bonds would change the interest rate. Secondly, information would be needed on how much investment or consumption changes in response to a given change in the interest rate.

Economists have been able to gather a little information on the response of investment to changes in the interest rate, although this general area of the relationship between interest rate changes and spending changes is still open to considerable controversy. Even less is known about the impact of an open-market purchase on the interest rate and the process that occurs in the economy when the interest rate changes.

More and more economists are coming around to the view that the monetary sector and its interaction with the rest of the economy is extremely complex. And to make exact predictions, as the simple model might tempt us to do, would be foolhardy.

MONETARY POLICY IN THE CONTEXT OF THE COMPLETE MODEL

The more complete model that explicitly includes money and the price level is a somewhat more adequate device to analyze monetary policy. Recall in our early discussion of the complete model, after we had incorporated price level, that in the event of an unemployment equilibrium, the model indicates that the economy would eventually regain full employment through a price decline. Here the ME/P line shifts down and to the right until it intersects EE/P at the full-employment level of NNP. But we also called to mind that the process of moving to the full-employment equilibrium may well involve years of high unemployment. In the context of fiscal policy, a government spending increase or a tax cut shifted the EE/P line to the right, eliminating the need for a painful price decline. Let us now consider how monetary policy might be used to achieve the same effect as a government spending increase or tax cut.

First we must determine how monetary policy, i.e., a change in the money supply, affects the complete model. From our discussion in Chapter 7, we know that the money supply enters through the monetary sector. If you refer back to Figure 7–8, you will recall that the ME line consists of equilibrium points between a given money supply and various possible money demand curves that correspond to various levels of income or NNP. Now an increase in the money supply can be represented by a shift to the right in the money supply line of Figure 7–8 (A). As a result we obtain a new set of equilibrium points lying to the right of the original points, that is, we obtain a new ME/P line lying to the right of the original line, as shown in Figure 9–1 (A).

FIGURE 9–1. Monetary policy in the context of the complete model—correcting for unemployment and inflation

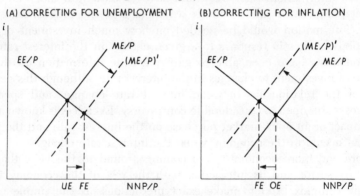

Notice that because of the increase in the money supply, the shift to the right of the ME/P line results in a lower equilibrium rate of interest in the economy. This is reasonable to expect. With more money available in the loan market, competition for money is less intense, and borrowers can shop around for more favorable rates. Then as the interest rate declines, investment, and perhaps consumption increases thereby increasing total spending and output in the economy. In other words, the overall equilibrium level of NNP increases. It is evident, then, that should the economy find itself in an unemployment situation, the appropriate monetary policy would be an increase in the money supply.

We should note as well that an increase in the money supply has the same effect on the model as a decrease in prices if the economy is experiencing unemployment. Both shift ME/P to the right and increase the level of real output in the economy. The major advantage of increasing the money supply is that full employment can be reached in a shorter time.

Of course, if the economy finds itself in the midst of an inflationary situation, as illustrated by Figure 9-1 (B), the appropriate monetary policy then would be to decrease the money supply. In this case, a decrease, or shift to the left of the money supply line would trace out a new set of equilibrium points lying to the left of the original set. In other words, we obtain a new ME/P line lying to the left of the original ME/P line. As a result the equilibrium value of real NNP declines. Providing the decrease in the money supply is large enough, the equilibrium level of NNP/P will decline until it reaches the full-employment level. At this point, the model implies there will be no inflationary pressure.

Of course the problems and complexities that beset monetary policy in the context of the simple model also apply to the more complete model. In particular, how much is it necessary for the monetary authority to change the money supply to obtain the desired change in NNP? The fact that the more complete model is a more adequate tool to describe monetary policy does not increase our empirical knowledge of the monetary sector and its relationship to the rest of the economy.

One additional problem of using monetary policy to control inflation is that the rise in the interest rate affects industries that rely on credit much more than it affects other industries. For example, the tight money policy during 1969 and 1970 hit the housing industry rather hard, particularly construction of single family dwellings. Thus an attempt to mitigate the inflation problem has contributed to yet another problem, namely the housing shortage.

THE INTEREST RATE AND INFLATION

As mentioned at the beginning of this chapter, a view held by some people during inflationary times is that the high rate of interest is the prime cause of inflation. As a result, some have proposed that the government take steps to reduce the interest rate. Two means are available: (1) impose a legal ceiling on the rate charged by lenders or (2) take monetary policy action that will result in a lower interest rate.

If it is illegal for lenders to charge an interest rate over a certain figure say, 7 percent, there is little choice but that the prevailing market rate of interest during inflation will be 7 percent. But if the percent increase in the price level is, say, 6 percent, we know from Chapter 2 that the real rate will be 1 percent. As you would expect, then, the interest rate ceiling that results in very low or even negative real rates of interest provides a strong incentive to borrow and invest in items that rise in value with the general price level. And the increased incentive to spend only adds to the inflationary pressure—just the opposite of what is intended.

If commercial bank reserves are not large enough to satisfy the increased demand for loans during the time of government imposed interest rate ceiling, it is necessary, then, for banks to ration loans. The ones to obtain loans, in this case, usually are the bankers' favored customers—large borrowers, friends, relatives, etc. The small borrowers, such as prospective home buyers or small businessmen, are the ones who generally suffer the most in this situation. Indeed, if the large borrowers have a strong influence with the government, still greater inflation may occur because it is in their self-interest to promote a still higher rate of inflation. Paying a negative real rate of interest on your loans is a relatively easy way to get rich, or richer.

The second means of obtaining a lower interest rate is to increase the money supply. As shown in Figure 9-1 (A), increasing the money supply shifts the ME/P curve to the right and as a result lowers the equilibrium rate of interest. But if the resulting equilibrium level of real NNP is larger than the full-employment level, as is the case during inflation, forces are set up in the economy for prices to rise even further. But, as you recall, increases in the price level shift the ME/P curve back up to its former high level, thereby pushing the interest rate back up. Again the government would have to increase the money supply more if it wanted to push the interest rate down once more to its desired low level. As you can see, the policy of maintaining a low interest rate through monetary policy can be accomplished only with round after round of increasing the money supply, which results in still greater inflationary pressure.

Starting at about the beginning of World War II and extending into the postwar years, the Federal Reserve embarked on a policy that came to be known as "pegging" the interest rate. In short, the objective was to maintain a low interest rate in order to minimize the interest charge on the large amount of government bonds outstanding. To carry out this policy, the Federal Reserve had to inject more and more money and reserves into the economy. And as we know from the preceding discussion, the inevitable result was a still larger amount of inflationary pressure on the economy. Although the "pegging" policy was not directly motivated by inflation, it still had the effect of causing more inflation. The exact same thing would happen if the government attempted to use monetary policy to push down the interest rate in a mistaken attempt to control inflation.

PRICE AND WAGE CONTROLS

During periods of excessive inflationary pressure the government has sometimes resorted to price and wage controls in an effort to stem the upward spiral of prices. In the United States at least such a policy generally is reserved for times of rather severe inflationary pressure such as during World War II. In recent years, many people have advocated a return to some form of price and wage controls to help "break the inflationary bubble." However, these suggestions have precipitated a considerable amount of controversy among economists, political leaders, and the general public.

Those who favor price and wage controls tend to place relatively little faith in the ability of traditional fiscal and monetary policies such as reduced government spending, higher taxes, or "tight money" to do the job. Some who favor controls may grant that traditional policy might eventually stem inflation, but the time required is too long to be acceptable to the general public.

Economists who oppose price and wage restraints will often point out that the imposition of controls does not remove the basic cause(s) of inflation. They argue that inflation is caused basically by either an excessive increase in spending, as represented by a substantial shift to the right in the EE/P line, or too rapid growth of the money supply, denoted by an excessive shift to the right of the ME/P line. Thus the imposition of price and wage restraints may suppress the symptoms of inflation but does not remove its underlying cause(s).

It is argued also that unless price and wage controls are applied universally, those prices or wages not affected will grow even more rapidly. In other words, it would be something like squeezing a balloon. If you push in at one place it will bulge out at another. But if all prices and wages are frozen, then it is argued that the economy is placed in a sort of "straitjacket." That is, there is no way for consumers to provide signals to producers through the price system.

In a market economy, resources are allocated mainly on the basis of market prices. If the price of one product rises relative to others, it is a signal to producers that consumers desire more of this product relative to others. And producers in attempting to increase profits by producing more of the higher priced product at the same time satisfy the desires of consumers. Similarly if the price of a resource increases, producers have an incentive to economize on its use by substituting lower priced substitute resources in its place. Thus the imposition of price and wage controls takes away the allocating function of product and resource prices.

It is pointed out as well that the inevitable consequence of price and wage controls are shortages in the product and resource markets. Hence some form of rationing must be instituted to divide the available output and inputs to all who would desire more than is forthcoming in the market at the controlled price. Also the existence of shortages tends to lead to black marketing and its ugly consequences. Thus the imposition of price and wage controls in addition takes away the rationing function of product and resource prices. A more thorough explanation of the allocating and rationing functions of prices is presented in microeconomics.

It would not be fair, of course, to imply that the backers of wage and price controls are ignorant of these consequences, or that they do not believe they are important. Rather they probably feel that the undesirable consequences of controls are still not great enough to overshadow the bad effects of inflation. The opponents of controls probably feel that this cure (controls) is even worse than the disease (inflation).

EFFECTIVENESS OF MONETARY POLICY

In the preceding chapter we mentioned that the effectiveness of fiscal policy depended to a large extent on the shape of the EE/P and the ME/P lines. The same is true for monetary policy. Monetary policy will be most effective if the ME/P line is relatively steep, as in Figure 9–2 (A). Here a change in the money supply changes equilibrium by almost the same amount, regardless of the shape of the EE/P line as long as it is downward sloping.

On the other hand, if the ME/P curve is relatively flat, a shift right or left in the curve has a relatively small effect on the level of equilibrium real NNP. Hence, monetary policy is relatively weak or ineffective, as shown in Figure 9–2 (B). The diagrams are drawn so that the horizontal shift in the ME/P lines is the same in both diagrams. But note how much more equilibrium NNP/P increases in response to an increase in the money supply when the ME/P curve is relatively steep.

FIGURE 9–2. The slope of the ME/P curve and the effectiveness of monetary policy

(A) MONETARY POLICY EFFECTIVE   (B) MONETARY POLICY INEFFECTIVE

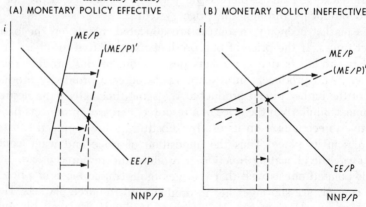

As mentioned in Chapter 7 the slope of the ME/P line depends to a large extent on the slope of the demand curve for money. If the demand curve for money is relatively steep, the ME/P also will be steep and monetary policy will be quite effective, as shown in diagram (A) of Figure 9–2. On the other hand a relatively flat demand curve for money implies a relatively flat ME/P curve and a somewhat ineffective monetary policy, as shown in diagram (B).

VELOCITY AND THE SLOPE OF THE *ME/P* LINE

It is possible also to relate the slope of the *ME/P* line to velocity. A steep demand curve for money means that velocity does not change very much in response to a change in the interest rate, i.e., people hold about the same amount of cash regardless of the interest rate. Thus we can say that monetary policy will be most effective if velocity does not change in response to a change in the rate of interest and NNP. On the other hand, if the demand curve for money is quite flat, velocity changes in response to a change in interest and as a result monetary policy is ineffective. In this latter case, for example, an increase in the money supply prompts a rather negligible increase in NNP/P because people just hold the added money instead of spending it.

FIGURE 9–3. Velocity and the slope of the *ME/P* line

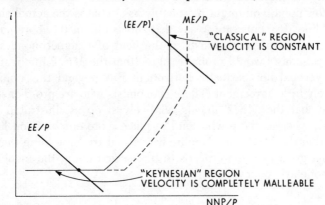

It is interesting to note, as well, that a very steep *ME/P* curve implies that the quantity equation of exchange is a good predictor of what happens to output of the economy when the quantity of money changes. Recall that the quantity equation is $M \times V = P \times Y$. Thus, if M increases, say, by 10 percent, money income of the economy also must increase by 10 percent if V remains constant. On the other hand, if V declines by 10 percent, the increase in M is exactly offset so there is no increase in money income. This latter case would be illustrated by a horizontal *ME/P* line.

Economists have found it convenient to summarize the relationship between velocity and the slope of the *ME/P* line by dividing the line into three regions, as illustrated in Figure 9–3. At the uppermost region where the line is vertical, velocity is a constant, and monetary policy is a powerful tool.[1] As shown in Figure 9–3, if *EE/P* intersects *ME/P* in this region,

---

[1] We should point out that in order to obtain a vertical *ME/P* line both the supply of money and demand for money curves must be vertical.

a given change in the money supply brings forth a comparable change in NNP/P, unless the economy is already at full employment. On the other hand, the lower-most region of ME/P is drawn horizontal implying the V changes in the same proportion and in the opposite direction of M. If EE/P intersects ME/P in this region there is no increase in NNP/P when M is increased because the horizontal portion of the line does not shift. The middle region is somewhat of a compromise between the two extremes. In this region velocity is fairly stable but is not a constant.

The vertical portion of the ME/P curve has come to be known as the "classical" region because of its close relationship to the quantity equation of exchange and the implied strength of monetary policy. As you recall, the classicists emphasized monetary policy a great deal. The horizontal portion of the ME/P line is sometimes called the "Keynesian" region probably because of the Keynesians' stress on fiscal policy and their lack of emphasis on monetary policy.

At this point, you might reasonably ask, what is the actual shape of the ME/P line? It seems safe to say that this is one of the more controversial questions that presently exists in the field of macroeconomics. Granted, most economists would probably agree that the ME/P line is neither perfectly vertical nor perfectly horizontal. But beyond this point, there is relatively little agreement. Those economists who are pro-monetary policy believe that the ME/P line is relatively steep as illustrated by Figure 9–2 (A), whereas those who tend to place more emphasis on fiscal policy argue that the ME/P line is quite flat. About the only thing that is certain is that a great deal more needs to be learned about the monetary sector and monetary policy.

TIMING OF MONETARY POLICY

There is one additional problem of implementing monetary policy that perhaps overshadows all the rest that we have mentioned—this is the timing problem. Recall that this was a serious problem for fiscal policy also.

Our models tell us that in the event of rising unemployment, the appropriate monetary policy is to increase the money supply. Or if the money supply is already being increased from year to year, the appropriate policy would be to step up the rate of increase so as to push the ME/P line to the right just a bit faster. Conversely, if inflation is the problem, we learned that the money supply should be decreased, or at least its rate of growth should be decreased. Keep in mind, though, that if inflation has built up a momentum, a reduction in the growth of the money supply may result in increased unemployment and continued inflation, at least for a time.

Neglecting for the moment, the other problems of monetary policy, the first order of business is to identify when the monetary authority should "step on the gas" and increase the money supply to combat rising unemployment or "apply the brakes" to ease inflationary pressure. As we pointed out in the previous chapter, it is not at all evident when these policies should be pursued because the economy is continually experiencing small ups and downs in economic activity. The critical problem, then, is to distinguish a small and temporary slowdown in economic activity from a full-fledged recession, or a small upturn from an inflationary spiral.

Because of the political implications of rising unemployment or inflation, there is a great deal of controversy regarding the state of the economy. At the first glimpse of rising unemployment, the political party that is not in power generally calls for a change of policies and leadership, claiming that the country is headed for a deep recession. On the other hand, the party in power likely will argue at the same time that the economy is experiencing a temporary downturn and soon will recover to its former state of high employment. It is evident, then, that the monetary authority cannot expect to always please both political parties at once, nor should it try. From this standpoint, it is perhaps fortunate that the Federal Reserve Board of Governors is somewhat of an autonomous body, to some extent shielded from conflicting pressures of the political parties.

But the Fed is still faced with the problem of when to take action. It must be aware, too, that action at the wrong time can be worse than no action at all. For example, if the Fed steps up the rate of increase of the money supply in the mistaken belief that the economy is headed for a downturn, the result will be a needless inflation in the months and possibly years to come. Or if it sharply curtails the rate of increase of the money supply, thinking that inflation is upon us when it is not, the result may well be a needless increase in unemployment in the future. As illustrated in Figure 9–4, the correct time to undertake an expansion of the money supply or increase its rate of growth, i.e., engage in an "easy money" policy, is at time T_0. Or if the economy is headed for an inflationary spiral, such as at T_1, the models imply that the Fed should cut back on the rate of growth of the money supply, i.e., engage in a "tight money" policy. The object of these policies, of course, is to smooth out the fluctuations in the economy, as illustrated by the dotted line beginning at T_0 in Figure 9–4.

LAGS IN MONETARY POLICY

Assuming that the Federal Reserve is able to accurately identify the correct time to ease up or tighten up on the money supply, as the case may be, an even more difficult problem is to predict the lag between the policy action and the time when this action has its major effect on the economy. In our discussion of the Keynesian models, we have implicitly assumed that changes in the money supply have their full effect in the immediate time period. But in reality this is not likely to be the case. When

FIGURE 9-4. The timing of monetary policy

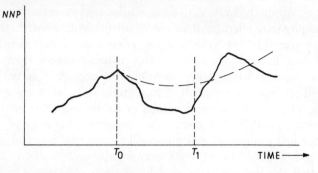

we consider that both the multiple expansion process of the money supply and the spending multiplier of the goods and services sector are involved with a change in the money supply, it is not too difficult to understand why time is required for the policy action to have its full effect. Professor Milton Friedman argues, in fact, that the lag in the effect of monetary policy is both long and variable.[2] For example, the major expansionary effect of a money supply increase may take three to four months at one time and six to eight months at another. If there is little chance of predicting the length of the lag involved in a policy action, there is little chance of accurately specifying when policy measures should be undertaken, or even what the appropriate policy should be.

RULES VERSUS DISCRETION: THE FRIEDMAN PROPOSAL

Because of the alleged long and variable lag in the effects of monetary policy, Friedman has proposed that the monetary authority would have a greater stabilizing effect on the economy if it would follow a simple rule of increasing the money supply about 4 to 5 percent per year to keep step with the growing economy, instead of periodically "stepping on the gas" and "applying the brakes" in response to downturns and upturns in economic activity.[3]

Notice, however, that Friedman is not saying that monetary policy is of little importance. Indeed he is saying that money is so important that large fluctuations in the money supply can cause large and damaging fluctuations in economic activity.

We can obtain a good idea of the uneven growth in the money supply that Friedman is concerned about from Figure 9-5. This graph in part

---

[2] Milton Friedman, "The Lag in Effect of Monetary Policy," *Journal of Political Economy*, Vol. LXVIII (December, 1960), pp. 617–21.

[3] Friedman, *A Program for Monetary Stability* (New York: Fordham University Press, 1959).

FIGURE 9–5.   Annual percentage changes in United States money supply* and money GNP, 1930–69

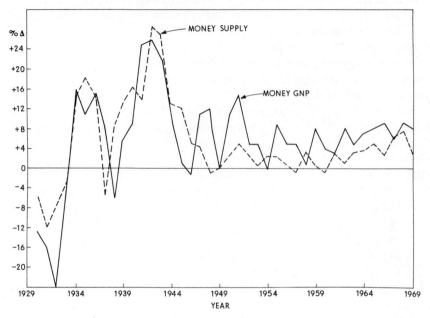

*Currency plus demand deposits.

shows the annual percentage change in the money supply for each year from 1930 to 1969. The positive numbers denote growth, and the negative numbers denote decline in the total money supply (currency outside banks and demand deposits). Similar fluctuations can be observed using the broader definition of money.

FLUCTUATIONS IN THE GROWTH OF THE MONEY SUPPLY

A quick glance at Figure 9–5 reveals that there has been considerable variation in the year-to-year change in the U.S. money supply over the past four decades. As you can see the major fluctuations came during the early 1930's, the era of the Great Depression, and during the World War II years. The large number of commercial bank failures during the early 1930's is generally given as the major reason for the drastic decline in the money supply at that time. In fact, many economists argue that had the Federal Reserve stepped in quickly and made emergency loans of reserves to the banks, there would not have been this large disturbance in the monetary sector. After a period of substantial increase in the money supply during the mid 1930's, it took another rather severe drop during 1937.

The most dramatic increase in the money supply came during World War II years. The sharp increase in government spending caused by the war was not matched by equal increases in taxes. As a result, the federal government's budget ran sizable deficits during this period. Part of the deficits were made up by borrowing from the public, i.e., selling government bonds, or war bonds as they were called then. The remainder of the annual deficits were made up by newly issued money that was used to purchase goods and services.

This is not to imply, however, that the federal government erred in following this policy. As we mentioned earlier, attempts to raise taxes by the full extent of the increased spending might have been even more disruptive and dampened incentives to work. Also borrowing from the public probably was pushed close to its upper limit. People living during the World War II years undoubtedly still remember the large-scale campaigns to sell war bonds. The only other alternative, then, was to issue newly created money to purchase war materials and pay the salaries of servicemen. In fact, most governments in times of war are forced to use the "printing press" to finance part of their war expenditures.

The post–World War II period brought a bit more stability in the growth of the money supply. Except for the Korean War, the money supply growth during the major part of the 1950's fluctuated in the range of 2 to 4 percent per year. The rate of growth of the money supply picked up rather sharply during the early 1960's and then leveled out around an 8 percent growth rate throughout the middle and latter part of the decade. However, 1969 brought a rather sharp contrast, exhibiting a relative decline in the money supply. Essentially this reflects the "tight money" policy of the Nixon administration in attempting to curb the inflation that gained momentum during the latter part of the 1960's.

Economists who believe that "money matters," i.e., believe that the ME/P line is rather steep, tend to argue that these fluctuations in the growth of the money supply contributed much to the economic instability that was experienced during these four decades. As evidence they point to the rather close relationship between changes in the money supply and changes in money GNP as shown in Figure 9–5. For example, they would argue that the sharp decline in the money supply during the early 1930's pushed the ME/P line to the left and as a result there was a decline in output and prices and an increase in unemployment. Conversely, they point out that the sharp increase in the money supply during the World War II years pushed the ME/P line sharply to the right, resulting in inflationary pressures in the economy. Similarly, it is argued that the relatively slow growth in money during the 1950's contributed to the rather sluggish economy during the latter part of that decade. Finally, it can be argued that the relatively high growth in the money supply during the major part of the 1960's was responsible for the high level of employment during this time as well as contributing to the inflationary pressure at the end of the decade. Notice, however, that there appears to be a one- to two-year lag between major changes in the growth (or decline) of the money supply and changes in the growth (or decline) of money GNP.

The proponents of the Friedman proposal which calls for a stable year-to-year growth in the money supply of perhaps 4 to 5 percent per year maintain that had such a policy been followed in the past, the economy would have enjoyed much more economic stability.

MAIN POINTS OF CHAPTER 9

1. In conducting monetary policy it can be argued that a more appropriate guide for action is the quantity of money rather than the interest rate. Maintenance of a stable interest rate can result in an unstable economy.

2. During a recession, the decreased demand for loans results in a decrease in the money rate of interest. In this situation the monetary authority should take action to push down even harder on the interest rate to induce increased spending by investors and consumers. A policy that attempted to hold the interest rate up at its initial level would just contribute to the recession.

3. During an inflation, the increased demand for loans tends to push the interest rate higher. To hold the interest rate down in this case just adds to the inflationary pressure. The correct policy here would be to push the interest rate even higher to reduce the incentive of the private sector to spend.

4. The three main tools that the Federal Reserve has at its disposal to change the money supply include (1) open-market operations (buying and selling government bonds), (2) changes in required reserve ratio of commercial banks, and (3) changes in the "discount" rate that commercial banks pay the Fed for borrowed reserves.

5. The Fed can increase the money supply by (1) purchasing government bonds from banks, institutions, or the general public; (2) reducing the required reserve ratio; or (3) reducing the discount rate. The open-market purchase of bonds is the main method of increasing the money supply. A decrease in the money supply is accomplished by selling bonds, decreasing the reserve ratio, or increasing the discount rate. The open-market sale is the primary method of decreasing the money supply.

6. The Federal Reserve can always buy the desired amount of bonds by increasing their price. An increase in the price of bonds is equivalent to a decrease in their interest return. The Fed also can sell the desired amount of bonds by decreasing their price, which is equivalent to raising their interest return.

7. Secondary tools of monetary policy include "moral suasion" and various credit controls.

8. Monetary policy in the context of simple Keynesian model is accomplished by the following chain of causation: Change in M $\rightarrow$ Change in i $\rightarrow$ Change in I and C $\rightarrow$ Change in aggregate demand $\rightarrow$ Change in equilibrium NNP.

9. The ultimate effects of monetary policy appear to be more difficult to predict than the effects of fiscal policy.

10. In the context of the complete model, monetary policy shifts the ME/P line, thereby changing the equilibrium level of real NNP. An increase in the money supply shifts ME/P to the right whereas a decrease shifts it to the left.

11. Attempting to reduce inflation by reducing the interest rate may result instead in even greater inflationary pressure.

12. Considerable disagreement has arisen over the desirability of price and wage controls as a means of curbing inflation. Opponents of this policy maintain that the problems created are as bad or worse than the inflation itself.

13. Monetary policy is most effective if the ME/P line is very steep which implies that velocity is relatively stable in the face of changes in the interest rate and NNP. Monetary policy is ineffective if the ME/P line is relatively flat or horizontal.

14. Perhaps the most difficult problem of implementing monetary policy is its timing. There are two facets of the timing problem: (1) the correct time to undertake policy action and (2) the time when this action has its major effect on the economy. Action taken at the wrong time or having an effect at the wrong time can be more harmful than no action at all.

15. Because of these timing difficulties Friedman has proposed that monetary policy would be most stablizing if the monetary authority would follow the simple rule of increasing the money supply 4 or 5 percent per year to keep step with the growing economy.

16. Economists who believe that "money matters," tend to argue that the fluctuations in the growth of the money supply contributed in large part to the economic instability that existed in the United States during the past four decades.

QUESTIONS FOR THOUGHT AND DISCUSSION

1. "During the Great Depression the money rate of interest declined substantially. This is an indication that the Federal Reserve followed the correct monetary policy at that time." Do you agree? Explain.

2. "The fact that monetary policy seems to have its effect on the economy through the interest rate is an indication that the Federal Reserve should try to maintain a stable interest rate in order to achieve a stable economy." Do you agree? Explain.

3. Explain how the Federal Reserve can regulate the supply of money to the economy.

4. "If the Fed undertakes a policy of 'moral suasion' during an inflationary period, it is an indication that commercial banks are acting against their own self-interest." True or false and explain.

5. Explain how monetary policy works in the context of the simple Keynesian model without money. Use a diagram in your explanation.

6. Explain how monetary policy works in the context of the complete Keynesian model with money. Include a diagram in your explanation.

7. During the inflationary spiral of the late 1960's, it was proposed by some people that the government take action to reduce the rate of interest. Using the complete model, analyze the consequences of this action.

8. "Price and wage controls are the best methods to control inflation." Comment.

9. Suppose two of your friends are having an argument. One says that monetary policy is of little use because a change in the money supply does not change total spending in the economy. The other argues the opposite. Can you point out the implications of their arguments?

10. The friend in Question 9 above who argues that monetary policy is not effective, also argues that when it is undertaken it can cause more harm than good. Is this argument consistent with his argument in Question 9? Explain. Is there any validity to this latter argument? Explain.

11. "Friedman's proposal of following a simple rule of increasing the U.S. money supply by 4 to 5 percent per year implies that money does not matter very much to the economy, hence there is no need to engage in an active or discretionary monetary policy." True or false and explain.

CHAPTER
10
POVERTY AND THE
DISTRIBUTION OF INCOME

The economic well-being of a particular individual or group in society depends upon (1) the size of the national output or income and (2) how the output or income is distributed. Our discussion of the problem of unemployment was concerned mainly with maximizing the size of a nation's output. Unemployed people or resources implies that the national output is smaller than it might otherwise be. Our concern in this chapter, however, is with the second factor—the way the national output or income is distributed among the people.

Specifically we will be concerned with the people who have been subsisting on a very small share of the output—the poor. First, we will look briefly at some of the problems of identifying the poor and measuring the distribution of income. Then we will turn to some of the policies and programs that influence the distribution of income in the United States, particularly how these policies affect the poor.

DEFINING POVERTY

At first glance it may seem odd to be concerned with such a seemingly obvious definition. Surely you might say, the poor are the people with little money. In general terms you would certainly be correct—additional cash in the pockets of the poor would go a long way in alleviating poverty. But how much additional cash? How low does a family's income have to be before the family is considered "poverty stricken"?

At the present time the "poverty line" is agreed upon by most to be in the neighborhood of $3,500 income per year for a family of four. A single individual living alone with an income of about half this amount would be considered to be on the edge of poverty. We should remember too that the demarcation line that defines the so-called poor is used purely for the sole of convenience of definition. A family a few dollars over the line is in reality not much better off than a family a few dollars below, although the former is not defined as poor while the latter is.

In addition, the definition of poverty has changed over the years, partly because of inflation and partly because of general economic growth. In the early 1960's, for example, when the nation became acutely aware of the current poverty problem, $3,000 income per year for a family of four was considered to be the cutoff point. Indeed, back in the late 1920's and early 30's, families with $3,000 per year income in today's prices would have been considered quite well off. The poverty line then was something less than $2,000 per year in current prices. Or if we compare the United States with other nations, even the more wealthy ones such as the western European countries and Japan, a $3,500 per year equivalent level of purchasing power would be considered quite comfortable in these countries. And in the underdeveloped nations, the equivalent of $3,500 per year income in current U.S. purchasing power would be considered a mark of absolute affluence.

It is quite evident, then, that poverty is a relative thing. It's definition depends to a large extent on the "public conscience." As the nation's overall average income rises, so does the accepted demarcation line between the "rich" and "poor."

Even recognizing the tendency of the definition of poverty to change over the years and from country to country, the selection of a single number to represent the poverty line is, as you might suspect, a gross oversimplification. Perhaps most important is the need to recognize the variety of circumstances and environments that people find themselves in. For example, we would expect a family with young children to require more income to maintain a certain living standard than a couple.

Looking at Table 10-1, it appears, in spite of the old cliche, that two cannot live as cheaply as one. However, comparing the single person with the married couple, it does appear that two living together can live much more economically than two living separately, which tells us something about the economic incentive for marriage. Also, as shown in Table 10-1, families with older children have to spend considerably more than a family with younger children to maintain the same standard of living.

Although the living costs quoted in Table 10-1 provide for a standard of living much above the poverty level, they do make it clear that different family circumstances require different incomes to reach a comparable living standard. For example, a college age, single person can live moderately well for about $3,300 per year. A family with three school age children will need over three times this amount to attain the same living standard—

Table 10–1. Estimated annual budget cost for a moderate living standard, urban United States, 1967

Single person, under 35 years old	$3,320
Husband and wife, under 35 years old:	
No children	4,480
One child under 6 years	5,560
Two children under 6 years	6,360
Husband and wife, 35–54 years old:	
One child, 6–15 years	7,440
Two children, older 6–15 years of age*	8,963
Three children, oldest 6–15 years of age	10,310

*Less personal taxes paid to state and local governments and family disability insurance
Source: *Statistical Abstract*, 1969, p. 349.

a fact worth remembering when the desire to reproduce becomes especially strong!

The place of residence also bears strongly on the amount of income needed to attain a given living standard. As shown in Table 10–2, it costs more to live in a large metropolitan area than in a smaller town. The largest difference appears to be in housing, although food, clothing, personal and medical care, and other items such as education and recreation cost more to buy in the larger cities. Transportation cost is the only item that is larger in the smaller towns and cities. This is not because autos or public transportation are higher priced in smaller towns; mainly it reflects the longer distances required to travel to work, shopping, etc.

Although the costs of maintaining comparable living standards for farm families are not shown in Table 10–2, we would expect these figures to be somewhat lower still, principally because of lower food costs. The Social Security Administration has estimated living costs for farm families

Table 10–2. Comparison of annual budget costs for a four-person family between metropolitan and nonmetropolitan areas—two living standards, spring, 1967

	Lower		Moderate	
	Metro	Nonmetro*	Metro	Nonmetro*
Food	$1,664	$1,550	$2,135	$1,973
Housing	1,331	1,179	2,302	1,909
Transportation	420	563	856	941
Clothing	546	504	777	718
Personal care	168	139	221	203
Medical care	488	412	491	415
Other consumption	306	244	570	476
Total Consumption	$4,923	$4,591	$7,352	$6,635
Other costs and taxes	1,071	973	1,891	1,687
Total Cost of Budget	$5,994	$5,564	$9,243	$8,322

*Places with population of 2,500 to 50,000.
Source: Department of Labor, Bureau of Labor Statistics, "Three Standards of Living for an Urban Family of Four Persons," *Bulletin No. 1570–5*, 1969, p. 15.

to be about 70 percent of urban families, although this estimate might be a bit low. The Bureau of the Census places this figure at about 85 percent of corresponding nonfarm lands.[1]

THE CONCEPT OF PERMANENT INCOME

In our discussion so far we have considered income only during a given year. If a family's income is below the poverty line for a particular year, the family is considered poor. But even taking into account the complexities mentioned in the previous section, defining poverty by a single year's income still involves some problems. We must consider, as well, variation or changes in income. Perhaps the most noticeable problem here is the year-to-year fluctuation in income. Consider two comparable families: one has a steady $4,000 per year income and the other has an income that fluctuates from, say, $3,000 per year to $9,000 per year every other year. Over a period of 10 years the $4,000 per year family is never included in the poverty group if the cutoff point is $3,500 per year. On the other hand, the second family would fall within the poverty group in 5 out of the 10 years, even though its average income over this 10-year period would have been $6,000 per year—$2,000 per year higher than the first family.

Thus, the incidence of poverty, as poverty is currently defined, can be reduced simply by reducing the variability of income. Indeed, the second family actually could suffer an absolute reduction in average income over a number of years and still be defined as "better off" simply because it escapes the every-other-year poverty classification. But it is hard to imagine that the second family would consider itself better off with a $2,000 per year smaller, although less variable, income.

This phenomenon is important to recognize because a society can be misled into thinking that its people are better off just because it succeeds in reducing the proportion of the population that falls into the poverty group in any one year. A more accurate measure would be the proportion of families that fell below the poverty line over a period of several years. In the above example, the second family would never be considered poverty stricken if income would have been averaged over a period of just two years at a time.

A related problem, and perhaps even more important, is the way in which a family, or person, views its long-term income potential. Most college students, for example, do not consider themselves poverty stricken even though their incomes might place them in this category. They know

---

[1] U.S. Bureau of the Census, *Current Population Reports*, Series P-60, No. 68, "Poverty in the United States, 1959 to 1968" (Washington, D.C.: U.S. Government Printing Office, 1969), p. 11. Also for a good account of the rural poverty problem, see *The People Left Behind*, a report by the President's National Advisory Commission on Rural Poverty, 1967.

that in a few years, or less, they will be able to enjoy a substantial increase in income. Thus, college students, tend to enjoy a much higher standard of living than, say, ghetto dwellers with comparable incomes but who have little or no hope of ever improving their lot. There can be little doubt, too, that the psychological effects of having a low income is much different between a college student and a ghetto dweller. The hope of someday breaking out of one's poverty conditions makes these conditions somewhat more bearable. In a sense, poverty is a state of mind as well as the state of one's pocketbook.

The fact that people tend to look at their long-run earning potential in making consumption decisions probably makes current expenditures on consumption a better measure of poverty than current income. For example, if you have a current income of $2,500 per year but expect to be making $10,000 per year in two years, your current consumption per year will likely be a great deal larger than someone who expects little or no increase in income. The idea that long-run average income, or permanent income as it is called, is an important determinant of current consumption was first brought out by Friedman in his book *The Theory of the Consumption Function*. This idea is generally referred to as the "permanent income hypothesis."

Another reason for paying attention to current expenditures instead of current income as a measure of poverty is to take account of people that live off of their savings. The phenomenon is particularly important for retired people. For example, it is not uncommon to observe an older person or couple selling off some property or stocks to pay for medical care, buy a new car, or take a trip. Indeed people save during their lifetimes for these very purposes. This is not to say, however, that there is no need to be concerned about poverty among our older people. Many are truly poor. The point is, there is a great deal of difference between the situation where a couple has $3,000 per year income and zero savings or wealth, and the case where a couple has the same income but $100,000 in wealth. The first couple is poor, the second is not.

THE DISTRIBUTION OF INCOME IN THE UNITED STATES

Although mere numbers can never reflect the depression and anxiety of the poor, it will be instructive, nevertheless, to look briefly at the extent of poverty in the United States. Also because of the difficulty of obtaining data, we are forced to largely gloss over the complexities and problems of measuring poverty that we have just considered.

It is necessary to bear in mind, too, that as long as the income of the nation is not divided up exactly equal between the people, some, by necessity, will have to be on the lower end of the income scale. Thus, in viewing figures on the distribution of income it is useful to look both at the dispersion of income between the lowest and highest income recipients and the number or percentage of people that fall into the various income levels.

In Table 10–3 we present the percentage of families that fall within 6 specified before income tax brackets for 1947, 1960, and 1968. To make the three years comparable, the 1947 and 1960 income figures were adjusted for changes in the general price level before the percentages were computed. Thus, any upward movement that is shown in family incomes is due to real economic growth rather than to inflation.

Table 10–3. Percent distribution of money income of families in the United States, selected years, constant 1968 dollars

Annual Income Level	1947	1960	1968
Under $ 3,000	26.0%	17.9%	10.3%
$ 3,000 to 4,999	28.1	16.3	12.1
5,000 to 6,999	21.8	20.1	14.5
7,000 to 9,999	14.2	23.3	23.4
10,000 to 14,999	10.0	15.7	24.9
15,000 and over		6.6	14.8
	100.0%	100.0%	100.0%
Median family income	$4,716	$6,604	$8,632

Source: U.S. Bureau of the Census, *Current Population Reports*, Series P-60, No. 66, "Income in 1968 of Families and Persons in the United States" (Washington, D.C.: U.S. Government Printing Office, 1969), p. 20.

From the figures presented in Table 10–3 we would have to conclude that the old adage "the rich get richer and the poor get poorer" does not hold true, at least for the United States. As shown, over one fourth of all U.S. families had incomes lower than $3,000 (in 1968 prices) in 1947. (If we would have computed the 1947 percentages using 1947 prices, over 49 percent of all families would have fallen in the $3,000 and under group.) But in 1968, as we see, only about 10 percent of all families were included in the $3,000 and under income group. The influence of economic growth is evident, too, in the upper end of the income scale. In 1947 only 10 percent of all families had incomes of $10,000 or more (in 1968 prices), whereas in 1968 the percent of families in this group increased to almost 40 percent. At any rate, the near doubling of median income from the end of World War II to the present reflects an across the board increase in incomes rather than just an increase in the incomes of the wealthy.[2]

We cannot tell from the overall upward movement of family incomes, however, whether or not the dispersion of incomes is becoming narrower or that poor families are getting a relatively larger slice of the pie. The

---

[2] Median family income is defined as that level of income where 50 percent of the families are below this level and 50 percent are above.

figures in Table 10–4 provide some indication of the relative distribution of incomes. Here we observe that if all families are ranked by income level from the lowest to the highest, the lowest 20 percent received only 5.7 percent of the total money income in 1968. However, it is interesting to note too that the lower income groups have increased their share of total income slightly during the post–World War II years. For example, the lowest fifth of the families increased their share of the income "pie" from 4.9 percent in 1960 to 5.7 percent in 1968. The middle income groups have obtained a slightly larger share of the nation's income as well during recent years. The increasing share of the lower and middle income families has come at the expense of the highest fifth, and particularly at the expense of the highest 5 percent of the nation's families, are shown in Table 10–4. Remember, too, that these figures are before tax income so if the higher income families are taxed at higher rates, the after-tax distribution would show less dispersion than is shown in Table 10–4.

Table 10–4.   Percentage share of total before tax U.S. money income received by each fifth of families and top 5 percent of all families, selected years

Family Group	1947	1960	1968
Lowest fifth	5.0	4.9	5.7
Second fifth	11.8	12.0	12.4
Third fifth	17.0	17.6	17.7
Fourth fifth	23.1	23.6	23.7
Highest fifth	43.0	42.0	40.6
Top 5 percent	17.2	16.8	14.0

Source: U.S. Bureau of the Census, *Current Population Reports*, Series P-60, No. 66, "Income in 1968 of Families and Persons in the United States" (Washington, D.C.: U.S. Government Printing Office, 1969), p. 22.

THE LORENZ CURVE

Economists have long used a device to describe the nation's income distribution that is perhaps a bit more illustrative than numbers such as are shown in Table 10–4—the Lorenz curve, after the man who developed it. The Lorenz curve is obtained by plotting the cumulative percent of the nation's income against the cumulative percent of the nation's families or individuals receiving this income. Generally income is represented on the vertical axis of the diagram and households or individuals on the horizontal axis, as shown in Figure 10–1.

Perhaps the easiest way to understand the Lorenz curve is to ask, what would the curve look like if the nation's income were distributed in a perfect equalitarian manner? In other words, suppose everyone received the same income. In this case, 20 percent of the nation's families would receive 20 percent of the income, 40 percent would receive 40 percent of the income, etc. Plotting these figures on a Lorenz curve diagram would result in a straight, upward sloping line, as shown in Figure 10–1.

FIGURE 10–1.   The Lorenz curve

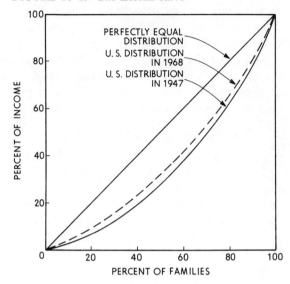

Of course, we know that no nation exhibits a completely equal distribution of income. The lowest 20 percent of the families generally receive substantially less than 20 percent of the income whereas the highest 20 percent of the families receive much more than 20 percent of the income. What does the Lorenz curve look like in a situation such as this? In this case if we plot the percent of income received by the lowest 20 percent of the families, say in the United States for 1947, we go up on the vertical axis only to 5.0 percent, according to the figures in Table 10–4. Proceeding on, we see that the cumulative income of the bottom 40 percent of the families, as shown in Table 10–4 for 1947, amounts to 16.8 percent of the total income for that year. Hence in plotting this combination, we choose the point that corresponds to 40 percent on the horizontal axis and 16.8 on the vertical axis. If we continued on in this manner for the 60 and 80 percent points on the horizontal axis, we obtain points that also lie below the straight, bisecting line. And by connecting these points, we obtain the Lorenz curve. Note that this curve lies below the straight line that depicts perfect equality.

We can conclude therefore that the more unequal the distribution of income, the more curvature there will be in the Lorenz curve. Indeed if all of the income of the country were received by just one family, the curve would be a rectangle, traced out by the horizontal axis and the right-hand side of the "box" shown in Figure 10–1. By the same token, if there is a trend towards a more equal distribution of income, the Lorenz curve will "flatten out" and move close to the straight, bisecting line. As mentioned, there appears to have been a slight trend towards a more equal distribution of income in the United States in recent times. Thus the Lorenz curve is somewhat "flatter" now than 20 to 30 years ago. This is illustrated in Figure 10–1, where the 1968 Lorenz curve lies closer to the perfect equality line than the 1947 curve.

Bear in mind, too, that the after-tax, disposable income should be reflected by a Lorenz curve that lies closer to the perfect equality line if the progressive income tax is doing its thing, that is, if the high-income families are taxed at a higher rate than their low-income counterparts.

THE GINI RATIO

Economists often use another term to describe the distribution of income—the Gini ratio or Gini coefficient. The Gini ratio is derived from the Lorenz curve diagram and is defined as the ratio of the area between the Lorenz curve and the perfect equality line to the total area below the perfect equality line. In terms of Figure 10–2 it is the ratio of area A over the total area $A + B$, i.e., the Gini ratio is equal to $A/A + B$.

FIGURE 10–2.   Deriving the Gini ratio

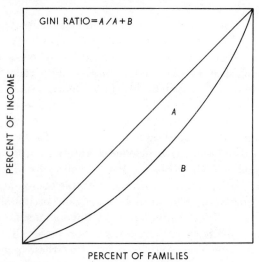

PERCENT OF FAMILIES

The size of the Gini ratio or coefficient can vary from zero to one. As a nation moves closer to perfect equality in its income distribution, the Gini ratio will approach zero. This occurs because area A, the numerator in the fraction, becomes smaller and smaller as the Lorenz curve becomes flatter and approaches the perfect equality line. Then at the extreme of perfect equality, area A disappears, or becomes zero, which means that the value of the fraction becomes zero. Conversely, as a nation moves toward complete inequality of the income distribution, the Lorenz curve approaches the boundaries of the rectangle and area *B* grows smaller and smaller. At the extreme of complete inequality, area *B* disappears so the ratio is equal to *A/A* or one.

Thus nations that have a relatively low Gini ratio have relative equality in their distribution of income. The advantage of using the Gini ratio is that it enables us to describe a nation's income distribution by a single number rather than a series of numbers such as Table 10–4 or as a diagram such as Figure 10–2. Of course, the Gini ratio also can be used to describe the income distributions of smaller groups of people such as states or municipalities.

POVERTY IN THE UNITED STATES

With a little reflection, it soon becomes clear that poverty is a relative concept. If every family in the world had an income of $3,500 per year, we would not likely consider $3,500 as the poverty line, nor would the concept of poverty be likely to come up. Everyone would be equally rich, or poor whichever you prefer. By the same token, even a millionaire might feel poor in a world of billionaires. It appears, therefore, that poverty will always be intimately tied up with the distribution of income. We have looked briefly at the income distribution of the United States, now let us take a somewhat closer look at poverty.

Although no one is immune from being poor, there are certain groups of people in society that tend to be poverty prone. This is not to say that certain groups of people prefer poverty to affluence; poverty is mainly the result of circumstances rather than preferences. Table 10–5 provides a partial listing of family characteristics that allow us to identify groups of people where the incidence of poverty is relatively high.

In determining the incidence of poverty shown in Table 10–5, the Department of Commerce attempted to take into account some of the varying circumstances mentioned earlier in this chapter such as differences in number of children and place of residence. For example, the poverty line for a four-member nonfarm family in 1968 was set at $3,531. This figure increases to $5,722 for a seven or more member nonfarm family. Also the lower cost of living on farms is taken into account as reflected, for example, by the poverty line of $3,034 for a four-member farm family in 1968. The substantial reduction in the poverty line for farm families is accounted for in large part by the lower cost of food on farms. In fact, the core of the poverty definition was the cost of a nutritionally adequate food plan as determined by the U.S. Department of Agriculture. Also annual revisions in the poverty line were based on price changes in this predetermined food budget.

Finally, in measuring the income of families in order to judge whether a family was above or below the poverty line, the following receipts were not counted as income: (1) receipts from the sale of property such as

Table 10–5.   Selected characteristics of families in relation to the incidence of poverty, 1968 and 1959

	Percent below the Poverty Line	
Selected Characteristic	1968	1959
1. Sex and race of head:		
White—male head	6.3	13.3
White—female head	25.2	34.8
Negro—male head	18.9	44.2
Negro—female head	52.9	72.0
2. Residence:		
Nonfarm	9.5	16.1
Farm	18.8	44.6
3. Age of head:		
14 to 24 years	13.2	26.9
25 to 54 years	8.6	16.0
55 to 64 years	8.2	15.9
65 and over	17.0	30.0
4. Size of family:		
2 persons	10.5	19.6
3 and 4 persons	7.1	12.8
5 and 6 persons	10.2	20.2
7 persons or more	24.7	45.6
5. Occupation group of head:		
Professional and managerial	2.6	5.0
Clerical and sales	3.7	5.7
Craftsmen and foremen	3.7	7.2
Operatives and kindred workers..	6.4	14.1
Service workers, including		
domestics	16.5	25.3
Nonfarm laborers	15.3	29.4
Farmers and farm workers	26.3	54.1
Armed forces	6.7	15.5

Source: U.S. Bureau of the Census, *Current Population Reports*, Series P-60, No. 68, "Poverty in the United States: 1959 to.1968" (Washington, D.C.: U.S. Government Printing Office, 1969), p. 4.

house, stocks, bonds or car; (2) bank withdrawals; (3) borrowed money; (4) tax refunds; (5) gifts; and (6) inheritances and insurance payments. On the basis of our previous discussion the omission of some of these items might be questioned, but at least it is important to know what is included in measured family income.

Looking first at poverty in relation to sex and race of head of family, we see that poverty is much more prevalent among fatherless families, especially among negro fatherless families. Over half of this latter group fell below the poverty level in 1968. Regarding residence, we see that the incidence of poverty is almost twice as high among farm families than their city counterparts, even taking into account the decrease in cost of living on farms.

As we might expect, poverty is more prevalent among the very youngest and very oldest families, although as we mentioned no account was made for the wealth or savings of this latter group. Again, as we might expect, poverty is more prevalent among the very largest families. Finally, we see that the occupation of the family head has an important bearing on the incidence of poverty. As expected, the higher income professional, managerial, and skilled craftsmen occupations result in the least amount of poverty. On the other end of the scale, farmers and farm laborers exhibit the most poverty, followed by service workers and nonfarm laborers.

Perhaps the most striking thing about Table 10–5 is the tremendous decline in the incidence of poverty from 1959 to 1968. All of the categories mentioned exhibited a reduction in poverty during this period. In fact, in many instances the percent of families below the poverty line dropped by a half or more. This phenomenon clearly demonstrates the influence of general economic growth on poverty. If everyone can be made a little richer, the poor benefit as well as the rich.

Of course, as we pointed out, society's concept of what constitutes a poor family or individual generally changes with continued economic growth. As the poverty line inches upward, the same families that escaped the poverty group in the 1960's may find themselves right back in during the 1970's. In large part, the income necessary to escape poverty turns on what goods and services society considers as necessities. Indoor plumbing was once considered a luxury, now it is a necessity, at least in the United States. Similarly, animal protein in the diet is considered a luxury in many underdeveloped nations while it is considered a necessity in the United States. Indeed, it is not difficult to imagine that in the years to come many present-day luxuries such as air conditioning and convenience foods will come to be considered as necessities.

MYTHS ABOUT POVERTY

In the United States at the present time it is taken for granted by most people that poverty is an undesirable thing and that society would be better off if it were eliminated. Strangely enough, this thinking did not always prevail. Throughout history a number of long-standing myths about poverty were commonly accepted, and perhaps still are accepted by some people today.

One such myth was that every society needed to keep a certain fraction of its population poor in order to have a source of labor for the disagreeable and menial tasks that had to be done. For example, it was thought that if no one were poor who would clean the streets, collect the garbage, or maintain the sewers? As societies have developed, however, this fear has been proven to be unfounded. First, the invention and adoption of machines have taken much of the drudgery out of many of these jobs and have completely eliminated others. Also people did not realize that a free functioning labor market would take into account the varying amount of disagreeableness in jobs and compensate the people who held undesirable jobs with higher wages. For example, the bank clerk who takes part of his salary in comfortable working conditions no doubt would be happy with the salary of the sanitary engineer (garbage man).

Another myth that might be more prevalent than we would like to admit is that poor people are inherently lazy and the only thing that keeps them working is the fear of starvation. Thus it is reasoned that these people must be kept poor in order for them to be industrious. What was often forgotten here was that relatively low wages provide poor people with very little incentive to work or to improve their lot. As an example, it is sometimes argued that some minority groups in the United States today are inherently lazy because they do not strive for more education in an attempt to improve themselves. But we must remember that discrimination in the labor market has prevented many of these people from capturing a return to their education, hence there was little incentive for them to invest in more education.

Still a third myth, that again is probably held by some people who are not poor, is that poor people have deliberately chosen to be poor because of the mental and physical cost involved in breaking out of the poverty class. The stereotyped "hillbilly" or skid row dweller is generally used as an example. Granted there will always be a few people in every society who wish to "drop out." But the mass exodus of people from the poverty level to the "middle class" in the United States and other developed nations provides a strong case for arguing that most people take advantage of opportunities to escape the grasp of poverty. Indeed, it is very hard to argue that the poor live a carefree and easy life. "Pounding the pavement" in search of even a temporary job or worrying about where next month's rent will come from would not be considered an easy life by most middle- or high-income people.

PUBLIC POLICY ON POVERTY

With the gradual abandonment of these myths about poverty, many nations have adopted specific policies or programs to reduce poverty. And some of these policies or programs involve a transfer of income or wealth away from high-income people to poor people. It is interesting to note that a society's decision to alter its income distribution involves the implicit assumption that the additional satisfaction or utility that poor people receive from additional income, more than offsets the loss of utility that the middle- or high-income people lose when their incomes are reduced. It should be pointed out, however, that economists have not been able to prove that the total welfare of society improves by a transfer of money from the rich to the poor. In order to prove this, it would have to be shown that the poor receive more satisfaction than the rich lose from this transfer of money. The basic question, then, is do the poor receive more satisfaction from extra money than the rich?

Suppose $100 is taxed away from a rich family and given to a poor family. Let us say that this tax prevents the rich family from having a lavish night on the town but allows the poor family to buy shoes for the children. Who gains more satisfaction? Offhand, it seems reasonable to believe that the poor family gains more than the rich family loses. But, as mentioned, in order to prove this we would have to show that the poor family has a greater capacity for enjoyment than the rich family. Since no one has been able to measure satisfaction or utilities directly, it is not possible to determine whether the shoes or the night on the town brings more satisfaction to their respective families. We must at least grant the possibility that the rich family could have received more satisfaction from the $100. The problem is one of determining who has the greater capacity for satisfaction from additional income.

In spite of the impossibility of solving this problem, at least to date, the people of the United States, and many other nations, have decided that the poor do gain more than the rich lose, at least for fairly small transfers of income. It is not so clear, however, whether society would accept a more drastic equalization of incomes than we now have. Given the fact that the people of the United States have decided collectively to help the less fortunate members of society, let us look at some of the public programs and policies that tend to, or at least are supposed to, help the poor.

IMPLICIT PROGRAMS THAT HELP THE POOR

Before turning to the more explicit poverty or income redistribution programs, we ought to mention that the extent of poverty is influenced a great deal by other circumstances in the economy as well. These include:

1. *General economic growth.* Although we do not generally consider economic growth as a program to help the poor, there can be no doubt that the across-the-board increase in incomes has greatly reduced the extent of poverty in the United States and in the other more highly developed nations of the world. This is clearly shown in Table 10–5 where the incidence of poverty during the 1960's has been reduced by a half or more for many groups. Remember, too, that these figures are based on a current definition of poverty. Had we used the poverty definition from the 1930's the incidence would have been even lower.

2. *A full-employment economy.* Since poor people make up a disproportionate large share of the unskilled labor force, a rise in unemployment hits poor people the hardest. In our discussion of unemployment in Chapter 2, we pointed out that the unskilled tend to be the first laid off. As we saw in Chapter 2, the unemployment rate among "blue-collar" workers rises faster than all workers during a recession, this in spite of the fact that the blue-collar category includes many skilled craftsmen that

do not face as great a threat of layoffs. Thus during recessions the poor tend to be hurt the most.

3. *A stable price economy.* The presence of an unexpected high rate of inflation also hurts the poor. For one thing, wage increases of poor people tend to lag behind the general rise in prices, which results in an absolute reduction in their already small real incomes. Perhaps even more important, the adjustment in government unemployment insurance and welfare payments, which sustain a large share of the poor, tends to lag even further behind prices than do wages. Also for the retired living on relatively fixed social security and retirement benefits, the rise in the cost of living makes it necessary for these people to reduce their standard of living even further.

4. *Public education.* Although we may not think public education as a policy or program to help the poor, there can be no doubt that such has been the case. The relationship of education to poverty is very clear. If we take a cross section of poor people we find them in many different situations. Some are white, others black. Some live in big cities, others in small towns or on farms. We find the poor in every region of the country and from divergent backgrounds. Indeed, the poor are far from a homogeneous group. If we tried to find a common characteristic that fitted most poor people, aside from a lack of money, probably the closest we could come would be their low level and poor quality of education.

The relationship between income and education is illustrated by Table 10–6. Here we see that at the lowest educational levels, median income is

Table 10–6.   Relationship between income and education, United States, 1967

Education Level	White Families		Nonwhite Families	
	Median Income	% below $3,000	Median Income	% below $3,000
Less than 8 years	$ 4,932	28.5	$ 3,670	40.3
8 years	6,608	17.1	4,897	28.4
1–3 years high school	7,971	9.5	5,083	25.1
4 years high school	8,962	5.3	6,665	14.1
1–3 years college	10,277	5.0	8,189	8.8
4 or more years college	12,770	3.3	10,485	4.4

Source: U.S. Bureau of the Census, *Current Population Reports,* Series P-60, No. 59, "Income in 1967 of Families in the United States" (Washington, D.C.: U.S. Government Printing Office, 1969), p. 44.

lowest and the incidence of poverty is highest. This is true for both white and nonwhite families. Notice, however, that nonwhite families suffer lower incomes and a higher incidence of poverty than their white counterparts—the fruits of discrimination.

The mere fact that income bears a close positive relationship to education does not guarantee, of course, that large numbers of poor people can use education to escape from poverty. Education is a very costly activity and not many poor people could afford to purchase much if they had to pay the full cost. Thus, if education is to be a major means of escape from poverty, a large share of its cost must be borne by the public. In public elementary and high schools, the entire operating costs are financed by tax revenues. In public colleges and universities, student tuition generally covers a third or less of the operating costs of the institutions, with tax revenue covering the major part of the remainder.

In spite of generous public support of educational institutions in the United States, it has been argued that the poor and lower middle class still subsidize the college education of the higher income people. The argument has some validity. Low-income people pay taxes to support public colleges and universities but utilize these institutions to a much smaller extent than the higher income people. This is especially true for poor people among minority groups.

One way to make higher education much more accessible and responsive to poor people is for the government to directly support or subsidize people (students) rather than educational institutions. One proposal is to give students vouchers that they could "spend" at the educational institution of their choice. This would have the advantage, also, of creating some competition between educational institutions which in turn should promote greater efficiency and higher quality of services provided. It should always be kept in mind that public educational institutions were set up to serve the public. In many cases these institutions have become rich and powerful in their own right and some have turned to serving their own interests instead of the public. Giving exclusive monopoly power to "public servants" involves the danger that the "servants" become the master and the public becomes the "servant."

EXPLICIT PROGRAMS TO HELP THE POOR

In addition to the points mentioned in the previous section, there are other programs and policies designed more or less to alter the income distribution towards more equality. These include:

1. *Minimum wage laws.* Since poor people tend to be on the low end of the wage scale, minimum wage laws affect the poor primarily. At first glance it may appear that minimum wage laws are a boon to poor people. After all, if a poor person cannot be paid less than $1.60 per hour, say, his income will be higher than if his wage were $1 per hour. What is often forgotten, however, is that the higher minimum wage can only benefit the poor person if he is working. If the market wage is lower than the minimum wage, the inevitable result will be a reduction in the employment opportunities for poor people. Indeed, it has been argued that a minimum wage law harms poor people as much as it helps them because of the

increased unemployment that it causes among the people at the low end of the wage scale.

2. *Farm programs.* Since poverty has been and still is relatively prevalent on farms and rural areas, various farm programs have been designed to bolster farm incomes. In large part these programs have taken the form of supporting the prices of various agricultural products above their free market levels. Again, it may appear reasonable to believe that such a program would benefit poor farmers. If a farmer can receive $2 per bushel for his wheat, for example, his income ought to be higher than if he received $1 per bushel. But one of the problems of such a program is that the setting of a support price higher than the market level reduces the quantity demanded of farm products (which includes foreign buyers as well). Thus the government has to set limits on how much farmers can produce in order to keep the surpluses at manageable levels. At any rate, the nation ends up using scarce resources to produce products that no one wants to buy.

An even more important problem of farm programs is that they end up helping large, high-income farmers to a much greater degree than they help poor farmers. A little simple arithmetic makes this point clear. A small farmer that produces 100 bushels of wheat for sale will gain $100 extra income if the price of wheat is raised from $1 to $2 per bushel by the support price. But the large farmer who sells, say, 10,000 bushels of wheat per year gains $10,000 in extra income from the program. It is becoming increasingly clear that present farm programs are causing a more unequal distribution of income among farmers.

The amount of government payments to farmers for 1963 are presented in Table 10–7. Here we see that over half of all government payments in 1963 went to the upper 10 percent of the farms. And the average payment per farm was over 40 times larger for the group with the largest farms than for the group with the smallest.

3. *Welfare programs.* Included under this general heading are a variety of programs specifically designed to help poor people, such as the Aid

Table 10–7.   Government payments to farmers in 1963

Farms with Sales of—	Distribution of Farms (Percent)	Government Payments		
		Total (Million (Dollars)	Per Farm (Dollars)	Distribution of Total (Percent)
$20,000 and over	10.7	918	2,391	54.5
10,000 to $19,999	16.6	398	670	23.6
5,000 to 9,999	17.0	213	350	12.6
2,500 to 4,999	13.0	80	173	4.7
Less than 2,500	42.7	77	51	4.6
Total	100.0	1,686	472	100.0

Source: T. W. Schultz, "Public Approaches to Minimize Poverty," in Leo Fishman (ed.), *Poverty Amid Affluence* (New Haven and London: Yale University Press, 1966).

to Families with Dependent Children (AFDC), hospital and medical care for the poor, school lunches, food stamps, etc. At the present time about $20 billion dollars per year in public funds go into these various programs, up from about $7 billion per year in 1960. Although these programs undoubtedly help the poor, they have undergone a growing amount of criticism in recent years.

First it appears rather strange that the real cost of welfare has more than doubled in the United States during the past decade while the incidence of poverty (measured without welfare payments) has declined by almost one half (Table 10–5). Many middle-income taxpayers are beginning to ask embarrassing questions. Moreover many poor people complain that too much of the money is eaten up in administering the programs and as a result not enough "welfare" reaches them. Thirdly, the present welfare programs give rise to a number of undesirable side effects. For example, there is the built-in incentive for breaking up families. Poor families with several children find that the income of the wife and children can be increased in many instances if the husband leaves home and the family goes on welfare. This is reflected in the substantial increase in the proportion of fatherless families among urban blacks—from 23 percent in 1960 to 29 percent in 1968. Indeed, there are more fatherless children living in New York City today than there are people of all ages in most other American cities.

Some welfare programs also have the effect of in a sense placing a 100 percent tax on additional income to the poor. For example, if the husband of a poor family finds a job that pays an after-tax wage equivalent to his wife and children AFDC payments and rejoins the family, the payments stop, leaving the family with the same net income with the job as without. Thus there isn't much incentive for fathers of poor families to take jobs and reunite with their families.

The present welfare program also provides a strong incentive for people to leave rural areas particularly in the South and migrate to the large northern cities. This occurs because of the much larger AFDC payments made by northern states. For example, the maximum monthly AFDC payment for a family of four is $55 in Mississippi and $332 in New Jersey. Again, with the urban congestion and pollution, it does not seem desirable to hasten migration to large cities, as the current welfare setup does.

4. *Social security and unemployment insurance.* These two programs are more straightforward and less controversial than the ones we have just discussed. Perhaps the major criticism of the social security program is that it also has elements of the 100 percent tax phenomenon. If a retired person wants to supplement his income with part-time work, he must be careful not to earn over the allowable maximum, else he loses his social security benefits. If these benefits are lost, it is equivalent to a 100 percent tax on his income up to the cutoff point.

5. *Progressive income tax.* Although the income tax is the major revenue source for government, the fact that the tax rates are intended to increase with income makes it also an income redistribution scheme. In fact, the government can obtain any income distribution that is desired simply by adjusting the tax rates. For example, if it wanted more equality it could increase the tax rates on high incomes and reduce them on low incomes. An income tax in its purest, unadulterated form is considered by many economists to be the fairest and least distorting tax that a government can levy.

Unfortunately, the U.S. income tax is not very "pure." It is "riddled" by a host of loopholes that allow certain people to escape the tax altogether and others to pay a greatly reduced tax. One very large loophole is the capital gains treatment. Here expenses incurred in the creation of capital gains can be written off against ordinary income while the gains are taxed at only one half the rate on ordinary income. Thus a person can reduce his tax by one half by taking his income as capital gains. Also the payment of the tax can be postponed indefinitely because capital gains are not taxed until realized.

Certain industries also enjoy special tax treatment. For example, in 1967 the nation's 15 largest oil refiners paid an average tax rate of only 8 percent on net income. Indeed, one company with a net income exceeding $145 million paid no federal income taxes whatsoever. Another with $893 million net income paid only 1.9 percent in federal income taxes.

Another unfortunate aspect of tax loopholes is that each year millions of dollars of man-hours are devoted to figuring out ways to avoid paying taxes. It pays for individuals to do so but it amounts to an absolute waste for the nation. It is also unfortunate that the ones who gain most from loopholes are the highest income people. The poor and middle-income people who have their taxes deducted from their wages have relatively little chance to take advantage of loopholes.

NEGATIVE INCOME TAX

The negative income tax is a relatively new proposal that has received a great deal of attention of late. It was first proposed by Milton Friedman in his 1962 book, *Capitalism and Freedom.* Since then the basic idea has been called a number of things including "income maintenance" or a "guaranteed annual income." The proposal is surprisingly simple. If society is really serious about helping poor people and wants to help them in the most efficient way possible, the best way is for the government to supplement their incomes by a so-called negative tax—a payment from the government to the poor.

Perhaps the easiest way to understand how the negative income tax plan might work is to look at a specific example. Suppose that under the ordinary income tax schedule, a family of four could earn up to $3,500 per year without paying any federal income tax. Next, let us consider the case of a poor family of four with a total income of $2,500 per year. This family would after the end of the year file an income tax return reporting that it had an income deficit of $1,000 ($3,500 − $2,500). Finally, let us assume that the negative tax rate or the refund rate is 50 percent. In this case the family would receive a $500 check (0.50 × 1,000) from the government, which in a sense is a negative tax—a payment from the government to a citizen instead of vice versa. Thus the family would end up with a total income of $3,000—$2,500 from its initial income plus $500 in "negative taxes."

It is important to recognize, too, that the negative tax rate would be something less than 100 percent. In other words, the government would not make up the entire difference between a family's initial income and the zero tax income ($3,500 in our example). For example, suppose the family had an opportunity to earn an extra $500 so that its initial before tax income would increase to $3,000. Now with a $500 deficit the government would mail a check for $250 giving the family a total income of $3,250—the initial 3,000 plus the $250 negative tax. Thus in this second case the family's after-tax income would have increased to $3,250. If the government would have made up the entire difference between the $3,500 base and the family's actual income, the total income would have been $3,500 in both cases. Hence there would have been no incentive for the family to earn additional income if it remained below $3,500. But as long as the negative tax rate is less than 100 percent, the family still has an incentive to earn money on its own. Thus one of the principal objections to the negative tax proposal, namely that people would have no incentive to work, is not valid. Of course, the negative tax rate and the base zero tax income could be set at any level desired as long as the rate is kept below 100 percent. The 50 percent rate and $3,500 income are just examples. Also additional refinements could be built into the plan such as allowing deductions from actual income for such things as medical expense before calculating the negative tax.

The arguments in favor of the negative tax are quite convincing. First, it would be possible to eliminate or at least reduce the variety of present programs that are overburdened with administrative expense and often treat different groups very unequally. The negative income tax would not suffer from either of these shortcomings. Secondly, poor people would not have to suffer the indignities and degradation that they are now subject to in the case welfare schemes that label the poor in full view of their neighbors. Also, programs that dole out a few dollars for this and a few dollars for that treat the poor as if they were second-class citizens that could not be trusted with money. To be poor is bad enough, but to suffer the indignities of the present welfare setup is more than some can bear.

It is estimated that the cost of the government of including every family in the United States under a negative income tax plan would run in the neighborhood of $10 to $15 billion per year, which is considerably less than the cost of current welfare programs.

MAIN POINTS OF CHAPTER 10

1. The definition of poverty depends to a large extent on the average income and wealth of the population. The higher the income, the higher the line of demarcation between rich and poor.

2. The family income necessary to rise above the poverty classification also depends on size of family and place of residence.

3. The extent of poverty in any one year depends upon the long-run expected income as well as current income. The idea that current consumption depends upon long-run expected income is known as "permanent income hypothesis."

4. The percent of families under the $3,000 per year income level has fallen from 26.0 percent in 1947 to 10.3 percent in 1968 in constant 1968 dollars.

5. During the past 20 years, the before-tax income distribution in the United States has tended towards greater equality.

6. The Lorenz curve shows the percent of total income received by a certain percent of the population. A straight-line Lorenz curve illustrates perfect equality. The more curvature of the Lorenz curve, the more unequal the distribution of income.

7. The Gini ratio is the ratio of the area between the actual Lorenz curve and the perfect equality line to the total area under the perfect equality line. A Gini ratio of zero denotes complete equality of income whereas a ratio of 1 denotes complete inequality.

8. In the United States poverty is more prevalent among black families, farmers, families in the very youngest and very oldest age categories, larger families, and those in the unskilled occupations.

9. Because of general economic growth the percent of families defined as poor declined substantially in all family classifications between 1959 and 1968.

10. Some past and present myths about poverty include: (1) every society needs poor people to furnish labor for menial and undesirable tasks, (2) poor people are poor because they are lazy, and (3) the poor have deliberately chosen to be poor because of the mental and physical cost of increasing their incomes.

11. Deliberate attempts to redistribute income from the rich to the poor involves the implicit assumption that the poor gain more from extra income than the rich lose.

12. In the United States the poor do benefit greatly from programs or policies not designed specifically as poverty programs. These include: (1) general economic growth, (2) full employment, (3) stable prices, and (4) public education.

13. Other programs or policies designed to more specifically help poor people include: (1) minimum wage laws, (2) farm programs, (3) various welfare programs, (4) social security and unemployment insurance, and (5) the progressive income tax.

14. The farm program and traditional welfare programs have come under increasing criticism in recent years because of their high cost and undesirable effects both upon the poor and the rest of society.

15. A relatively new proposal put forth by Professor Milton Friedman is the negative income tax plan. Under this plan, families below a specified income level would receive a "negative tax" or payment from the government.

16. An important feature of negative income tax plan would be a negative tax rate of less than 100 percent. This would allow families to increase their total income without having their negative tax payments decreased by a like amount. Hence there would still be an incentive for poor people to improve their incomes on their own.

QUESTIONS FOR THOUGHT AND DISCUSSION

1. "A poor family in the United States also would be considered poor in India." Do you agree? Why or why not?

2. Sometimes it appears as though families become poorer as they grow older even though their incomes are rising. Do you think there is any substance to this observation? Explain.

3. The high rate of poverty among aspiring artists, actors, and actresses is well known. Why do you suppose people persist in choosing these lines of work? (Hint: Also consider how poverty is measured.)

4. Consider two families: one made up of two college seniors just recently married and the other a couple in their late 50's. Both couples have incomes of $2,500 this year. Which is poorer and why?

5. Consider two groups of people: one group is made up of the students in your economics class and the other are the people that regularly attend concerts on campus. Which group would likely have the most unequal income distribution. Draw hypothetical Lorenz curves for each group. Which would have the highest Gini ratio?

6. It is sometimes argued that professors prefer to be poor. Ask your professors if this is really true.

7. Suppose your economics professor has an annual income 10 times greater than yours. Can you convince him that you would gain more than he would lose if he gave half of his annual income to you? How about $10? Would he believe $1?

8. Because of campus disturbances in recent years, some people have argued that students should pay a higher share of the cost of operating a college. What long-run effect would this likely have on the income distribution of the country? Why?

9. Compare the service you obtain from a local retailer in your neighborhood with that from your college administration. Do you notice a difference? Can you think of a reason for the difference if there is one?

10. Do you believe the minimum wage laws help or harm poor people? Why?

11. Compare the negative income tax proposal with the farm program and welfare programs as a means of helping poor people.

CHAPTER
11
INTERNATIONAL TRADE AND FINANCE

Our discussion thus far has centered mainly on the national economy and the problems of unemployment and inflation. In this chapter we will broaden our perspective somewhat and look at the international economy, specifically at the phenomenon of trade between nations.

We should bear in mind throughout the discussion that nations exist because of artificial boundaries that men have devised. Were it not for border guards, barricades, check points, etc., we could travel across national boundaries without being aware that we had done so. The artificial and temporary character of nations or national boundaries is aptly illustrated by their continual formation and dissolution throughout history. For example, we now think of East and West Germany as separate countries, whereas just a few decades ago they were a single country. What was once trade between two people or two business firms, now has become international trade between people located in different countries.

The main point to be made here is that international trade is just trade between two people, business firms, or groups of people who happen to find themselves enclosed within different national boundaries. Too frequently we lose sight of this simple fact and consider international trade as trade between two countries or governments. Of course, governments have a great deal to say as to whom we buy from and sell to, and at what price, as we shall see more vividly later in the chapter.

THE BASIS FOR TRADE

Perhaps the easiest way to understand the basis of all trade is to consider why each of us as individuals engages in trade. If people did not trade with each other everyone would have to be self-sufficient. However, the extreme inefficiency of self-sufficient people is well documented throughout history, starting with the cave men. It didn't take people long, even the most primitive people, to discover that by specializing in one or a few activities, their total productivity could be increased greatly. For example, in tribal societies it is well known that certain people made the utensils, others hunted, and still others cared for the domestic animals and crops. These people knew that output of the entire tribe was increased when even a modest amount of specialization took place.

The opportunity to increase output also accounts for present-day trade between people whether it be people in the same neighborhood or people of different regions of a country, or different countries. In the United States, for example, it would be foolish for people in the northern part of the nation to attempt to grow their own citrus fruits—the output of the entire nation is increased when people in the South and West produce the nation's fruit, part of which is traded with the people of the North for items produced there. A trade barrier between North and South surely would reduce the output of the entire country because each region would have to undertake production for which it was not well suited. The same reasoning applies to trade between countries. (In the discussion that follows we will speak of international trade as trade between two countries. But keep in mind that in reality it is trade between people living within different national boundaries.) If the United States attempted to produce its own coffee, for example, it would have to forego the production of a relatively large amount of other products because of the resources that would have to be devoted to relatively inefficient coffee production.

The examples in the preceding paragraph illustrate what is perhaps the most obvious reason for the increase in total output or productivity resulting from trade—differences in climate or natural resources. Citrus fruits and coffee require specific climates so it makes sense to produce these products in the areas that have the appropriate climate. Similarly, the extraction of minerals or petroleum can take place only where nature provides these resources. Other examples include the location of a fishing industry in a specific area because of the proximity to a large body of water, of the existence of lumbering because of abundant tree growth. It wouldn't make much sense for the Great Plains to produce lumber and the Northwest to produce corn, for example.

In addition to differences in the natural endowment, specialization and trade takes place because of the past establishment of traditions and institutions that favor a certain industry. For example, Japan has become well known for its light manufacturing industries. Germany for its machines and tools, Sweden for its high-quality steel, Switzerland for its watches, etc. Traditions of workmanship and knowledge are passed down from generation to generation, giving the nation or region a distinct advantage in certain kinds of production.

Also the existence of a particular industry often gives rise to other supporting industries and institutions. For example, trade centers or markets are established where buyers and sellers can get together. Or financing institutions develop that cater to a particular industry because of the specific knowledge required. Also if a large share of the people are employed by an industry, it is common for the public schools to offer training that is specifically applicable to the industry. Economists refer to the increase in productivity that occurs because of the formation of other supporting industries or institutions as "external economies." In other words, an industry may become more productive as it becomes larger because of the existence of other supporting industries and institutions.

It is sometimes argued too that the people of certain regions or nations have some innate ability or characteristic that makes them better suited for certain occupations. For example, the Japanese have gained a reputation for being nimble and able to assemble tiny components of their products. The Germans and Swiss, on the other hand, often are thought of as possessing a characteristic of preciseness which makes them well qualified to produce tools and instruments. It is not clear if such traits are inherent in the population, or if they are learned or acquired through generations of people doing the jobs that require these traits. At any rate, if differences in skills between populations do exist, regardless if they are inherent or acquired, it is reasonable to expect that a nation or area will be better off if it accentuates the activities that it is comparatively good at.

COMPARATIVE ADVANTAGE

It is fairly easy to see how specialization and trade can be beneficial to areas or nations because of special advantages in the production of certain goods or services. As mentioned these advantages may stem from climatic conditions, natural resource endowments, human skills, etc. It is possible, however, to find areas or even nations that seem to have been "shortchanged" by nature and as a result do not possess special advantages vis-a-vis other areas or nations. In these cases, will there be any incentive for the more productive nations to trade with their less productive neighbors? After all, in order to have trade between two nations, or even two people, it is necessary for both to gain from the transaction. If one trader gains and the other loses, the loser will refuse to trade.

We are indebted to an early English economist named David Ricardo for first shedding some light on this question. Using the production of cloth and wine in Portugal and England as an example, Ricardo demonstrated that even though Portugal might be able to produce each unit of wine and cloth more "efficiently" than England, it still was to the advantage of Portugal to engage in trading these two commodities with England. The incentive for trade to take place in this situation is much less obvious than the examples we discussed earlier where each country has a special advantage in one of the commodities.

The key to understanding the basis for trade in this latter situation is found in the concept known as "comparative advantage." Perhaps the easiest way to understand this concept is to construct a simple example. Let us use the United States and the United Kingdom as our two countries, and wheat and wool as our two products. If you wish you may assume that the United States is more "efficient" in both, or vice versa. We will see a bit later that any difference in the level of absolute "efficiency" between the two countries does bear upon the problem.

In Table 11–1 we present some possible levels of output for each com-

Table 11–1. Examples of production possibility schedules for wheat and wool in the United States and the United Kingdom

Possibility	United States		United Kingdom	
	Wheat	Wool	Wheat	Wool
A	480	0	120	0
B	320	20	80	10
C	160	40	40	20
D	0	60	0	30

modity in each country. Notice that when wool is increased in each country the output of wheat declines and similarly if more wheat is produced the quantity of wool must decline. This tells us that each country has a limited amount of resources and, therefore, each cannot simultaneously increase the production of both commodities. Economists often refer to these figures as production possibility schedules.

Using the figures in Table 11–1, we can calculate the cost of wheat and wool in the two countries. First notice that should the United States wish to increase its wool output from 0 to 20 million bales it must give up 160 million bushels of wheat. In other words, each bale of wool costs 8 bushels of wheat in the United States. In the United Kingdom we see that each additional bale of wool costs only 4 bushels of wheat. Thus in comparing the two countries we would say that wool is expensive in the United States and cheap in the United Kingdom in terms of the wheat given up to obtain it.

The cost of wool can be obtained in the same manner. Moving up from the bottom of the table we see that the United States gives up 20 million bales of wool to obtain 160 million bushels of wheat—0.125 bales of wool for each bushel of wheat. In the United Kingdom the first 40 million bushels of wheat are obtained by giving up 10 million bales of wool—0.25

bales of wool for each bushel of wheat. Thus we can conclude that in terms of wool, wheat is cheap in the United States and expensive in the United Kingdom. These costs are summarized in Table 11–2.

Table 11–2.   Costs of wheat and wool

	United States	United Kingdom
Cost of wool in terms of wheat	8 bushels	4 bushels
Cost of wheat in terms of wool *	0.125 bales	0.25 bales

*Notice that the wheat costs are the reciprocals of the wool costs and vice versa.

Because wool is relatively cheap in the United Kingdom compared to the United States, economists would say that the United Kingdom enjoys a comparative advantage in the production of wool vis-a-vis the United States. Similarly, the comparatively low cost of wheat (in terms of wool) in the United States gives the United States a comparative advantage in the production of this product. Notice that in our derivation of comparative advantage we did not say anything about the absolute efficiency of wheat and wool production in the two countries. The important distinction is the relative efficiency of producing one product versus the other. In the United States, wool production is relatively inefficient (in this example) because a relatively large amount of wheat must be given up to obtain the wool. In the United Kingdom, wheat production is relatively inefficient because much wool must be given up to obtain the wheat.

THE GAINS FROM TRADE

So far in the example we have illustrated a situation where the United States has a comparative advantage in wheat and the United Kingdom has a comparative advantage in wool. So what? We will now show that because of comparative advantage, each country, by cutting back on the production of its high-cost product and increasing the output of its low-cost product, and then trading part of its "cheap" product, can end up with more of both products. The only thing required for this little "slight-of-hand" trick is that the trading price be someplace between the production costs in both countries.

In our example, the production cost of a bale of wool is 8 bushels of wheat in the United States and 4 bushels of wheat in the United Kingdom. Suppose the two countries could agree on a "middle-ground" price of say 6 bushels of wheat for each bale of wool it buys from the United Kingdom. Notice that this is a good deal for the United States because in order to obtain more wool by producing it domestically, it would have to give up 8 bushels of wheat per bale of wool. Similarly this price implies that

United Kingdom pays one sixth of a bale of wool for each bushel of wheat. Again this is a good deal for the United Kingdom because by producing more wheat domestically it must give up one fourth of a bale of wool for each bushel of wheat. Hence there is a mutual advantage for both countries to trade.

Let us now illustrate how both countries can end up with more of both products after trading. As an initial situation suppose both countries are producing at possibility B as shown by Table 11–1. In this situation, the United States is producing 320 million bushels of wheat and 20 million bales of wool, while the United Kingdom is producing 80 million bushels of wheat and 20 million bales of wool.[1] Now let us suppose the United States cuts back on its production of wool by 5 million bales. The 8 to 1 cost ratio tells us that the United States can expand its wheat output by 40 million bushels. Also suppose the United Kingdom cuts back on wheat production by 32 million bushels. The 4 to 1 cost ratio in the United Kingdom tells us that they can expand wool output by 8 million bales. (We will discuss how these changes might be initiated in the section on international markets.)

Table 11–3.   Illustrating the gains from trade

	United States		United Kingdom	
	Wheat	Wool	Wheat	Wool
Before trade	320	20	80	10
After trade				
Domestic production . . .	360	15	48	18
Add imports		+6	+36	
Subtract exports	−36			−6
Total	324	21	84	12

To complete the example, let us suppose the United States sells 36 million bushels of wheat to the United Kingdom in exchange for 6 million bales of wool. Recall that the agreed upon price was 6 bushels of wheat for a bale of wool. After the transaction is complete, note that the United States now has 324 million bushels of wheat (360 − 36) and 21 million bales of wool (15 + 6). Also the United Kingdom now has 84 million bushels of wheat (48 + 36) and 12 million bales of wool (18 − 6). In other words, both countries now have more wheat and more wool. This delightful phenomenon happened because each country increased the output of the product in which it had a comparative advantage and then traded part of this increased output to the other country for the product if found expensive to produce. The results are summarized in Table 11–3.

---

[1] Keep in mind that these figures only represent an example and are not intended to illustrate the actual production of these two products in the United States and the United Kingdom.

INCOMPLETE SPECIALIZATION

In the preceding example, it turns out that the total output of wheat and wool in the United States and the United Kingdom is maximized if the United States specializes in wheat and the United Kingdom in wool. But in reality complete specialization would not likely take place.

In order to make this example as simple as possible, we left out a number of complicating factors. Even in a simplified form, international trade examples have a tendency to become complex and confusing. One simplification is that in the production possibilities schedule shown in Table 11–1, we assumed that wheat could be transformed into wool, or vice versa, at a constant cost over the entire range of possibilities. In the United States, for example, we assumed that the cost of obtaining an additional bale of wool was 8 bushels of wheat regardless of the amount of each produced. We made the same assumption for the United Kingdom, only here we assumed a constant ratio of 4 to 1.

In reality we would not expect the same cost ratio to prevail over the entire range of production possibilities. For example, in the United States there are certain parts of the country such as mountainous or hilly areas where wool production can be carried out without much sacrifice of wheat because wheat could not be grown on the hills anyway. Thus the first few million bales of wool likely could be obtained quite economically in terms of wheat given up. But then as more and more of the nation's resources are devoted to wool production, more and more of the productive wheat land is taken over by this activity. Hence at relatively large amounts of wool produced, additional wool becomes more costly because more and more wheat is given up to obtain the added wool. The same is true for expanding wheat production. Trying to grow wheat in the high mountain plateaus will reduce wool output considerably but would add relatively little to wheat output. Hence wheat becomes expensive.

In this more realistic situation of increasing costs, we would expect that beyond some point it would not pay to trade. For example, the United States might continue to produce a little wool domestically because the first few million bales might be produced as cheaply (in terms of wheat) as in the United Kingdom. Similarly, the United Kingdom might continue to produce some of its own wheat because of certain areas that can produce wheat very economically.

We also should consider transportation costs. In order to move the products of one nation to another additional resources are required to provide the transportation services. With increasing costs at some point the comparative advantage might become so small that it would not be large enough to offset the added costs of transport. This would be particularly important in the case of heavy or bulky products. We don't observe much international trade in cement blocks, for example.

The extent of a nation's trade with other countries is influenced also by political and military considerations. If the government of one nation is not on "speaking terms" with the government of another nation, there will not likely be trade between the two countries. It is unfortunate that ideological differences between the political leaders of nations are allowed to determine whether or not the people of the respective countries can trade with each other. As we saw in Table 11–3, the output available to the people of both nations can be increased because of trade.

Also national policies aimed at achieving "self-sufficiency" are common, particularly among developing nations. The implication is that a nation is better off if it produces most of everything it consumes. Again, as we saw in the preceding section, this will not be true if the nation has a comparative advantage in one or more products. An obvious exception, of course, is in military goods. No nation wants to rely on other nations to provide the products for its war machine—another cost of war.

INTERNATIONAL MARKETS

We should recognize, of course, that international trade does not take place through barter, no more than trade between individuals. For instance, in our previous example the United States would not exchange 6 bushels of wheat for each bale of wool that was imported. Rather purchases and sales of wheat and wool would take place between firms in each country. It is not uncommon to find firms specializing just in the import or export business.

It is not difficult to visualize how international trade is initiated. Suppose some enterprising American while reading international price quotations notices that the price of a bale of wool in the United Kingdom is equal to 4 bushels of wheat but that it takes 8 bushels of wheat to be worth the equivalent of a bale of wool in the U.S. market. What a splendid opportunity to make an easy buck! He can buy wool in the United Kingdom, offering a bit more than the 8 to 1 ratio. After paying the transport charges, the difference, which might be the equivalent of 2 or 3 bushels of wheat for each bale of wool, would be pure profit for the importer of wool.

Of course, the same thing could be done with wheat. The import-export firm could buy wheat relatively cheap in the United States and sell it in the United Kingdom where it is relatively expensive. Again the difference between buying and selling price, less transport charges, would be a pure profit. Indeed this kind of activity has made millionaires out of a number of people. This is not to say that such import-export activity is harmful. On the contrary, it is very beneficial. The consumers of wool in the United States can enjoy a more abundant supply at a lower price. The same thing is true for the consumers of wheat in the United Kingdom.

There are some additional effects of opening up of trade. The producers of wheat in the United States will likely enjoy an increased price of their product because of the additional demand of consumers in the United Kingdom. Similarly, wool producers in the United Kingdom will not likely complain about the strong demand and rising price for their product. With these price increases, U.S. wheat producers and U.K. wool producers both will find it profitable to increase their output, as illustrated in Table 11–3. The only "fly in the ointment" is that U.S. wool producers and U.K. wheat producers might find the prices of their respective products declining because of the increased supply of these products from abroad. We will say more about this problem when we discuss tariffs and quotas.

If the two governments allow free trade to take place in wheat and wool, before long the relative prices of these two products will come closer together in the two countries. In other words, as more wheat comes into the United Kingdom the price of wheat relative to wool will likely fall, say from 4 bushels of wheat per bale of wool to perhaps 5½ bushels per bale. By the same token, as wool becomes more plentiful in the United States, the wheat/wool price ratio will tend to decline from say 8 to 1 to perhaps 6½ to 1. We would not expect the relative prices to exactly equalize in the two countries, however, because of the transportation cost of bringing wool into the United States and wheat into the United Kingdom.

EXCHANGE RATES

At this point you might ask, how do firms doing business abroad pay or receive payment for the items they buy and sell? An American seller of wheat, for example, would not want to be paid in English pounds because this money would be of little use in the United States. Conversely, sellers of wool in the United Kingdom need to be paid in pounds. This little problem is taken care of quite nicely by the financial institutions in the respective countries who are authorized by their governments to do business abroad. Some of the large New York banks have checking accounts in the larger London banks, and vice versa. Thus an English exporter of wool, for example, upon receiving a check from an American import firm drawn on a New York bank, presents this check at a London bank and receives payment in pounds. Ultimately the account of the U.S. import firm in his New York bank is decreased when the check is returned to the United States.

We must recognize, of course, that American dollars are not exchanged on a one-for-one basis with English pounds or other currencies. The currency of each nation has either an official or market exchange rate, or both, with the currencies of all other nations. For example, at the present time one English pound is exchanged for roughly $2.40 in American dollars. Thus, if a New York bank deposits $2,400 American dollars (in check or currency) in a London bank, the account of the New York banks is increased by 1,000 pounds. The exchange rates between U.S. dollars and the national currencies of a selected number of other countries for 1967 are presented in Table 11–4.

Table 11–4. Exchange rates: units of foreign currency per U.S. dollar, 1967, selected nations

Country and Currency Unit	Exchange Rate	Country and Currency Unit	Exchange Rate
Argentina (peso) 350.00		Israel (pound)	3.500
Canada (dollar) 1.0809		Japan (yen)	361.900
France (franc) 4.908		Mexico (peso)	12.490
Germany (D. mark) 3.999		Sweden (krona)	5.165
Greece (drachma) 30.000		United Kingdom (pound)	.4155
India (rupee) 7.505		Vietnam (piastre)	117.500

Source: *Statistical Abstract, 1969,* p. 852.

In countries that maintain legal or official exchange rates with other currencies, particularly U.S. dollars, it is not uncommon to observe a difference between the "official" and the "market" rate of exchange. We will discuss later in the chapter how market rates of exchange are determined and what effect exchange rates have on international trade. At this point we might just mention that a divergence between the official and the market rate can result in a "black market" in currency.

For example, suppose the market rate of exchange for Vietnamese piastres is 220 piastres per U.S. dollar as opposed to the official rate of 117.5 per dollar. This creates an incentive for Vietnamese entrepreneurs to search out Americans who are willing to exchange their dollars "unofficially," for something more than the official 117.5 piastres per dollar but less than 220. By using U.S. dollars to buy on the black market, these Vietnamese in effect can obtain goods and services cheaper than if they used piastres. Americans, of course, also are tempted to exchange on the black market since they can obtain more piastres per dollar, hence more Vietnamese goods and services per dollar.

It is unfortunate when a government tries to maintain an official exchange rate significantly different than the market rate, especially if it makes a serious attempt to enforce the legal rate. Scarce resources must be allocated to an expanded police force; otherwise productive people are put in jail or executed and, as we will see later, the country may suffer a reduction in trade with other nations, hence a reduction in the economic well-being of its people.

QUOTAS AND TARIFFS

Throughout the history of the world extending up to the present, most governments have attempted in some degree to reduce imports into their respective countries by imposing various trade restrictions in the form of quotas and tariffs. As the name implies, a quota simply limits the amount of a good that can be brought into a country. A quota may be set up to exclude a good entirely or allow the import of a certain amount per year. A tariff, on the other hand, is in effect a tax on an imported good. As a result of tariffs, the prices of imported goods to domestic consumers are increased over what they would otherwise be. And, as you would expect, the higher prices discourage domestic buyers from purchasing imported articles. Thus trade is diminished.

From our discussion of the gains from trade, we saw that trade is mutually beneficial to the nations involved. If this is true, then why do governments persist in setting up barriers to trade? The advocates of tariffs and quotas have used numerous arguments to justify the existence of these barriers. Most are based on rather questionable economic reasoning. Let us review some of the more common arguments for trade restrictions.

1. *Tariffs as a revenue source.* Governments, of course, generally are on the look out for sources of revenue, particularly for ways to "fleece the goose with the least amount of squawking." It might seem logical, therefore, to impose a tax on foreign producers, i.e., let foreigners help pay the country's taxes. But in reality the people of the nation imposing the tariff end up "paying" the equivalent of the tax anyway. This occurs because the tariff has the effect of reducing the real output of the country so the people have less goods and services to consume. The general income tax (without loopholes) is a less costly method of financing government expenditure because it tends not to distort the economy and thereby reduce real output.

2. *Tariffs to equalize for low cost foreign labor.* A common argument for tariffs in the United States is that the wages of labor in foreign countries are but a fraction of U.S. wages, therefore, foreign products can be made more cheaply and drive U.S. products off the market. A basic flaw in this argument is that it makes no mention of why U.S. workers receive higher wages. In market economies the wage of a worker is determined ultimately by his productivity. If a person is paid $30 per day, he has to produce at least $30 per day in order for his employer to pay his wages.

Workers in other nations who happen to be paid a fraction of U.S. wages find themselves in this unhappy situation because their output is so small—a fraction of the output of U.S. workers. Mainly this stems from the fact that low paid foreign workers have a relatively small amount of capital (machines, tools, etc.) to work with. Also their skills may be lower than U.S. workers. Both of these factors explain why foreign workers, especially those in underdeveloped countries, earn such low pay. The main point is that well-paid labor does not imply high-cost products. The important factor in determining the cost of a product is the price of labor and capital in relation to their productivities. A U.S. worker may earn three times that of a foreign worker, but if his contribution to output is over three times that of the foreign worker, the U.S. worker is actually the "cheaper" of the two. Indeed as we will see in Table 11–7, the United States sells more to the developing nations, those with the lowest paid labor, than it buys from them.

Of course, it is to be expected that the low-wage countries may have a comparative advantage vis-a-vis the United States in the production of certain items just as the United States has a comparative advantage in other items. In these situations it pays to engage in trade. As we pointed out in a previous section, both countries gain by trading.

Carried to its logical conclusion, the low-wage argument would imply also that no trade should be allowed between nations at all. As you recall, trade takes place because of comparative advantage. If tariffs are employed to offset comparative advantage, there is no incentive to trade. And as you also recall, the effect of this is to reduce the total output available to the countries involved and to the world as a whole.

3. *The "infant industry" argument.* Sometimes people attempt to justify tariffs on foreign products in order to reduce competition to a newly established domestic industry. The argument is that small industries should be given protection until they can grow large enough to take advantage of "economies of scale" and thus produce at a lower cost some time in the future.

The problem with this argument is that an industry should not come into existence unless it can earn a rate of return on its capital that is comparable to other nonsubsidized industries.[2] If the return to its capital is lower, the economy could enjoy a larger real output by investing in other industries. For example, if the rate of return to other additional investment in the economy is 10 percent, then the rate of return to the "infant industry" over the long run should also be at least 10 percent. If it takes a tariff to achieve a 10 percent return, we know that the true rate of return is less than that, indicating that the economy is misinvesting its resources. If the return is relatively high, as is often implied, then it should not need a tariff to become established. The high profits in the latter years should be great enough to compensate for any losses in its early years.

4. *Tariffs for retaliation.* It has been argued that although tariffs and quotas on imports are undesirable, a nation often is "forced" to retaliate against other nations which have set up trade restrictions of their own. But it can be argued that a government which retaliates by increasing its tariffs really does not have the economic well-being of its people in mind. For the imposition of a tariff by a nation reduces the products coming into that country, thereby reducing the total amount of goods

---

[2]A possible exception to this rule occurs when the industry in question results in external effects on other industries, i.e., lowers their production costs.

and services available to its people. Just because a government chooses to reduce the economic well-being of its people is not reason why another government should follow suit. Retalitory tariffs are analogous to two governments trying to best each other, each saying that I can deprive my people from more things than you can deprive your people from.

5. *"Buy American."* Quite frequently we see bumper stickers or advertisements urging us to buy American-made products. Apparently the objective is to keep American dollars at home. But why? As we pointed out in Chapter 5, money is just a convenient tool for exchanging goods and services. The important things are the real goods and services that are available to society, not the number of pieces of paper called money that it has. The amount of money in a society can be increased simply by the government "cranking up" the printing presses.[3]

In our discussion so far we still haven't presented a convincing argument for tariffs and quotas. But we cannot deny that they are extremely popular throughout the world. Thus, there must be some reason for having them. To be perfectly honest, tariffs and quotas can result in a short-term gain for specific industries. In our wheat and wool example, the entrance of foreign wool in the United States or foreign wheat in the United Kingdom likely would have reduced the price of wool in the United States and the price of wheat in the United Kingdom, or at least kept prices lower than they would otherwise be. By placing tariffs or quotas on these products and reducing imports, U.S. wool producers and U.K. wheat producers probably would enjoy higher prices.

Thus, when advocating trade restrictions, industry spokesmen should, to be perfectly honest, admit that tariffs or quotas will help them by keeping the prices of their products higher than they would otherwise be. Efforts to increase tariffs or lower quotas often increase during downturns in economic activity, as we have observed in the late 1960's and early 1970's. The object, of course, is to keep out foreign products so as to maintain higher domestic prices. The problem, of course, with being honest about trade restrictions, at least in a democracy, is that the public may not be as willing to grant special favors to specific industries if they realize that these special favors work to the detriment of the rest of society. Thus numerous excuses or rationalizations are thought up, such as those we have just discussed, to justify trade barriers.

It should be stressed also that trade restrictions can at best provide short-term benefits to the industries that they are designed to help. In the long run, many of the people in the protected industries probably would have been better off to leave and enter industries in which the nation has a greater comparative advantage. By doing so their incomes might be in-

---

[3]Keep in mind, though, that large fluctuations in the quantity of money can have important effects on the real output of an economy.

creased even more because of their greater productivity in other lines of work and their larger contributions to the total output of the nation. Tariffs and quotas often serve to delay adjustments that eventually come about in the long run anyway.

DUMPING

Occasionally a nation will try to sell more of its products abroad by setting the export price lower than the domestic price, with the government reimbursing the producers for the difference. This practice has come to be known as "dumping." The United States often has been accused of this practice in disposing of its surplus agricultural products abroad.

Domestic industries that must compete with subsidized imports, of course, condemn this practice. Consumers in the recipient nations may receive some temporary benefit because of more ample supplies and lower prices of these products. It has been argued, however, that in the long run the recipient nations are probably harmed because of the distortion of their domestic production. The United States P.L. 480 program is sometimes cited as a good example. By supplying food grains to underdeveloped nations at less than world prices, the price of food in these nations was maintained at artifically low levels. Hence there was little incentive for the domestic agriculture in these nations to become more productive and to increase output.

From the standpoint of the "dumping" nation, there is little economic justification for this practice. For instance, suppose it costs the United States $2 per bushel to produce the wheat that it sells abroad for $1 per bushel. The difference between the cost and selling price is pure waste. In this example, the total output of the nation, and the world, could be increased if less resources are devoted to the production of wheat and more to the production of other products that consumers value more highly. If the United States is really interested in helping the "starving" people abroad, then a much more efficient and equitable program would be to provide them with purchasing power that they could use in the world market to buy whatever they choose. Too often, programs implicitly designed to help special interest groups have been disguised under the cloak of help for the needy.

UNITED STATES TRADE

It will be of some value to look briefly at the magnitude and characteristics of U.S. trade with other nations. The figures in Table 11-5 provide an indication of the magnitude of U.S. exports and imports. In the majority of years since the Great Depression, the United States has exported a larger value of merchandise to other countries than it has bought from

Table 11–5. U.S. exports and imports of merchandise, selected years, 1969 prices

Year	Exports (Millions $)	Imports (Million $)	Imports as a Percent of GNP (Percent)
1930	8,616	6,807	3.4
1940	10,852	6,915	2.7
1950	15,422	13,884	3.2
1960	24,147	18,270	2.9
1968	35,506	35,396	3.8

Source: *Statistical Abstract, 1969*, p. 783.

them. In recent years, however, the export surplus, if any, has become quite small.

Perhaps most noticeable is the very small amount of imports relative to GNP. Most Americans, it appears, do "buy American." In fact, U.S. citizens consume a small share of their total goods and services in the form of imported items compared to most other nations of the world. We should not conclude from these figures, however, that Americans are more "isolationist" or distrustful of foreign goods than other people. For it is necessary to bear in mind that the United States is a large and diverse nation compared to most other countries. A good deal of the trade that takes place between regions or states in the United States would be considered international trade in other countries.

Table 11–6 provides a little information on the major items traded by the United States. Notice in particular that manufactured items including chemicals, machinery, and other manufactured goods make up over two thirds of all U.S. exports. These general categories also make up the largest share of imports, although a somewhat smaller percentage.

It is possible to observe, of course, the same type of item being exported and imported, although not necessarily to or from the same country. For example, the United States may sell electric generating equipment to India and buy similar equipment from West Germany. It all

Table 11–6. United States exports and imports, 1968 (millions $)

	Exports	Imports
Food and live animals	$ 3,890	$ 4,577
Beverages and tobacco	702	786
Crude materials, inedible, except fuels	3,541	3,347
Mineral fuels and related materials	1,056	2,529
Animal and vegetable fats	274	158
Chemicals	3,289	1,135
Machinery and transport equipment	14,462	7,991
Other manufactured goods	6,085	11,508
Other transactions	929	1,221
Total	$34,227	$33,252

Source: *Statistical Abstract, 1969*, 799–802.

depends on the preferences of buyers in the various importing countries. Also we should recognize that the large general categories in Table 11–6 include a great many diverse items, many of which are found only in exports and not in imports, and vice versa. Thus, we cannot use these aggregative figures to infer anything about comparative advantage of the United States vis-a-vis other countries.

The figures in Table 11–7 tell us something about who are the major trading partners of the United States. As we might expect, there is not as

Table 11–7.   United States trade statistics by continent and nation groups, 1968 (million $)

	Exports to—	Imports from—
Africa	1,269	1,121
Asia	7,580	6,913
Australia and Oceania	1,026	694
Europe	11,151	10,332
North America	10,645	11,164
South America	2,742	2,880
Communist nations, or areas	217	201
Developed nations	23,384	24,040
Developing nations	10,813	8,863

Source: *Statistical Abstract, 1969*, p. 808.

much trade with the developing nations as with the more highly developed, industrialized economies. Also note that U.S. exports to the developing nations are smaller than imports from these nations. The opposite is true for the developed nations. It is interesting to note, too, that the United States buys somewhat more from communist nations than it sells to them, although both figures are tiny compared to the totals.

A simple but often forgotten point is that from the standpoint of the entire world exports must always equal imports during any given period of time. A dollar of exports by one nation must always be a dollar of imports to another, just as a sale by one person is always a purchase by someone else. Of course, for an individual nation exports need not equal imports during any given year.

A country is said to have a "favorable" balance of trade if it sells more than it buys from other countries, i.e., exports exceed imports. It is perhaps unfortunate that this term came into such general use because it does not have much, if any, economic justification. As mentioned in Chapter 3, the error of this thinking is made clear by considering the limiting case where a nation sells everything it produces to other countries but buys nothing in return, leaving exactly zero goods and services for the people to consume—not a very "favorable" situation by most definitions of the word. Somehow people have fallen into the habit of thinking that foreign currencies, or gold, are more desirable than real goods and services.

BALANCE OF TRADE VERSUS BALANCE OF PAYMENTS

In discussing international trade and finance, it is necessary to distinguish between a nation's "balance of trade" and its "balance of payments." In the narrowest sense, the balance of trade is sometimes thought of simply as the difference between value of exports and imports of merchandise. Of course, as shown in Table 11–8, international trade includes a good deal more than just merchandise trade. For example, during 1969, the United States spent 4.9 billion in other countries for military purposes, $3.4 billion on foreign travel, and $3.6 billion for transportation services provided by foreign firms. Including the value of services traded together with income from (or payment to) investments, this adds nearly $20 billion to the United States trade during 1969. In other words, a broader definition of the balance of trade would include the exports and imports of both goods and services.

We should recognize, however, that the total amount of money coming in and going out of the country during a given year includes more that is represented by trade transactions. This brings us to the balance of payments. Notice in the lower part of Table 11–8 that during 1969, several billion dollars left the United States for various purposes such as remittances and pensions to people in other countries, government grants to foreign nations, and investments for new capital formation in other countries. Although this outflow of dollars was partly offset by foreign investments in the United States ($4.1 billion), there remained a net outflow, which is referred to as a balance of payments deficit. Thus we see that even though the United States experienced a balance of trade surplus of $1.9 billion in 1969, it still ran a balance of payments deficit of $7.2 billion.

During the 1960s, the U.S. balance of payments deficits typically have been in the range of two to three billion dollars per year. The 1969 deficit was somewhat higher than normal for this period. A major factor causing the large balance of payments deficit in 1969 was a large reduction in the foreign capital flow item (foreign investment in the United States). During 1968 this figure amounted to $8.7 billion compared to the $4.1 billion for 1969 as shown in Table 11–8.

We should keep in mind that a U.S. balance of payments deficit does not mean that the nation has not "paid its bills" or cannot do so. It just means that the U.S. government and U.S. citizens spent more in foreign countries than these countries or their citizens spent in the United States during the year in question.

An inevitable result of this situation is that foreign governments, their financial institutions, or citizens of foreign countries hold more U.S. dollars at the end of the year than at the beginning. There is no reason, of course, why foreign holders of U.S. dollars must keep these dollars. This brings us to a discussion of the use of gold.

Table 11–8.   U.S. balance of payments, 1969
(billion dollars)

Exports of goods and services		+55.5
Merchandise	+36.5	
Military sales	+ 1.5	
Transportation	+ 3.1	
Travel	+ 2.1	
Investment income	+ 8.8	
Other services	+ 3.5	
Imports of goods and services		−53.6
Merchandise	−35.8	
Military expenditures	− 4.9	
Transportation	− 3.6	
Travel	− 3.4	
Investment income payments	− 4.5	
Other services	− 1.4	
Balance on goods and services		+ 1.9
Remittances and pensions	− 1.2	
U.S. government grants and capital flow	− 3.8	
U.S. private capital flow	− 5.3	
Foreign capital flow	+ 4.1	
Errors and unrecorded transactions	− 2.9	
Balance of payments		− 7.2

Source: *Federal Reserve Bulletin*, July, 1970.

GOLD—THE INTERNATIONAL MONEY

Gold is often called the international money because it is used at the present time to "settle accounts" between nations. Perhaps the easiest way to understand how gold is used is to consider a simple example. Suppose during a given year U.S. citizens purchase $100 million worth of goods and services from the United Kingdom while people of the United Kingdom during this same year buy $95 million of U.S. goods and services. When the books are balanced at the end of the year, financial institutions in the United Kingdom find that they now have 5 million more U.S. dollars than they held at the beginning of the year. It is possible that these financial institutions will decide to hold these extra U.S. dollars as added foreign currency reserves. On the other hand, if U.S. dollar reserves in the United Kingdom are already deemed adequate, the Bank of England may decide to send these dollars back to the United States.

To understand what happens in this case, we should point out first that nations holding membership in a world organization known as the International Monetary Fund (IMF) have agreed to always stand ready to buy or sell gold in exchange for their respective currencies to any qualified firm or agency at a specified exchange rate. At the present time, the price of gold in terms of U.S. dollars is set at $35 per ounce.

Returning to our example, if the Bank of England appears on the "doorstep of the United States with 5 million U.S. dollars in hand," the United States is obligated to take these dollars and in return give the Bank of

England $5 million worth of gold. In actual practice, the physical transfer of gold from the United States to the United Kingdom may never take place. The Federal Reserve Bank in New York may just add the appropriate number of bars to the Bank of England's "pile."

THE U.S. GOLD OUTFLOW PROBLEM

It is easy to see now that if other countries accumulate dollars because of U.S. balance of payments deficits and these countries decide to exchange their dollars for gold, the United States will have its gold reserves drawn down. This is, of course, what happened during the 1960's. As shown in Table 11–9, the U.S. gold reserves have declined by about one half during the past 10 to 15 years.

Table 11–9.   U.S. Gold reserves, selected years

Year	Gold Reserve (Billion $)
1949	$24.5
1954	21.8
1959	19.5
1964	15.4
1969	11.9

Source: *Economic Report of the President, 1970*, p. 282.

From the attention that the gold outflow phenomenon has received in the press, it goes without saying that the U.S. government is concerned about it. Why? For one thing, the government is required by law to maintain a certain amount of gold as reserves against its paper money. It is feared, therefore, that should gold reserves fall below the legal minimum, the money supply will have to be reduced and depression will follow. This fear is largely unfounded, however, because Congress has from time to time reduced the gold reserve requirement to allow for expansion of the money supply in the face of declining gold reserves.

Another concern over the loss of gold is that the United States might not be able to maintain its international liquidity. It is pointed out that foreigners now hold more dollars than the United States holds in gold. Thus if foreign holders of U.S. dollars all demanded gold in exchange, the United States could not satisfy their demands and its commitment to the IMF. Of course, we must remember that fractional reserves are nothing new or unusual; every commercial bank in the United States is in the same position in that they could not pay off all of their depositors at any point in time.

But we might ask, why would foreign holders of U.S. dollars desire to turn in their dollars for gold? After all, when it came time to pay for imports from the United States they would need to just reacquire dollars.

The main incentive to exchange dollars for gold comes from the belief that the U.S. government will at some near date raise the price of gold in terms of dollars, so that it will take more dollars to withdraw each ounce of gold. For example, the U.S. might raise the price of gold from $35 to $40 per ounce.

DEVALUATION

Raising the price of gold in terms of a nation's currency is called devaluation—the nation's currency becomes less valuable relative to gold. Returning to the U.S. case, why does the prospect of devaluation spur foreign dollar holders to turn in their dollars for gold? A simple example will make the reason clear. Suppose a foreign bank holds $350,000 in U.S. dollars. Exchanging these dollars for gold at the $35 per ounce price gives the bank 10,000 ounces of gold. Now if the United States should raise the price of gold to say $40 per ounce, i.e., devalue, this bank can turn in its gold and obtain $400,000 in return—a pure profit of $50,000 made from the devaluation. Thus it is not so much a matter of preferring gold to dollars that prompts the "flight from dollars" but the prospects of quick and easy profits made possible by devaluation. After the profits were made these people would still end up with dollars. In the "dollar crisis" of the late 1960's many foreign holders of dollars felt that the United States would devalue, but so far it has been able to hold out, keeping the gold price down to $35 per ounce.

Why is the United States so reluctant to devalue? After all, there is nothing sacred about the $35 per ounce gold price. For one thing, there seems to be a profound psychological block against changing the price of gold. The thinking seems to be that the U.S. dollar would no longer be as "sound" if its exchange rate for gold were altered. However we should bear in mind that the price of other commodities both in terms of dollars and in terms of gold are continually changing without any "damage" to the dollar or to the "soundness" of other commodities.

It is important to recognize, however, that devaluation changes the price relationships of internationally traded commodities. Again the effect is easiest to understand using an example. Suppose the United States devalues, raising the price of gold from $35 to $40 per ounce. This means that if the British pound, for example, stays tied to gold at its previous exchange rate, it will now take more U.S. dollars to buy a British pound; $2.74 per British pound compared to the previous exchange rate of $2.40 per pound. Or looking at it the other way around, it now takes a smaller share of a pound to buy a U.S. dollar. This means, in effect, that U.S. goods become cheaper to foreign buyers because foreign money gains purchasing power relative to dollars. By the same token, dollars lose purchasing power in other countries because after devaluation more dollars are required to purchase other currencies.

In terms of our previous wool and wheat example, suppose the price of wool in the United Kingdom is 5 pounds per bale and the price of wheat in the United States is $1.50 per bushel. Before devaluation it takes $12 to buy the bale of wool (5 pounds × the $2.40 exchange rate). After devaluation the same bale of wool sells for the same 5 pounds in the United Kingdom, but it now costs $13.70 (5 × 2.74) to an American buyer. Similarly before devaluation it took 0.625 British pounds to purchase a bushel of wheat in the United States ($1.50/$2.40). After devaluation it would take only 0.547 pounds to buy it ($1.50/$2.74). Thus we can conclude that devaluation by a country stimulates its exports to other nations because the country's goods in effect become cheaper to foreign buyers. Also devaluation dampens imports because the goods of other nations become more expensive to the nation in question.

It is sometimes argued that devaluation is undesirable because it causes disruptions in world trade patterns. For example, a U.S. devaluation makes U.S. wheat become cheaper than Canadian wheat, thus Canadian wheat producers will find it more difficult to sell their product. In this sense devaluation is "disrupting," just as a reduction in the price of Fords would be disrupting to General Motors. However, whether devaluation is more disrupting or damaging than other means of reversing balance of payments trends is another question. If a nation finds itself a persistent loser of gold reserves, it may resort to restricting imports by quotas or tariffs and placing restrictions on spending in other countries. In this case total world trade diminishes and entire countries involved are likely to lose, not just specific industries.

Occasionally a nation will revalue its currency upwards in terms of gold. This was done fairly recently by West Germany. The motivation for this action usually stems from inflationary pressure in the country in question because of excessive growth in aggregate demand compared to the productive capacity of the country. By revaluing its currency upwards, the country in effect makes its products more expensive to foreign buyers thereby reducing exports and aggregate demand. Also imports tend to be increased because the country's currency unit now can command a larger amount of other currencies, which in effect reduces foreign prices. For example, Volkswagons now are more costly to American motorists but U.S. feed grains are less costly to West German farmers. The overall result is an increase in the goods and services available to the people of West Germany.

FIXED VERSUS FLEXIBLE EXCHANGE RATES

At the present, IMF member nations are committed to maintaining a fixed exchange rate between their respective currencies and gold. Exchange rates can, within certain limits, be changed through administrative decision. However, a decision to devalue a nation's currency usually comes after a prolonged period of anticipation by other nations either because of balance of payments difficulties of the nation in question or because of its unemployment or inflation problems. Because of the publicity connected with devaluation decisions, they often do cause disruptions in world trade as well as giving rise to speculative activity.

Some economists advocate freeing exchange rates from administrative control, allowing them to seek their own market level. If, for example, foreign holders of U.S. dollars wished to decrease their holdings by turning in their dollars for gold, as described earlier, there would be a tendency for the price of gold in terms of dollars to increase because of the increased demand for gold. Eventually an equilibrium would be reached where the price of gold rises to a point where everyone is satisfied with the amount of dollars they hold. The main advantage of flexible exchange rates is that there is no need for extreme pressures to build up before exchange rates are allowed to change, often in an abrupt fashion. As mentioned these pressures often give rise to tariffs and trade restrictions which have the effect of diminishing trade and reducing the economic welfare of the people.

In general, international bankers and trade authorities seem to be opposed to flexible exchange rates. Their argument is that they would lead to unnecessary fluctuations and "undue" speculation in the international market. Whether or not this is a valid argument is an empirical question. It should be kept in mind, though, that the markets for other internationally traded commodities seem to behave in an "orderly" fashion without administrative control over prices.

"PAPER GOLD"

Because world trade has grown more rapidly than world gold stocks, it has become apparent in recent years that gold would have to be augmented by another form of international money. In 1968, the "Group of Ten" nations of the IMF agreed to create a new international money through the IMF called "Special Drawing Rights (SDR's) or "paper gold" that can be used to settle accounts between nations much as gold is used. It is anticipated that the SDR's will gradually supplement and perhaps eventually replace gold as the international money. Just as paper money and checks have replaced gold in domestic transactions, we may be witnessing the beginning of the end for gold as the international money.

The advantages are clear. First, with the decreased demand for gold, its price should fall and less resources would be devoted to the rather futile activity of digging it out of the ground and then reburying it in vaults. Also the IMF will be able to control the amount of international reserves and as such their size will not be subject to outside disturbances such as the drying up or discovery of gold fields.

MAIN POINTS OF CHAPTER 11

1. International trade is, in reality, trade between people who happen to find themselves within different national boundaries.

2. Trade allows people to specialize in what they do best, hence in‑creases their productive capacity.

3. The most noticeable basis for trade stems from differences in the natural endowment such as climate, minerals, water, etc.

4. A nation or area will enjoy a comparative advantage in the produc‑tion of a product if it gives up less of alternative products than do other nations or areas that produce the product.

5. By increasing the output of products in which it holds a comparative advantage and then trading these products for items it finds expen‑sive to produce, a nation can enjoy more of both types of products.

6. Because nations or areas are not homogeneous we do not observe complete specialization taking place. In other words, because of in‑creasing costs, a nation may lose its comparative advantage in a product as output of the product expands. Also as comparative ad‑vantage becomes smaller, transport charges may eventually offset the cost advantage, especially for heavy or bulky products.

7. As long as the international price of a product is somewhat higher than its price in a low cost country and somewhat lower than its price in a high cost country, there will be an incentive for someone to initiate trade. As trade takes place the price of the product will tend to equalize in the two countries, except for transportation costs.

8. The number of units of one currency that is required in exchange for a unit of another currency is known as the exchange rate. The "official" government exchange rate between two currencies may or may not be equal to the "market" rate of exchange. When the two rates differ substantially, there is a strong incentive for a black market in currency to appear.

9. Governments have used a variety of rationalizations to impose trade quotas and tariffs. These include (1) tariffs as a revenue source, (2) tariffs to equalize for low paid foreign labor, (3) tariffs to protect "infant" industries, (4) tariffs ·for retaliation, and (5) trade restric‑tions to encourage people to buy domestic products. In large part these rationalizations are based on questionable economic reasoning. To be honest, advocates of trade restrictions should cite as their pri‑mary reason, the desire for short-run gains for specific industries or special interest groups.

10. Dumping refers to the situation where a country sells products on the world market for a lower price than exists in its domestic

market, with the difference between the two prices made up by the government.

11. Imports account for only 3 to 4 percent of U.S. GNP. The largest share of U.S. exports are manufactured products, and the largest share of U.S. trade is carried on with the more developed nations of the world.

12. The balance of trade refers to the difference between value of exports and imports of goods and services. The balance of payments includes the difference between exports and imports but also includes the inflow and outflow of money due to remittances and pensions, grants to foreign countries, investment in other countries, and foreign investment in the country in question. In recent years the U.S. has been experiencing balance of trade surpluses but balance of payments deficits.

13. Gold is often referred to as an international money because it is used to settle accounts between countries. Because the United States has experienced persistent balance of payments deficits in recent years, the number of U.S. dollars held by foreign people has increased. The United States has been losing gold because holders of U.S. dollars have decided to turn them in for gold, motivated perhaps by the expectation of a U.S. devaluation.

14. Devaluation refers to an increase in the price of gold in terms of a nation's currency. If other currencies are not devalued at the same time, devaluation increases the prices of other currencies vis-a-vis the currency in question. This in turn has the effect of increasing the import prices of foreign products and reducing the export prices of domestic products, thus dampening imports and stimulating exports.

15. At the present time the exchange rates between the currencies of the major trading nations are set by government edict. Thus rather extreme pressures must build up before exchange rates are altered. Also instead of changing exchange rates nations may resort first to trade controls and restrictions.

16. The major trading nations of the IMF recently agreed to create a new international money called Special Drawing Rights (SDR's) or "paper gold" that can be used to settle accounts between nations much as gold is used today.

QUESTIONS FOR THOUGHT AND DISCUSSION

1. It has been suggested by an extremist group that California separate itself from the rest of the country because its economy already is as large as most other countries. Suppose this was done and then trade barriers were put up to restrict trade with the remaining United States. What

would happen to the prices and consumption of products not now produced in California? What would happen to prices of products produced exclusively in California? Also speculate on what effect California's separation would have on the economic well-being of people in California?

2. Montana is said to have a "comparative advantage" in beef production and Washington State in lumber production. What is meant by this statement?

3. Why doesn't Washington produce all the lumber used by Montana and Montana produce all the beef used by Washington?

4. The common market was established to reduce trade barriers and increase trade between countries in Europe? Why was increased trade a desirable goal?

5. From an economic standpoint, do you think it was wise to keep Britain out of the Common Market? Why or why not?

6. "A country like Iceland that lacks abundant natural resources probably doesn't have a comparative advantage in anything at least in regard to the United States." Do you agree? Explain.

7. Suppose you were in a position to advise the ruler of a small African nation on economic matters. Also suppose that one of his goals for the country is self-sufficiency in the production of every major commodity. Would you try to talk him out of this goal? Why or Why not? What kind of an example could you present to him?

8. American citizens travelling abroad, sometimes are approached with offers to buy U.S. dollars from them at a rate of exchange higher than the official rate. From this situation what can you infer about the market exchange rate relative to the official rate in these countries?

9. The United States has considerable trade barriers against foreign petroleum. If these barriers were eliminated, what would happen to the price of gasoline in the United States? Why do you suppose these barriers aren't done away with?

10. Distinguish between "balance of trade" and "balance of payments."

11. "An excess of exports over imports represents a 'favorable' balance of trade." Do you agree?

12. Explain how U.S. balance of payments deficits are related to the U.S. gold outflow problem?

13. "A flight from dollars by foreigners is an indication that U.S. dollars are no longer considered a 'sound' money." Do you agree?

CHAPTER

12

ECONOMIC GROWTH AND DEVELOPMENT

In this the final chapter on macroeconomics, we will look briefly at the relatively recent phenomenon of economic growth. We say recent because from the standpoint of world history, several thousand years elapsed during which the economic well-being of most of the world's population remained at a relatively low level. Indeed in most nations of the world the largest share of economic growth has taken place within the past two centuries.

At the outset it will be useful to define rather specifically what is meant by economic growth. We will define economic growth as a long-run sustained increase in the per capita real output of a society. Occasionally growth is defined in terms of total output of a nation, but for our purposes, growth in the per capita context will be the most useful concept. For lack of a better measure, real output generally is gauged by one of the output measures discussed in Chapter 3—GNP, NNP, etc.—adjusted by changes in the general price level. However, we should keep in mind the biases of these measures discussed in Chapter 3 also.

GROWTH AND THE QUALITY OF LIFE

Up until fairly recently, most people thought of economic growth as a desirable goal. In fact throughout a large part of the post–World War II period, nations seemed to have been engaged in a kind of contest to see who could grow the most rapidly. The contest was especially noticeable between the nations with communistic governments and those with more democratic forms of political organization.

This is not to say, though, that economic growth has now become totally undesirable. Most nations still rank economic growth as a high pri-
ority goal. But in recent years, in the United States at least, a growing
number of people, especially young people from upper middle- and high-
income families, have begun to question the wisdom of striving for a high
rate of growth. They point to the growing amount of pollution, congestion, and social instability as evidence of the consequences of growth.
Some have even suggested that a more desirable goal would be a no-
growth economy, implying that the United States is "rich" enough already.

Upon closer examination of their argument, it becomes apparent, however, that the advocates of a "no-growth" economy really do not mean
that at all. What they appear to be saying instead is that people now are
consuming enough automobiles, appliances, "luxuries" of various types,
etc., but not enough of other things such as clean air and water, a chance
to see the blue sky once in a while, and the opportunity to enjoy more
peace and serenity. In other words, the no-growth advocates really want
growth in the output of such things as pollution control devices, parks,
etc.—goods and services that improve the environment.

Perhaps a reason for some of the confusion about a no-growth economy
is that many things that people once considered "free" goods, such as
clean air and water, blue skies, green grass, and the sight of a bird, now
are no longer free. In an industrialized society many of these items become economic goods in the sense that alternative goods and services
must be given up to obtain them. For example, if we want cleaner air and
water around industrial cities, some of the resources that formerly were
devoted to the production of industrial products now must be devoted to
the production of pollution control devices.

There may be a few people who would be willing to give up some of
their present consumption to obtain more quality in their environment.
Surely there are more people, however, who would prefer to retain their
present level of consumption and obtain a higher quality of environment
through the growth of the economy. Indeed it seems reasonably safe to
say that most people in the United States would prefer both more conventional goods and services and a higher quality environment.

Thus the question of growth versus no-growth turns out to be for most
people a question of the most desirable mix of output. At this point it is
not clear how much of other goods and services society is willing to exchange for a better environment even if they can have more of both kinds
of goods through economic growth. So far the poor and lower middle-
income people have not expressed a great deal of enthusiasm over the
proposals of the "environmentalists." Apparently, the poor are in no mood
to give up much of what little they now have to obtain more "quality" in
their environment. It's nice to be able to look at blue sky and clear water,
but it's even nicer to have food on the table, a decent house, and clothing
for the family.

Perhaps the main point to be made here is that there is really no contradiction between economic growth and "quality of life." Indeed it is the phenomenon of economic growth that has freed man from a lifetime of struggle against famine, disease, and the elements, and allowed him to set his sights on more comfortable and enjoyable existence.

ECONOMICS: THE DISMAL SCIENCE OF THE 1800'S

For the most part, economic growth is taken for granted by many people living today, especially those in the developed nations. But this was not always the case. After the world had experienced thousands of years of relative stagnation in per capita real output, few people, if any, living much over 200 years ago ever imagined the existence of such a phenomenon as sustained economic growth as we know it today.

After Columbus made his famous trip and the new world gradually opened up, it soon became apparent that new lands and resources could add appreciably to the economic well-being of the established nations. It was at about this time that economics began to emerge as a discipline. And a major economic issue of time was economic growth. One of the first economics books, and perhaps still one of the most famous, is Adam Smith's *Wealth of Nations*, published in 1776. In the main, Adam Smith was rather optimistic about the chances for economic growth provided the government allowed markets to allocate goods and services to their most productive uses. He envisioned growing supplies of both capital and labor leading to a growing level of real output over time.

About 25 years later a clergyman by the name of Thomas Malthus came out with a book, *Essay on the Principle of Population* (1798). To be sure, Malthus was something less than optimistic over the future of mankind. He is perhaps most remembered for his famous population growth example. Malthus argued that population has a tendency to grow geometrically over time—1,2,4,8,16,32,64, etc.—unless checked by a shortage of food. And, according to Malthus, in the long run the shortage of food would serve as the ultimate check on population growth. Even if new lands were brought into production, it would only be a matter of time before the population grew enough to bring everyone down once again to a subsistence level.

Malthus, to strengthen his argument, also introduced his now famous "law of diminishing returns" in which he argued that as more and more labor is applied to a fixed amount of land, beyond some point the extra output attributable to an extra unit of labor will begin to decline. Because of the fixed amount of land in the world, the expanding population would insure that beyond some point, each additional person would not be able to produce enough food to sustain life. Consequently, a point would be reached where population growth would stop as everyone (at least the masses) teetered on the edge of starvation.

To say the least, Malthus' ideas had a pronounced impact on the thinking of the time. It wasn't long before the optimism of Adam Smith's ideas began to give way to the pessimism of the Malthusian doctrine. More and more economic writers took the Malthusian view that mankind was in for a rough time indeed. Because of the prevailing pessimism among economists, the economics profession became known as the "dismal science" during a large part of the 19th century.

NEW TECHNOLOGY AND THE UNEXPECTED DIVIDEND

Having the benefit of over 170 years of hindsight, we can now say happily that Malthus' dire predictions have not materialized, at least for the United States and the more highly developed nations of the world. Indeed, instead of famine the major agricultural problems of these nations have been overproduction and food surpluses. Why have these nations managed to escape the plague of long-run diminishing returns in the production of food? We know that their populations have grown considerably and that their total land areas have remained about the same or even declined. For example, in 1950 the total land in farms in the United States (50 states) amountd to 1,162 million acres. By 1964 this figure had been reduced to 1,100 million acres. Indeed in 1969 the federal government paid farmers not to grow crops on about 58 million acres of farmland.[1]

It is interesting to note too that the number of people engaged in the production of agricultural products also has declined substantially in the United States. At the end of World War II (1946), the U.S. farm population totaled 25 million people. By 1969 the farm population had been reduced to about 10 million people. These substantial reductions in both land and number of farmers become even more impressive when we consider that the total U.S. population increased from 141 million people in 1946 to over 200 million in 1969. Thus we see that in the United States, not only has a given land area supplied the food for a greatly increased population but that the amount of land used to produce food and the number of farm people has in fact declined. For the United States, at least, Malthus couldn't have been more wrong.

But we are still faced with the question of why was Malthus wrong. First, we should bear in mind that Malthus considered only two major resources in the production of food—land and labor. What he failed to consider was the host of new resources or inputs that have come on the scene since his time. Here we have in mind such things as new, improved varieties of crops such as hybrid corn, better and cheaper sources of commercial fertilizer, new and improved pesticides and herbicides, and the tremendous increase in tractors and equipment of all kinds. In addition,

[1] U.S. Department of Agriculture, *Agricultural Statistics, 1969*, p. 541

and perhaps most important, man himself has become a new and improved resource because of the increased skills he has acquired through research and education. These new, man-made resources along with greater knowledge have enabled mankind to greatly increase the production of food from a given land area.

Of course, we should not criticize Malthus too severely for failing to foresee the additional output that new technology has made possible. During his lifetime the primary inputs in the production of food were labor and land. Indeed, diminishing returns will occur in any situation where there is the mere application of additional labor to a fixed amount of land. It is only the application of additional, complementary resources that makes labor and land more productive, thereby offsetting the phenomenon of diminishing returns. To be sure, the law of diminishing returns is still employed to a considerable extent in the study of microeconomics.

You may have recognized also that Malthus' pessimistic predictions about the future of mankind have been more nearly borne out in the underdeveloped nations of the world. In many of these nations food shortages and malnutrition have continued to be the major problems facing the people. Indeed, in some of these nations people are still perishing because of a lack of food. We will return to a more thorough discussion of the problem of achieving economic growth in the underdeveloped nations a bit later in this chapter.

TECHNOLOGICAL CHANGE

Our discussion thus far has centered mainly on the effects of new technology in the production of food particularly in reference to the Malthusian doctrine of diminishing returns. We should be aware, however, that new technology has had pronounced effects on virtually every sector of the more highly developed nations. Indeed the developed nations are characterized by the widespread use of new technology.

The utilization of new and improved resources to achieve a larger level of output in the economy has come to be known as technological change. For a long time economists have been aware of the increased output that could not be explained by the increased use of conventional resources such as land, labor, and traditional forms of capital. The additional or unexplained output was then attributed to the phenomenon of "technological change." However, the more basic question still remains, namely, what are the causes or sources of technological change? Using the phrase "technological change" as a label for the additional or unexplained output is really nothing more than giving a name to our ignorance.

In more recent years economists have begun to address themselves to the more basic questions of identifying the sources of technological change. There is still a great deal to be learned in this area, but at the present it is possible to at least make some general statements. At the most general level we can say that the basic source of new technology, or technological change, is new knowledge. By unlocking some of the secrets of the universe, man has been able to create new inputs or resources that are more productive than his traditional resources. Hence, it has become possible to increase output without increasing the use of traditional resources. Thus we observe an increase in output per unit of input because traditional measures of inputs tend not to reflect the improved quality of inputs or the completely new inputs that have come on the scene.

THE PRODUCTION AND DISTRIBUTION OF KNOWLEDGE

At this point it is legitimate to ask what are the sources of new knowledge? The nations that have been most successful in acquiring new knowledge have done so through formal, structured research and development activities. Man has learned a few new things in his normal day-to-day activities, but the contributions of learning by doing have been relatively small compared to the contributions of scientists and engineers.

A very important step in the acquisition of new knowledge by a society is the transmission of this knowledge from research workers to the general public. Knowledge that only exists in the minds of scientists or perhaps in scientific journals is of little value to society until it is disseminated to the general public and put to widespread use.

The dissemination or "trickling down" of new knowledge is in most cases a complex process. New knowledge seems to first find its way into professional journals, then into textbooks, most likely at the upper levels of school first, and then gradually out into society as graduates begin to utilize it. For example, the concept of hybridization developed by Mendel was understood only by professional geneticists not too many years ago. Now it is found in undergraduate biology texts and is common knowledge to plant breeders. As knowledge becomes more widely known and accepted, it seems also to become simplified so that what was initially understood only by a few scientists and teachers later becomes understandable to more and more of the general public, providing, of course, the knowledge proves useful to the public.

SOURCES OF ECONOMIC GROWTH

Although we do not as yet have a generally accepted theory of economic growth, such as the Keynesian theory of national income determination, economists have identified several factors that appear to be important in contributing to growth.[2] At the same time, we should also bear

[2] See for example, Edward F. Denison, *The Sources of Economic Growth in the United States and the Alternatives before Us* (Washington, D.C.: Committee for Economic Development, 1962).

in mind that a great deal remains to be learned about economic growth.

You will notice in the discussion to follow that the word investment is used repeatedly. We should stress at the outset that investment appears to be the "name of the game" as far as economic growth is concerned. By investment we mean the allocation of resources to the production of additional resources which themselves contribute to the increased output of future goods and services. In other words, in order for a society to increase its output of goods and services, i.e., achieve economic growth, it must increase its productive capacity. But we should also stress that investment per se may not necessarily lead to economic growth. Rather it must be investment that contributes substantially to the output of goods and services—economists refer to it as high payoff investment.

1. *Investment in knowledge.* From our preceding discussion, it should come as no surprise that investment in the production and distribution of knowledge is considered an important source of economic growth. Although our "knowledge" about the contribution of knowledge is still relatively meager, most of the evidence points to the fact that investment in knowledge-producing activities, i.e., research and development (R&D), has paid off handsomely especially for the more developed countries of the world.[3] In fact, one characteristic that the more highly developed nations share in common is their substantial investment in research and development activities.

2. *Investment in human capita!.* In recent years economists have begun to look upon education as an investment in human beings, i.e., the production of human capital. Perhaps most basic is the ability to read and write. Again we have evidence that achieving the equivalent of an elementary level of education as a bare minimum for everyone in society has paid off highly for the developed nations. In countries where a substantial share of the population is illiterate, we also observe a relative low level of per capita output of goods and services, hence a low living standard. Moreover, as the wealth and output of the developed nations increase, a larger share of their people tend to attain higher levels of education which in turn results in still higher levels of per capita output of goods and services.[4]

3. *Investment in nonhuman capital.* Without knowledge and without tools, man is a very unproductive creature. Thus the production of machines, tools, buildings, etc., also is a major factor contributing to the output of nations. The more capital a person has to work with, the more productive he tends to be. At the same time we should point out that the

---

[3] For a more thorough discussion of the economic effects of R&D, see Willis L. Peterson, *Principles of Economics: Micro* (Homewood, Ill.: Richard D. Irwin, Inc., 1971), chap. 12.

[4] For a more thorough discussion of the economic effects of education, see Peterson, *op. cit.,* chap. 11.

kind of capital produced will have an important bearing on the payoff to the investment. It is becoming more evident that the highest payoff is achieved by producing capital that utilizes new knowledge. For example, doubling the number of bullocks and wooden plows in India would not likely add very much to India's food production. In fact this might actually decrease the food available to the people when we consider the increased food requirement for the animals. But if India would invest an equal amount of resources in the production of modern tillage and harvesting equipment and in improved varieties of crops together with more fertilizer production facilities and irrigation equipment, the payoff in increased food output likely would be much greater.

For most countries, these three major sources of economic growth are likely to be very complementary with each other. For example, the payoff to investment in the production and distribution of knowledge can be expected to be much greater when accompanied by increased education and investment in nonhuman capital. Indeed, much of the new knowledge that is produced requires new forms of nonhuman capital to be useful to society. Similarly, investment in education probably pays off more handsomely if accompanied by investment in R&D and in additional nonhuman capital. Thus we would expect the payoff to investment to be greater where all three areas are emphasized, instead of just one or two.

COSTS OF ECONOMIC GROWTH

First, we need to remind ourselves that there are two basic kinds of goods and services produced in any society: (1) consumption goods and (2) investment goods. If a society insisted on producing only consumption goods and services, i.e., people did not save any of their income, there would be no resources available for investment goods. And, according to the preceding discussion, there would be no chance for economic growth to occur. The fact that most societies have chosen to devote a portion of their resources to the production of investment goods means that they decided to forego a certain amount of their present consumption in order to have more consumption goods in the future.

Thus in one sense we can consider the cost of economic growth as the consumption goods and services we have to give up in order to undertake investment. As members of the present generation, we should be thankful that past generations decided to forgo part of their possible consumption goods in order to produce investment goods, else we would probably still be living in caves, cloaked in animal skins and sustaining ourselves on roots and raw meat.

The fact that a certain amount of present consumption must be given up in order to achieve economic growth presents a serious problem to the underdeveloped nations. If the major part of a nation's resources are required to produce just the necessities of life—food, clothing, and shelter—there isn't much chance to forgo much consumption goods in order to invest. And if investment is small, the resulting economic growth will tend to be small. Since the end of World War II, many of the developed nations have attempted to provide investment goods such as technical assistance (knowledge) and a small amount of machines and other forms of nonhuman capital to their less developed neighbors, but progress has been slow. The fact that a large share of the people in underdeveloped nations tend to have a small amount of education makes it difficult for them to assimilate large doses of modern technology and capital.

In recent years there has been an increase in concern over what might be considered another cost of economic growth, namely the pollution, congestion, social unrest, and other problems that accompany an industrialized society. Part of the difficulty, which we alluded to at the beginning of this chapter, involves obtaining a meaningful measure of economic growth. If in fact the environment has deteriorated significantly over the years, then using GNP to gauge the economic well-being of society may result in an overstatement of economic growth. However, as we said, this does not mean that economic growth is undesirable. In order to obtain a more pleasing environment without giving up the consumption goods and services we now have, we must have continued economic growth.

CROSS-COUNTRY COMPARISONS

At this point it will be useful to compare the record of various nations in achieving economic growth. In Table 12–1 we present the 1967 GNP for 14 representative countries ranging from the most highly developed to the least developed. Also the average annual growth in per capita GNP for a recent period is shown.

There are two major points to be gleaned from Table 12–1. First, notice the extreme variation between countries in the per capita output of goods and services. The people fortunate enough to be born in the nations on the upper end of the scale enjoy about 40 times the annual amount of goods and services available to the people of the poorest nations.

The second point to note is the wide variation between countries in the annual growth of per capita GNP shown in the second column. Again in this case the people living in the richest nations have been able to achieve much larger annual increases in per capita output than the inhabitants of the less developed countries. Indeed during the three-year 1963–66 period the average Indian citizen experienced a slight decline in output of goods and services. In this case population grew faster than total output. In terms of absolute growth, all of the nations of the lower end of the GNP scale, with the possible exception of Mexico, exhibited a rather meager increase in per capita output. In order for the poor nations to catch up

Table 12–1.   Estimates of per capita gross national product in U.S. dollar equivalents, 14 selected countries

Country	1967	Average Annual Change 1963 to 1967 (Dollars)
United States	$4,037	$218
Sweden	3,041	214
Canada	2,805	171
West Germany	2,021	96
United Kingdom	1,977	94
Austria	1,452	91
Japan	1,158	119
Mexico	528	36
Brazil	333*	11†
Philippines	278	6
Cambodia	146*	8†
Pakistan	125*	10†
Indonesia	99*	4†
India	88*	−1†

*For year 1966.
†Average annual change, 1963 to 1966.
Source: *Statistical Abstract, 1969*, pp. 828–30.

they must achieve a larger average annual absolute growth than their richer neighbors. Considering their small base values of per capita GNP, this requires an extremely high percentage rate of growth—something most poor nations have not been able to achieve. In a relative sense, at least, it appears the rich are getting richer and the poor are getting poorer, as far as nations are concerned.

GROWTH IN THE UNDERDEVELOPED WORLD

Because of the extremely low level of per capita output in the less developed countries together with their relatively small annual growth, the problem of achieving economic growth is both more critical and more perplexing than is the case for the richer nations. Of course, the general statements about the sources of new knowledge and the need to invest in activities that increase knowledge and education as well as the need for new forms of nonhuman capital to achieve economic growth apply to both the so-called developed and underdeveloped nations. However, because of the critical nature of the problem in the underdeveloped nations, it will be useful to consider these in somewhat more detail.

First, we should bear in mind that the attainment of economic growth is a matter of life and death for many people in countries where the supply of food is extremely limited. Without food today there is no tomorrow to enjoy the fruits of economic progress. It becomes apparent, then, that underdeveloped nations are faced with a dilemma. The acquisition of new knowledge, increasing the level of education and the production of new forms of nonhuman capital are long-run phenomena, taking perhaps several generations to bear significant results. Yet there is a critical short-run problem of staving off famine. Also an adequate food supply is necessary for people to be able to work and be reasonably productive.

To survive the difficult short-run future, most underdeveloped nations have attempted to adopt knowledge and technology of the developed nations to their situations. These efforts have been moderately successful. Certain knowledge such as the concept of hybridization, the technology for harnessing power such as electricity, the internal combustion engine, jet propulsion, the know-how for nitrogen fixation and chemical production, etc., can be applied in any locality. On the other hand, certain technology particularly that which is biological in nature, such as new varieties of crops, must be developed in the area in which it is to be utilized. Hybrid corn that grows beautifully in Iowa is a dismal failure in Mexico or Argentina.

It is very important also to consider the profitability of new types of technology. It is a mistake to conclude that new resources which are profitable in the developed economies also will be profitable in the underdeveloped countries. A major consideration is differences in wage rates between nations. Laborsaving technology that is extremely profitable in countries where labor is relatively scarce and wages are high can at the same time be unprofitable in countries where labor is abundant and wages low.

THE IMPORTANCE OF AGRICULTURE

From our preceding discussion, it becomes apparent that agricultural development is a prerequisite for economic growth of the underdeveloped nations.[5] It becomes even more apparent when we consider that in the least developed nations upwards of 75 percent of the population are directly engaged in the production of agricultural products. In order for the nation to increase its output to any significant degree, the major sector in the economy must, of course, increase its output too.

Because plants represent cheaper or more efficient sources of carbohydrates and protein than animals, initial agricultural development efforts have concentrated on developing higher yielding varieties of crops, particularly rice and wheat. The term "green revolution" has been used to describe the impact of higher yielding varieties in developing nations. However, it is widely recognized that new, higher yielding varieties of crops by themselves will not be enough to attain a highly productive agriculture. In order for these new varieties to reach their potential, there

---

[5] For easy to read books on the problem of agricultural development, see T. W. Schultz, *Transforming Traditional Agriculture* (New Haven, Conn.: Yale University Press, 1964); and A. W. Mosher, *Getting Agriculture Moving* (New York: Agricultural Development Council, 1966).

must be an accompanying increase in complementary inputs such as fertilizer, management skills, and sometimes irrigation water.

Shortly after the end of World War II when development efforts began in earnest, many underdeveloped nations made the serious mistake of de-emphasizing agriculture. Government policies were instituted to draw resources out of agriculture, particularly manpower, to facilitate a more rapid development of the industrial sector. This was an easy mistake to make in view of the fact that all of the developed nations are highly industrialized.

In part, government policies to draw manpower out of agriculture were based on the mistaken belief that a portion of the agricultural labor forces in underdeveloped countries were redundant, i.e., contributed virtually nothing to the output of agricultural products. The error of this thinking was made clear when their agricultural output began to decline as labor was withdrawn. Hence efforts to promote industrial development in some cases just intensified the food problem. In recent years it has become more apparent that a more balanced growth of both the agricultural and non-agricultural sectors is required.

THE AGRICULTURAL ADJUSTMENT PROBLEM

Even though it has proven to be a mistake to prematurely withdraw labor from agriculture, we should not conclude that the number of people employed in agriculture should remain unchanged in the long run. As agricultural development occurs and the supply of food increases more rapidly than the growth in population, the inevitable result is a decline in food prices and in agricultural wages relative to nonfarm wages. This serves as an incentive for people to leave agriculture and take employment in other nonagricultural industries. Thus as a nation continues to develop there is a continual migration of people from farms to cities.

Of course, the people who leave agriculture add to the economic well-being of society by their employment in the production of nonagricultural products. There have been some people in the United States who have advocated policies to keep people from moving off farms. They often cite the characteristics of rural life—clean living, hard work, etc.—as reasons for maintaining the rural population intact. What is often not considered, however, is the cost that society would have to bear to maintain an artificially large farm population, namely, the other amenities of life that transplanted farmers could be producing were they not induced to stay on farms.

There has been a growing concern of late over the agricultural adjustment that underdeveloped nations will have to undergo as they attain greater productivity in agriculture. As we said, during the adjustment period millions of farm people leave agriculture to higher paying employment in cities. The basic concern is whether or not there will be sufficient jobs in cities to absorb the influx of additional labor.

Considering that the people of developing nations are a long way from being completely satisfied, there should be ample opportunities for producing more goods and services that people will want to buy. During the period of most rapid migration, however, we would expect increasing unemployment in cities as the labor market adjusts. Governments can play an important role during the adjustment period, however, by providing job information to migrants and also providing vocational and technical training to those lacking in marketable skills.

Strange as it may sound, the enactment of minimum wage laws may be a rather undesirable policy from the standpoint of helping migrating farm people. For if the minimum wage is higher than the contribution of potential employees, employers have no choice but not to hire these people. Because migrating farm people tend to be those with the least amount of skills useful in industry, hence on the lower end of the wage scale, minimum wage laws tend to increase their unemployment.

THE POPULATION PROBLEM

Improvement in the economic well-being of the average person in a developing country depends on two factors: (1) growth in the total output of the economy and (2) growth in the population of the country. The per capita output of a nation can increase only if total output increases more rapidly than population. For example, if population is growing at the same rate as total output, the economic well-being of the average person remains unchanged. In this case, per capita output could be increased by a reduction in the population growth and/or by an increase in the rate of growth of total output.

An unfortunate characteristic of most underdeveloped nations is that they exhibit a relatively high population growth. As more and more people press against the land area and other resources of these nations, the pressimistic predictions of Malthus are more nearly borne out. Hence, in recent years there has been an increased awareness of the need for the underdeveloped nations to practice some form of population control.

The extent of the population growth problem in the less developed nations is illustrated in Table 12–2. Notice that the population growth rates of some of the representative developed nations shown in the left-hand column are less than half of the population growth rates of the selected less developed countries shown in the right-hand column.

It is an established fact that as people attain more education and higher incomes they tend to reduce the size of their families, hence reduce the population growth. However, the explanation for this phenomenon is still an open issue. Explanations for population growth differences between nations or areas are largely economic and sociological in nature.

Table 12–2.   Annual population growth rates, 1963–67, 14 selected countries

Developed	Percent	Less Developed	Percent
Austria	0.5	Brazil	3.0
Canada	1.9	Cambodia	2.2
West Germany	1.0	India	2.5
Japan	1.0	Indonesia	2.4
Sweden	0.9	Mexico	3.5
United Kingdom	0.6	Pakistan	2.1
United States	1.3	Philippines	3.5

Source: *Statistical Abstract, 1969*, pp. 828–30.

On the economic side, it is argued that children constitute an economic asset to poor people, especially those residing in rural areas. The reuse of clothing, together with the relatively small expenditure on education, housing, and health services, make the rearing of an extra child in a poor family a relatively inexpensive proposition. Moreover, if the family makes its living from agriculture, by the time a child is 11 or 12 years old he (or she) can make a substantial contribution to the family's income. Indeed it is not unreasonable to believe that the contribution of an extra child to a family's income can in many cases offset the added expense of rearing the child—hence the child becomes an economic asset. Children also constitute a kind of social security for parents as well, especially in poor countries with little or no old-age assistance or welfare programs.

As a population becomes more urbanized and as people attain more education, the cost of rearing children increases. For one thing, more highly educated parents desire to provide a high level of education for their children as well. Generally more highly educated parents would prefer to provide a good education for two or three children rather than a poor education for five or six. Also there is less opportunity for children to contribute to the income of urban families, at least until they are in the 16- to 18-age bracket. In this regard, it is fairly evident that rural areas have a "comparative advantage" in the rearing of children.

Sociological differences between populations also have been used to explain population growth differences. For example, in some societies a large family has been considered a status symbol. Indeed this seemed to be the case in rural areas of the United States in the not too distant past, although it is less evident today.

The fact that a substantial proportion of people in underdeveloped countries are both poor and reside in rural areas makes the problem of population control in these nations very difficult. The emergence of new birth control devices in recent years has made it technically possible for people to voluntarily limit the size of their families providing they can afford the devices and have information on their use.

Of course, the mere availability of birth control measures does not insure their use; people must want to reduce the number of children. Considering that such action may constitute a short-run economic loss to the family, we have little basis for optimism. If governments of underdeveloped nations are determined to reduce population growth, they may have to institute policies that make children more expensive. These policies might range from removing any existing incentives to have more children to more drastic means such as placing a tax on children, or even requiring a permit to have children. Of course, as underdeveloped nations become more urbanized, the economic cost of children will tend to increase, which should serve as an incentive to reduce family size.

INCOME REDISTRIBUTION

A common characteristic of most if not all underdeveloped nations is a relatively unequal distribution of income. We tend to observe the vast majority of people existing on a very low income and a relatively few people enjoying a lavish standard of living. In the main, these unfortunate situations have come about because of special favors or outright grants of land or property bestowed by past governments to a few privileged families or royalty.

In recent times governments of some underdeveloped nations have made progress towards redistributing some of the wealth, particularly land, and providing more equal opportunity for the people. The importance of a more equalitarian distribution of income and opportunity to economic growth should be emphasized. For a situation in which a few are very rich and the masses are very poor is not conducive to economic growth. The very rich have little to gain and much to lose by any change in the existing political-economic structure. The very poor in this kind of a situation have little hope and even less means of improving their lot, hence they continue to live as they have for generations or even centuries.

Needless to say, the kind of situation described above where the bulk of the people are poor and a few are very rich tends to foster a great deal of resentment and even outright hatred on the part of the masses towards the privileged few. Frequently the outcome of such an environment is violent revolution. Unfortunately, in the aftermath of such revolution poor people sometimes find themselves suffering under just another form of political and economic repression.

ECONOMIC INCENTIVES

It is becoming increasingly clear that economic incentives play a critical role in the growth and development of a nation. If people are not allowed to reap the rewards of their individual efforts, there is little incentive for each individual to put forth the effort required to increase his output of goods and services. And, of course, the total output of any society is just a summation of the output of all the individuals in that society.

The importance of economic incentives has been clearly demonstrated by the communistic countries. The old communistic ideal of "from each according to his ability, to each according to his need" does not seem very consistent with human nature. Recognition of the importance of economic incentives has prompted some change in communist policy towards more material incentives such as group bonuses for workers, athough as yet these efforts have met with limited success.

The lack of economic incentives has proven to be especially costly in the case of agricultural production for many developing nations. Because of low agricultural productivity and resulting high food prices, governments of some developing countries have imposed price ceilings on food. The end result of such a policy, however, is to actually reduce food supplies or at least dampen further output of agricultural products. With artificially low prices for their products farmers have little incentive to invest in output increasing inputs such as irrigation, land reclamation, fertilizer, improved seeds, machinery, etc.

There is a growing recognition among communistic governments that the lack of economic incentives in agriculture has contributed a great deal to their continual problem of food shortages, even in those countries with the most advanced technology such as the Soviet Union. In spite of (or because of) huge collective and state farms which are supposed to take advantage of economies of scale and the influx of mechanization and fertilizer, the average Russian housewife still finds a very meager supply of very poor quality products at the grocery stores. We can obtain some insight into a probable source of their difficulty by the fact that the small plots of land given to farm workers for their individual use produce about 30 percent of the food supply in the Soviet Union but take up only about 3 percent of the land area. To an otherwise landless farm worker, a small plot of land he can call his own becomes his personal "gold mine" and he treats its accordingly.

POLITICAL STABILITY

In the preceding discussion we have argued that economic growth is obtained through high payoff investment in research, education, and the host of new, more productive inputs that increase man's ability to produce. But in order for man to be willing to invest, either in himself or in nonhuman inputs, he has to be reasonably sure he will be able to capture a return to his investment. Needless to say the threat of nationalizing private property or having people and property destroyed in armed conflict is not conducive to investment for economic growth.

An excessive allocation of resources to the military establishment also is a drag on economic growth. Past experience has shown that a military dominated society tends to draw the country's best educated people either into the military or into activities that serve the military. In addition, labor and other resources that would otherwise produce consumer and investment goods and services produce instruments of war instead, to say nothing about the destruction of people and property caused by war. Also it is not conducive to economic growth for young men to spend their years of learning on the rifle range or building fortifications instead of acquiring skills that make for a more productive society. It cannot be overstressed that economic growth depends critically on peace and harmony both within and between nations. Hopefully more of the world's political leaders will someday become aware of this fact and place their own political ambitions and desire for power below the desire to improve the living conditions of their fellow human beings.

MAIN POINTS OF CHAPTER 12

1. From the standpoint of world history economic growth is a relatively recent phenomenon, most of it occurring within the past two centuries.

2. There is really no contradiction between economic growth and the "quality of life." Unless society is willing to reduce its present consumption of goods and services, the quality of the environment cannot be increased unless growth occurs.

3. The optimism for economic growth and the future of mankind expressed by Adam Smith in his book *Wealth of Nations* was dampened somewhat by Thomas Malthus. In his book, *Essay on the Principle of Population*, Malthus argued that mankind was destined to an existence of hunger and poverty as an expanding population pressed against the fixed land area of the world.

4. To strengthen his argument, Malthus also set forth his well-known "law of diminishing returns" in which he argued that as more and more labor is applied to a fixed amount of land, beyond some point the extra output attributable to an extra unit of labor would begin to decline. And eventually population would grow until the masses teetered on the edge of starvation.

5. Because of the gloomy predictions of Malthus and his followers, economics became known as the "dismal science."

6. Malthus' dire prediction for the future of mankind has not been borne out in the highly developed nations of the world because of new and improved inputs which have complemented labor and land to increase man's productive capacity.

7. The term "technological change" describes the phenomenon of increasing output per unit of input. It occurs because quality improvements in traditional inputs or completely new inputs that have been adopted are not fully reflected in the input measures.

8. The most important determinant of economic growth is high payoff investment. For the developed nations this has proven to be investment in the production and distribution of knowledge, in education, together with investment in capital that utilizes new knowledge.

9. Currently the annual per capita output of the richest nations in the world is about 40 times greater than that of the poorest nations. Also the annual growth in per capita output is much greater for the more highly developed nations, indicating that the poorer nations are falling further and further behind their more highly developed neighbors.

10. To a certain extent, underdeveloped nations have been able to utilize knowledge and technology from the developed countries, although not all knowledge can be successfully transferred between countries.

11. Because agriculture is by far the dominant industry in the underdeveloped nations and also because of serious food shortages in these countries, a necessary condition for growth is the achievement of a more productive agriculture.

12. As was true for the United States and other developed economies, the attainment of increased productivity in the agriculture of underdeveloped countries will necessitate a large-scale migration of people from farms to cities. Once agriculture is able to provide an abundant food supply, this migration is a desirable goal because people are available to produce the nonfood items demanded by society.

13. Unfortunately the less developed nations also exhibit the highest rate of population growth. As a result the total output of these nations must increase at an even faster rate in order for per capita output to increase.

14. The poorest nations also tend to exhibit a relatively unequal distribution of income and wealth. This condition is not exactly conducive to economic growth because the rich generally have little to gain and much to lose by any change in the political-economic structure of the country.

15. Economic incentives that reward people on an individual basis for increasing output also are important for economic growth.

16. Political stability and peace contribute to economic growth by increasing man's willingness to invest both in himself and in new non-human inputs. Also valuable resources do not have to go to support a large military establishment.

QUESTIONS FOR THOUGHT AND DISCUSSION

1. Consider your present level of consumption of goods and services. How much would you be willing to give up so that resources otherwise used

to produce these goods and services could be employed in producing a cleaner environment?

2. If you have traveled abroad, did you observe more or less pollution than in the United States in the cities of relatively poor countries? Elaborate.

3. Why have the gloomy predictions of Malthus not come true in the so-called developed nations of the world?

4. "Economics was known as the dismal science because its textbooks were boring." Comment.

5. In the United States output per unit of input has increased in most industries. What is this phenomenon called? Does it mean that society is getting something for nothing? Explain.

6. Identify a new input in an industry you are most familiar with that could give rise to technological change.

7. At their recent rate of growth (in dollars per year) how long will it take the world's poorest nations to achieve the current per capita output of the United States? Do you think they will ever catch up to the United States? Why or why not?

8. Suppose you are having a nightmare where you find yourself director of economic planning for a large underdeveloped country. What do you think the government could do to foster economic growth in this country? Consider both short-run and long-run policies.

9. Referring back to Question 8, which sectors or industries would you consider as most important in terms of contributing to overall growth of the economy. Elaborate.

10. "Because the developed nations of the world are industrialized, the best way for underdeveloped nations to achieve growth is for them to build up industry at the expense of agriculture." Comment.

11. Why does migration of people from farms to cities go hand in hand with economic growth?

12. If you were a head of state of an underdeveloped country with a high population growth, how would you attempt to reduce the population growth?

13. If you were a head of state of an underdeveloped country with a very unequal distribution of income and wealth, how would you go about trying to equalize incomes and wealth somewhat?

INDEX

This book has been set in 10 point and 9 point Caledonia, leaded 2 points. Chapter numbers are in 14 point and 30 point Bodoni Bold, and chapter titles are in 18 point Bodoni Bold. The size of the type page is 27 by 45½ picas.